THE WORLD COURT

THE MACMILLAN COMPANY
NEW YORK · BOSTON · CHICAGO · DALLAS
ATLANTA · SAN FRANCISCO

MACMILLAN & CO., Limited
LONDON · BOMBAY · CALCUTTA
MELBOURNE

THE MACMILLAN CO. OF CANADA, Ltd.
TORONTO

THE
WORLD COURT

By

ANTONIO SANCHEZ DE BUSTAMANTE *y Sirven*

Judge of the Permanent Court of International Justice · Vice-
President of the Institute of International Law · Member
of the Permanent Court of Arbitration at the Hague
Professor of International Law at the University
of Havana · Member of The American
Institute of International Law

Translated by

ELIZABETH F. READ

for the American Foundation

New York

THE MACMILLAN COMPANY

1925

THE AMERICAN FOUNDATION
Maintaining
THE AMERICAN PEACE AWARD

Committee of the American Peace Award

PREFACE

We have faith that Judge de Bustamante's book on the Permanent Court will greatly aid American readers in understanding the World Court in its true perspective. Judge de Bustamante's distinguished scholarship and his long connection with progressive attempts to arrive at a better international understanding eminently qualify him to present the story of the Court to Americans. As a Judge of the Court itself, as a Member of the Hague Court of Arbitration and as Vice-President of the Institute of International Law he has for many years been closely in touch with the development of the principles of arbitration and law as methods of settling international disputes.

LOOKING AT THINGS INTERNATIONALLY

AN INTRODUCTORY WORD

We are amazingly fond, in these days, of differentiating between what we so loosely call "domestic questions" and "foreign questions." We vociferously urge the solution of the former, and appear indifferent to the latter.

A prominent United States Senator said to me not long ago, "I am more interested in the tax problem than I am in The World Court."

"Why?" I asked.

"Because the one is a domestic question vitally concerning my constituents, and the other is not," he answered.

"Which one is domestic?" I ventured.

"Which?" he repeated in astonishment. "Why the tax problem, of course. The World Court certainly is not."

"Why not?" I persisted. "I mean The World Court."

"Why, man, it is foreign," he exclaimed.

"I don't quite see that," I ventured back. "The World Court was essentially our idea. We proclaimed it for years: we argued for it: we labored for it and finally it was worked out, very largely, by the best American brains. It is of American origination: it came into the world consciousness because of American intiative: it is American in its conception and American in its reflection of our strong national belief in courts of justice. Just wherein is it foreign? If The World Court were to sit in Washington instead of at The Hague, would you call it foreign? Because an institution deals with world-problems do we say it is foreign and exclude the United States, remembering that we said to the world: We will show you what we mean by a World

Court; we will frame its procedure, outline its jurisdiction and then we will invite the nations of the world to join it. The only part of that proclamation we have overlooked is to join the Court ourselves."

"I am ready to grant all that," was the rather handsome answer. "All the same, The World Court is a child of The League of Nations."

"How can it be?" I asked. "We advocated and plead for a World Court years before The League of Nations was ever thought of. The World Court is essentially the child of America. The League's part was to bring America's child into being, doing for the United States what the United States couldn't do for itself."

It is exactly this entire question of the relation of The World Court and The League of Nations, so maliciously muddled up with us for political reasons, which Judge de Bustamante makes as clear as crystal in this book. No one when he has finished reading the present work of the writer can honestly say again that The World Court is an agency of The League of Nations,—that is, if he is open to intelligent conviction, particularly as he is being written to by a Judge of The World Court, a member of the old Hague Court, and a man who has given the best part of his life to the study of international relations and how far law can take the place of war.

To return to my friend, the Senator.

"Now, as to your tax matter," I asked, "how do you make that out a domestic question? Where did the taxes arise?"

"In the Congress, because of the war," was the answer.

"Did we begin the war?" I ventured.

"Of course not."

"Then our tax question is not of American origination as is The World Court? In other words, our taxes were forced upon us as the result of a foreign war imposed upon us by foreign conditions. Yet you speak of it as a domestic question with no foreign relation."

I ventured further. "Let us put it this way: which of the questions that you call 'domestic' and that bulk so largely upon our national attention at present has no foreign relation?"

"The farm question," was the Senatorial answer.

"Hold on," cut in a Northwestern miller sitting by. "The foreign market is *some* factor in our business, believe me."

And, passing to industrials, a manufacturer of steel in the group, a maker of automobiles, a cotton grower, a financier, all, within an hour, traced the relations of foreign conditions to our domestic output in such a direct and convincing manner as to leave the gentleman of the Senate without much room to turn around.

The Senator is, by no means, alone in this attitude toward the foreign relations to our domestic questions. The same is precisely true of the average man who is so quick to dismiss the problems of the nations across the sea as "foreign to American interests." He fails to see that we have scarcely a "domestic" problem today that is not tied up to foreign conditions and markets. We do not realize that we are no longer a nation apart. We cannot be. Surely we were taught in the War that we cannot sit idly by and fiddle while Europe burns. Our once boastful "splendid isolation" is a thing of the part. What concerns Europe, in a vital sense, concerns us. By the same token, our self-termed "domestic questions" are no longer "domestic": they have their roots deep down in conditions overseas. We boast of our power, forgetting that the more powerful a nation becomes the more directly related it becomes to the affairs of the rest of the world. There is no such thing in these days as a nation "going it alone."

All this means that we must cultivate an international mind. We must expand our interests. We must stretch the walls of our minds and broaden and enrich them with the problems of other peoples. And we must become of them. Not politically. That is not asked or contemplated in any question before the American people today. We must not only take a distinct but a large part in those great humanitarian problems that mean for the greater happiness of the peoples of the world: the security of their homes and lives and that justice that speaks for fair dealing and right living. For exactly in proportion as these conditions are better brought about among other peoples, so will they reflect upon our lives and the security and sanity of American living.

Most certainly should the people of the United States stand for every move and step that means peace and the abolition of war. It is our heritage so to do. And The World Court is a step in that direction. There must be a tribunal to which we can go, if needful, for the settlement of those misunderstandings which may arise at any time in the closer relations among the nations of the world to which all peoples are destined. Easier modes of travel, the spread of the wireless, the radio and the inventions of science are rapidly making of the world a closer community. While these results of progressive minds make for distinct material and spiritual advantages, they may likewise prove to be easier roads to differences of opinion. There must be a way to settle these, and there are only two ways to settle any misunderstanding. The one way is to fight. With that method we are through. We have suffered enough from a means which belongs to the cave-men and not to civilized beings. The other way is to talk over a difference and arrive at a peaceful solution.

This is where The World Court comes in: as a tribunal to which we can go and yet not be bidden: a judicial institution with no political entanglements: a Court which has confounded its enemies by doing the very thing which they said it could and would not do: refuse the bidding of The

Council of the League of Nations when its opinion was sought: a Court presided over by a group of jurists whose integrity not even the most violent opponent of The World Court has for a moment questioned.

This is the Court which, perhaps for the first time, is now told about in this book in such a readable manner that all can understand, by a writer peculiarly qualified to do so, since he is, as I have said before, a Judge of The World Court. The most significant reason why this book has a direct appeal to American readers is that it answers so well and so simply the questions about the Court that are uppermost in the minds of American voters: what the purpose of the Court really is, what its jurisdiction is; whether a nation rich as the United States can be dragged before it; what is the true relation of the Court to The League of Nations; whether it is true that the Court has power to render "secret" advisory opinions; whether the Judges "represent" their own countries in the Court; whether Great Britain, by reason of the votes of its dominions, could dominate the election of Judges and thus influence the decisions of the Court; whether the Court's decisions could be used for political purposes. It is all so comprehensive: so clear: so needful.

There is excellent temper and restraint in Judge Bustamante's arguments when he discusses the potentialities of the Court. He makes no extravagant claims for it. It cannot prevent war any more than did the Supreme Court of the United States prevent war between the North and the South. But what it *can* do is to take in its kindling stage the question that threatens to burst into a blaze, look into it carefully, weigh both sides, and show why it isn't worth a conflagration and how simply it can be settled. Just as all our Courts prevent bodily conflicts.

With clarity and sanity does Judge de Bustamante tell us that here is the first attempt at a permanent international Court that has in it the possibility of substituting law for war. That is more than the world has ever had before;

it is the wish of every American citizen that the Government of the United States shall encourage actively and maintain this ideal.

Less it cannot do for its own child. With less the American people will not be satisfied.

EDWARD W. BOK.

October, 1925.

TABLE OF CONTENTS

CHAPTER I

THE HISTORICAL ANTECEDENTS OF THE COURT

CHAPTER II

THE THEORIES AND PROJECTS OF STATESMEN AND WRITERS

CHAPTER III

COLLECTIVE PROPOSALS

CHAPTER IV

THE HAGUE PEACE CONFERENCES OF 1899 AND 1907

CHAPTER VII

THE ADVISORY COMMITTEE OF JURISTS; THE COUNCIL AND THE ASSEMBLY OF THE LEAGUE OF NATIONS

CHAPTER VIII

THE JUDGES: THE METHOD OF ELECTION; THEIR QUALIFICATIONS, RIGHTS AND DUTIES

CHAPTER X

The Financial Situation of the Court

CHAPTER XI

The Jurisdiction of the Court

CHAPTER XII

PROCEDURE AND JUDGMENTS

CHAPTER XIII

SANCTIONS

CHAPTER XIV

THE ADVISORY FUNCTION OF THE COURT

CHAPTER XV

The Work of the Court

CHAPTER I

1. Man longs naturally for progress; instinctively dissatisfied with his present existence, he struggles to make it better; and at the same time, in order to support the reforms he is planning by the things he has experienced, he tries to prove that what he is pursuing really exists, and that his dreams are of something he is trying to resurrect, not to create anew. As a great orator once said, man stands, paradise behind him and before him, between a great recollection and a great hope.

It is only natural, therefore, that every important idea or institution links the ages together like a chain; its periods of success, always more or less accidental, alternate with periods of persecution and reaction, more or less sincere. The conception of organized justice between the people of the world has obeyed this common law. It too has its history; some of the incidents in it, whether triumphs or defects, are clear beyond dispute; others were not as distinct as some of their observers thought they were. This chapter, which deals particularly with matters of fact, will prove what has just been said.

2. Certain Roman writers and some of the seventeenth century publicists believed that the Greek amphictyonies, particularly those of Delphos and Thermopylae, represent the first successful attempt to set up a permanent court of international justice. This much is true,—that the birth and the growth of joint institutions was made much more possible there by the fact that the tribes in these councils were of the same race and religion, lived near each other, and had to defend themselves against the same powerful ene-

1

mies. But these amphictyonic groups, formed for the two purposes specified in their famous oath—to mitigate the laws of war and to defend their shrines and sacred places, acted sometimes as judges, sometimes as arbitrators; at times they prevented wars, and at other times they brought about war, when their decision could be carried out only by force. Except for the great historians of Greece of the nineteenth century, like Grote and Curtius, the most authoritative writers, such as H. Burgel [1] and R. Rader [2] have proved that the facts now in our possession do not warrant us in saying that these councils constituted an international court of justice, but merely indicate that they administered justice only in the form of temporary arbitral agreements, justice not seeming as important then as the specific purposes for which the councils were formed.

3. Rome encouraged and practiced arbitration, frequently to its own advantage. For those who were not Roman citizens special courts were set up, in which a universal, not Roman, law was applied; Rome was not influenced by any international considerations in establishing these courts, for regard for other nations did not enter into the Roman policy of domination, and in fact was not compatible with what this sovereign people regarded as its historic mission; but it ended in the *Recuperatores,* and in giving the *fetiales* and the *praetor peregrinus* authority to apply the alien's law, instead of the Roman law, to aliens. It was pride, not a sense of justice, that made them create a court for aliens and a law of nations (*jus gentium*).

Whether these institutions should be regarded as extremely significant or not, they never governed the Roman people in its relations with other nations, near or distant. They were only a part of the domestic or internal law of Rome, only one of the instruments by which this power finally brought to realization its early dream of dominion over the whole world.

[1] Die pylaeisch-delphische amphiktyonie, Munich, 1877.
[2] L'arbitrage international chez les Hellénes, Christiania, 1912.

4. The Roman Empire broke into two parts; the oldest and really Roman part was destroyed in the fifth century by barbarian invasions. Before its overthrow it had been transformed by a new religion; persecuted and even proscribed when it arose, with neither the form nor character of an official cult, it was inspired by the same determination as the world-wide empire in which it arose, of ruling the conscience of the whole world.

When the barbarians invaded the empire, the Christian religion was passing through one of the most difficult crises in its history; it was rent asunder by the teaching of Arrius, which concerned nothing more nor less than the question whether the Father and the Son were equal or different in the monotheistic dogma of the Trinity. The enemies of Rome, who wanted to destroy her and then divide the spoils, took the heterodox side, because that put them into open opposition to the Roman center, which defended the orthodox principle of the Nicean creed that Father and Son were consubstantial. Thus, without being aware of it, the chiefs very quickly were united behind one faith, by successive and almost natural conversions to the pure Roman doctrine.

Thus, above all the political differences between the victors and the vanquished, there was one bond between men of the same stock and those of different races. Although their material wants were opposed and often incompatible, they had one faith in common, which resulted naturally in their regarding, as the proper judges of their disputes, the spiritual directors who represented the supreme power of the Catholic Church. As the world emerged gradually out the barbarism of the invasions, and from the feudal disintegration into which victory gradually was transformed, the resulting ethnic and religious fusion led to their submission in spiritual and often in material affairs to the supremacy, then uncontested, of the Roman pontiffs.

5. In the post-feudal period of the Middle Ages, and at the beginning of the modern era, the Popes were often called on to act as arbitrators; but they never made themselves the judicial power of the world, and, indeed, they did not try to win that power. For two reasons such an attempt would not have been successful. One grew out of the fact that the faithful were also the subjects of temporal sovereigns, and that the nature of the disputes that arose, in which these sovereigns were involved, often made it necessary for the Papacy to insist that it was not only supreme over the nations, but was the lord and master of every prince and every people. This is clearly shown in the famous bulls that mark each step of these politico-ecclesiastical struggles of the Middle Ages, especially in the *Venerabilem, Ad apostolica* and *In cena dominis* bulls. In struggling to maintain order within the Papacy against emperors and kings, the Popes were able, for example, to force Henry IV to come to the gate of Canossa; but this very fact made it impossible for them ever to be accepted as the supreme judge of all nations, when they had shown themselves the enemies of certain rulers.

Moreover, this phase of history resembles in a way the policy of Greece, of developing all the ethnic or religious similarities between groups of peoples, in order to unite them and then launch them, as a unit, against a common enemy—the barbarians in Greece, the Turks in Europe in the Middle Ages and the beginning of the following period. From the Crusades on the Church used all its authority in preparing for war against the infidel, though well aware, perhaps, that the habitual and authorized use of force would be likely to lead the strong to use the same methods for settling disputes between Christians, instead of trying to have them settled by law. Thus, sometimes encouraged, sometimes opposed, and with no practical method of application, international justice was overwhelmed in the struggle for supremacy which marked the development of monarchies in Europe, in what may be called the first act of modern history.

Nevertheless, in spite of what has just been said, the conception of the international authority of the Papacy had so much influence that even the most powerful monarchs, like Charles the Fifth and Francis I, submitted themselves to it. In the treaty which the impenitent rivals made at Madrid in 1526, after the defeat at Pavia—a treaty of somewhat doubtful validity—it was expressly agreed in Article 49 that the execution of the treaty should be entrusted to the ecclesiastical jurisdiction. At the same time, however, they limited the ecclesiastical power by stipulating that neither monarch should try to induce the Pope to set him free from the oaths and agreements he had made.

6. It was not easy to reconcile these struggles for domination, in their military, political, and even spiritual aspects, with the triumph of law; justice between the nations could not make any progress during this period. Very soon, however, the Reformation, with its prompt success in several European countries, destroyed the religious unity of the world, and the papal supremacy fell with it; the Thirty Years War, caused partly by quarrels over religion, and the Treaty of Westphalia at its close, reduced the exhausted great powers to a common level. Here it was that the conception of the equality of nations entered into the science of international law, and the notion of the balance of power entered into the practice of it, thus unconsciously laying new and serviceable foundations for international justice. Under their shelter arbitration came to life again; arbitration is a defective form of justice, but it is an elementary stage that prepared the way for the true judicial power. From the Treaty of Westphalia down to the beginning of the nineteenth century, occasional arbitrations are the only signs to be found of the evolution of international justice.

7. And yet, at the beginning of modern times, a new world had been discovered and colonized. Toward the close of the eighteenth century, one part of Anglo-Saxon America had become an independent nation, and by the beginning of the nineteenth century almost all of Latin America had followed its example. These nations, with great natural resources and scanty populations, with cultivation and without a past, now politically cut off from Europe, were almost all democracies; they took as their domestic policy, or as

their international platform, the essential elements of a republican form of government: equality and justice. When
European nations became involved in difficulties with these
countries, they could not settle them by force of arms,
because they found themselves face to face with the Monroe
Doctrine, applying to the whole of Latin America, and for-
bidding intervention, occupation, or the acquisition of territory by any European power. With force thus ruled out,
law had to be developed to take its place.

The free exchange of ideas and of systems of government which the French Revolution introduced in Europe encouraged the development of legal procedure for adjusting
disputes. In spite of two very strong periods of reaction
under Napoleon and the Holy Alliance, thrones had to fight
against revolutions, and in many cases yielded to them.
Then came charters, popular constitutions, parliaments
and cabinet government, all more or less transplanted from
across the Channel, but always animated by the ideal of
justice and of the recognition of rights. This judicial spirit
spread, sometimes with difficulty, into other lands, leading
by and by to arbitration and other fundamentally similar
forms of conciliation or collective international regulation.

Arbitral adjustments, frequent between American republics and by no means rare between European nations, have
also been used to adjust questions between the old world
and the new, as in the Alabama case, forever famous. The
following table, however incomplete it may be, indicates the
triumphal march of arbitration:

From 1789 to 1840, there were 23 arbitrations, or 1
every 2 years.

From 1841 to 1860, there were 20, or 1 a year.

From 1861 to 1880, there were 44, or 2 a year.

From 1881 to 1900, there were 90, or over 4½ a year.[1]

8. Not only was there this increase in the number of cases
submitted: there is another far more important development, in the nature of the cases submitted. In the first

[1] La Fontaine, Pasicrisie internationale, Berne, 1903. See Anales de la
Corte de Justicia Centro-Americana, 1911.

international arbitrations specific cases were submitted, by a special agreement for that particular case, called a *compromis*. The next step was the insertion in treaties of a clause providing for the arbitration of certain clauses or categories of disputes. Then came special arbitration treaties making a general agreement to arbitrate any questions that might arise, with certain specified exceptions. Finally international agreements were made which set up a tribunal to adjust differences, acting in a sense automatically and whether the parties wished it or not. Although these different phases varied according to the countries making these agreements, the swift progress of this movement is noteworthy, as well as the fact that each step in making arbitration more easy or more customary was a step toward the establishment of permanent international justice.

Another thing that helped in the spread of this general principle, both in law and in public opinion, was the tendency to set up temporary or permanent commissions to adjust boundary questions and the navigation of international rivers, or to act as the executive organ of international administrative unions and bureaus, like the Universal Postal Union, the International Telegraphic Union, and the Union for the Protection of Literary and Artistic Works.

Before discussing the results of the Hague Conferences of 1899 and 1907, it will be well to consider the doctrines and proposals of philosophers, statesmen and publicists of modern times who paved the way for the organization of international justice.

CHAPTER II

THE DOCTRINES AND PROPOSALS OF PUBLICISTS AND STATESMEN

9. THE first concrete proposal for an international court, so far as we now know, was made during the Middle Ages. A French jurist, Pierre Dubois, preoccupied, like all the cultured men of his time, with the idea of uniting Christendom against the infidel, thought that if justice were adopted instead of warfare as the method for adjusting international disputes, the peace, and therefore the unity, of the world would be secured.[1] There is one general observation that applies to this writer and to many others: that the reason why the judicial settlement of disputes has seemed opportune or necessary has rarely been because they wished to make law the rule of life, but usually because it appealed to them as a remedy for the evils of warfare, which weakened one part of the world at odds with another part that it regarded as its natural and inevitable foe: *"Quia omne regnum in se divisum, desolabitur."*

This author proposed that a council of princes and prelates should meet, on the call of the Pope, to take all necessary legislative measures for having ecclesiastical or civil arbitrators choose three judges from among the prelates and three for each of the parties to a dispute; the personal situation of judges was to be such that they would not be open to hate, or love, or fear, or ambition, or any other similar motive. After these judges had heard the parties and witnesses and had examined the evidence, with or without the assistance of technical assessors, they were to render a just judgment; an appeal from the judgment might be made to the Pope, thus made the supreme judge of all Christendom.

[1] Petrus de Bosco. De recuperatione Terrae Sanctae. Ed. Langlois, Paris, 1891.

8

The sanctions proposed for enforcing the judgments are worth mentioning. In addition to spiritual penalties, less dreaded then, according to Dubois, than material punishments, he proposes that those who have troubled the peace of the world should be sent to the Holy Land, where they could exercise their warlike propensities against the infidels, and that nations at fault should not be allowed to import anything, in order to starve them into submission. The vagueness of these proposals and the impossibility of carrying them out does not need comment; but it was not so much a question then of drafting a practicable treaty, as of sowing seed that would bear fruit in the course of time. And it would not be fair to expect from a fourteenth century enemy of the Mahomedan religion what one may expect from a twentieth century jurisconsult. Justice in foreign affairs will probably not be perfect until it is well advanced in domestic affairs; and national conceptions of justice when Pierre Dubois made these daring suggestions were not up to the standards of today.

10. Two students of this question in the next century, Georges Podiebrad, King of Bohemia, and Antonio Marini, who suggested the idea to him, may be passed over with mere mention. Not until the sixteenth century were any such proposals made as those of Albert Gentili,[1] one of the illustrious founders of the science of international jurisprudence, who lived in the very dawn of this science. According to him, questions of principle, sometimes less obscure and less important than personal litigations, could be submitted to a tribunal, provided only the judges were chosen with more regard to their competence and integrity. They could apply the Justinian Code, supplementing it, if necessary, by the precepts of reason, summed up in the three famous Roman principles: *"honeste vivere, alterum non laedere, suum cuique tribuere."* This represents another step forward in jurisprudence between the nations, in that the rules of law are stated that should be applied in the solution of disputes. This celebrated Italian did not know

[1] Albericus Gentilis. De jure belli, libri tres. Han, 1598.

that the new and important rules of law he was elaborating in his book would displace the inapplicable useless Justinian Codes, in international relations.

11. William Penn,[1] writing at the end of the seventeenth century, showed a tendency to work out an actual plan for the organization of an international tribunal. Penn hoped to see all the sovereigns of Europe organized in a permanent Diet, where each nation would be represented in proportion to its economic importance. International disputes that could not be adjusted by diplomacy were to be laid before this great assembly, but the pleadings were to be held before a section of ten of its members. In case one of the rulers refused to submit a claim to the assembly, or to accept its decision, or did not carry it out within the time set, or went to war over the controversy, all the other rulers were to unite their forces to compel it to submit and to carry out the judgment, as well as to make good all costs and damages.

12. The proposal of Abbé de Saint-Pierre,[2] so often referred to, follows the same general lines. Article 8 provided that no ruler should have recourse to arms or commit acts of hostility against any nation unless it had been declared an enemy of the Society of Europe; any nation that had cause to complain of another or had a claim against another was to direct its agent to present a memorial to a Senate, composed of twenty-four representatives of the European powers, and sitting in the City of Peace; the Senate was to try to adjust the difference by a commission of mediation; if no agreement was reached, an arbitral decision was to be given, by a majority vote on preliminary questions, and then by a three-fourths vote. One very curious provision was that the decision could not be given until

---

[1] William Penn. Essay on the peace of Europe, 1693.
[2] Charles Irénée Castel, Abbé de Saint-Pierre. An abstract of a plan for perpetual peace, invented by Henry IV, approved by Queen Elizabeth, by King James, her successor, by republics and various other powers, applicable to the present state of affairs in Europe, shown to be of infinite advantage to all men now living or to be born, in general and particular, for all rulers and ruling houses. Vol. III. Utrecht, 1728.

each nation had received instructions or orders from its head and had made them known to the Senate. Any government that refused to carry out a decision would be declared an enemy of the Society of Nations, which would declare war to extermination against it. All costs would be paid by the rebellious nation, which would also lose all of its territory that had been subdued.

These plans all have one feature in common: that they make justice depend on a semi-political association of all the Christian states of Europe, and that the judicial power, far from being independent, is regarded as a consequence or even as an instrument of diplomatic relations. Perhaps, in the state of the world at that time, this condition seemed indispensable to these writers, in order to have the decisions carried out with sufficient force to overcome the indifference or the arrogance of the nations that lost their case.

13. Toward the end of the eighteenth century an illustrious philosopher, also a utilitarian, wrote several things of real interest on international law, of which the world has known for a long time, but which have only recently been published.[1] There is a plan among them for universal and perpetual peace, based on fourteen assertions; the thirteenth is as follows: "The maintenance of stable peace could be greatly faciliatated by the organization of a joint court of justice for the settlement of differences between nations, even though the court could not exercise any coercive power." In this joint court, he adds, the necessity for war should not be based on opinions that were contradictory or took different points of view. The decision of the judges, whether just or unjust, leaves the credit and the honor of the contracting nations unimpaired.

Each power is to send two representatives, one a judge, the other a deputy judge. The joint assembly is to give its decision and have it circulated profusely in each of the nations in the controversy; if either nation rebels it is to be placed after a given period under the ban of Europe.

[1] Jeremy Bentham. Principles of international law. MS., 1786-89. Works published by W. Tait, Edinburgh, Essay IV. A plan for a universal and perpetual peace. Vol. II, p. 537 et seq. 1843.

Obviously, he thinks, there could be no danger in agreeing that as a last resort each nation would furnish a contingent to help carry out the court's decrees; but it would be preferable, and probably sufficient, if the treaty creating the court provided for liberty of the press, since the use of force, he thinks, could be avoided in many cases if the court's opinions were given unlimited circulation.

The importance, and even the daring, of some of these ideas cannot be denied; some of the questions they raise have not been settled yet. For this reason they deserve to be considered as an example of the power of the thoughts of men superior to the time in which they lived, serving as a beacon for the generations that followed them.

14. In the middle of the nineteenth century another English writer, John Stuart Mill,[1] enumerated the necessary conditions for a federal form of government, in discussing political law; he said: "The supreme court of the federation will render decisions on questions of international law. This is the first instance of what is really one of the greatest necessities of civilized society, a genuine international court."

This statement, slipped in incidentally in a work on another subject, proves that a very definite opinion on this question had been formed and was becoming general, and that this conception had passed from the restricted realm of specialists, and had become the general belief in juridical circles. Moreover, it involves a direct connection—referred to more frequently later, and perhaps foreseen by Bentham—between the federal jurisdiction and the true international jurisdiction between sovereign states.

15. At a conference on ways of preventing war in Europe, held on February 28, 1871, Sir J. R. Seely gave very strong reasons why it was necessary to substitute justice for war—although he exaggerated somewhat the timeliness of organizing a world federation, like that of the United

[1] John Stuart Mill. Considerations on representative government. London, 1861.

States of America; then, in stating the conditions under which a permanent tribunal should be established, praising the idea, he made this significant statement, which will be referred to subsequently:

"Interests must not be represented in a tribunal. A good tribunal is not one where both parties are represented, but one where neither party is."[1]

16. One of the most complete and farsighted of the projects worked out in the nineteenth century is that of Edmund Hornby. He asserts, in the first place, that it would be possible to obtain judges abundantly qualified and willing to devote their talents to developing universal respect and confidence in the Court, provided they were appointed for a reasonably long term, such as six years; were freed from any national obligation to their own state during their service; were eligible for reëlection; were given salaries and pensions that would save them from seeking national appointments afterward; and were given a standing which, while it would make them unable to accept other honors, offices or appointments during the rest of their lives, would satisfy their highest aspirations.

The task of perfecting a system of international jurisprudence was to be entrusted to them; they would devote their lives to making it perfect, not merely through study or research, but by testing most carefully the application of generally accepted principles to the cases that came up before them.

Although appointed by governments, they were not to represent them, nor to hold any mandate from them. Having nothing to hope or to fear from the officials that appointed them, they would seek their only recompense in the confidence and esteem they would derive from being entirely in the service of the great interests of humanity. The Court was to fix its own procedure, in such a manner that the issue decided in its sentence would be clear and distinct. It would have the right to suggest and itself to

---

[1] The possible means of preventing war in Europe. Lecture delivered by Sir J. R. Seely, K. C. M. G., Litt. D, February 28, 1871.

procure any evidence it considered necessary. In order to avoid the danger that certain of the judges might influence the final decision, a rigid system was provided making obligatory the full and free statement of individual opinions, so that the decision would really be that of the Court, either unanimously or by vote of the majority. Dissenting opinions were to be stated separately, and might be published after a time, if it seemed advisable.

The reasons on which the decisions were based were not to be given in full detail until they had been executed. The court, however, had nothing to do with their execution; its duty ended when its clerk announced the result. Moreover, the parties were to be informed that in order to obtain compliance with the judgment, they might suspend or break off diplomatic relations, impose fines, invade or occupy the enemy's territory, and, as a last resort, declare war.

The judges were forbidden to hold any communication, direct or indirect, with the head, or the government, or the press of any nation, in their official capacity, or to live within the territory of the power that appointed them. During nine months of the year they were to live in the place where the Court had its seat, or not more than twenty miles from it, at the most. Their only title was to be that of Senator, and in every country they were to take precedence of every one except the head of the nation.

The place where the Court resides, Hornby continues, ought to be neutralized and made extra-territorial; all the persons living there are to be subject to its jurisdiction, unless it should prefer to hand them over to the legal authorities of the nation in whose territory its seat is situated. The government of this nation is to collect and distribute the necessary funds for the Court, which the adhering states are to pay in the proportion agreed on.

The judges, of whom there are not to be less than thirteen, are to be jurists by profession, statesmen, diplomats, or judges. They are to choose their president each year, appoint the secretary, and organize their bureaus.

Each adhering nation is to nominate one judge, who may

or may not be a citizen of the nation that names him. If this is not done, the Court will make the nomination, when it is necessary to do so in order to bring the number up to thirteen. Each judge is to take a solemn oath to discharge his obligations.

After giving several rather detailed rules of procedure, which it is not necessary to give here, the author proposes that the sentences be given in the following manner: As soon as a case has been argued and studied, each member of the Court is to draft a preliminary statement and send it, marked with some particular symbol, to the secretary; the secretary is to send copies to each judge, and each judge, with all these anonymous opinions before him, is to prepare his final draft; this draft is sent to the secretary, with no identifying marks except the particular symbol, and the secretary is to prepare a joint draft for the majority, which the majority is to discuss, alter and approve; this constitutes the sentence, which is final and without appeal. The complete judgment is to be published, with all the supporting documents, as soon as it has been carried out.

This plan gives the Court various other functions, some of which came to light again in the Treaty of Versailles. In addition to hearing cases and giving decisions, the Court is to be ready, on the request of two or more nations, to give extra-judicial opinions on questions of law or the interpretation of treaties, for the purpose of preventing future disputes. It is also to suggest modifications or amendments in international law to conferences and congresses, and is to award the title of doctor of international law to persons already doctors of general law who pass an examination at the national universities.

Hornby thought Switzerland was the place most suitable for the Court's work. A proper building was to be constructed for it there, with an endowment of £1,000,000 sterling, paid proportionately by the adhering nations.

Aside from certain features of this plan which are open to criticism because excessive or impracticable, and those that recent history makes it impossible to accept at present, an elevated common sense runs through it, and it shows profound knowledge of national and international life. Later on in this book, the detailed study of the organization and working of the Permanent Court now in existence will verify these comments on Hornby's plan.[1]

17. A. B. Sprague also proposed certain rules and made some interesting observations. His plan, published in 1876, calls for a Court that shall be variable, yet permanent, elastic and yet having cohesion; to obtain this combination of qualities, he tries to find something in between judges with life tenure taking cognizance of all cases, and temporary judges appointed only for the one case which they are to decide. His solution is to have each nation appoint permanently one or more members of the Court; but the sections called upon to make the decisions are to be composed of judges chosen from among them, by agreement between the contracting parties.

The author is trying to make obligatory jurisdiction coexistent with arbitral jurisdiction, by keeping the arbitral system, but with appeals to a Permanent Court for any thing relating to the interpretation of an international code.[2]

18. M. Arthur de Marcoartu, who organized the contest won by the North American writer, Mr. Sprague, whose plan has just been discussed, points out, in an essay published in the same book, the advantages that all the nations would derive from an international assembly ensuring peace and stabilizing international relations. He prophesies what was to happen nearly fifty years later: "The régime of the internationalism of the future calls for a judicial power to apply and impose the legislation passed by the Assembly; this function can be confided to a high supreme international tribunal, composed of special judges *elected by this same legislative body,* with certain qualifications which the elected persons must possess."

[1] E. Hornby. Report on the necessity of a permanent court of arbitration. Official bulletin of the Sixth Universal Peace Congress, at Antwerp, 1894.
[2] A. B. Sprague. Internationalization. London, 1876.

19. Let us pass over a series of writers whose proposals, more or less useful, no doubt, would fill volumes; the bibliography at the end of this book will give some idea of their number. This chapter, however, ought to include some brief mention of the writings of an English internationalist which had a wide and lasting effect. This is James Lorimer; first in a magazine article, and afterward in a book, he advocated a new world-wide juridical organization, one element of which was to be a permanent judiciary power.

According to him, the Court should have two chambers, one criminal, and the other civil. An international ministry would appoint the judges from among the judges of the highest national courts, and later from the ministry itself. There were to be fourteen judges, six of them belonging to the six great powers of his day. They were to have life tenure, and were to be given high personal position; their functions were to be considered incompatible with any other legislative or political duties. The Court would be competent to hear all questions of international law referred to it by the parties or by the international ministry, and also any appeals which any state might authorize from the decisions of its national judiciary on matters of private international law.

There was also to be a public prosecutor and a body of international advocates regulated by the Court.[1]

20. Count L. Kamarowsky, author of an interesting and very useful book on an international court, cannot be passed over in silence. His book was published toward the end of the last century.[2] His thesis was that the idea of sovereignty demonstrates, in principle, the possibility of establishing an international justice, and that the principle of community between peoples makes an urgent necessity of this principle. A whole series of practical necessities, not merely diplomatic but also military and economic needs, are

[1] James Lorimer. The Institute of International Law. Vol. II, Book V. The Ultimate Problem of International Jurisprudence, p. 186 et seq., Edinburgh and London, 1884.
[2] L. Kamarowsky. Le Tribunal International (Traduction francaise). Paris, 1887.

involved with it. In order to satisfy these needs, justice must be organized, in a collegiate form, independent, sitting in public, with two forms of jurisdiction, and divided into departments or sections according to the nature of the cases of which they have cognizance.

He thought it would be preferable to have the judges appointed by the national governments, on the recommendation, however, of the academies and faculties of law, and after a body of aspirants had been organized; these candidates were to be men of wide and careful preparation, with practical experience; they must have served for a certain time as clerk of a court and in other capacities that would have made them familiar with the nature and character of public affairs. In short, they were to possess the qualities that Heffter says diplomats should have: probity and loyalty, enough energy to maintain whatever is just, incorruptibility beyond the reach of temptation, and a decided vocation. As to their age, he thinks they should be over 35 years old when nominated, and that when they are between 65 and 70, the Court should invite them to retire.

The jurisdiction of this high court over the nations was voluntary, except as changed by special agreements to compulsory jurisdiction for certain classes of disputes. Its competence related only to the foreign affairs of states, never to their domestic affairs, and only to the juridical aspects of their foreign affairs. It was to be divided into four services. The first, diplomacy, was to take cognizance of conflicts between the different organisms of the relations between peoples, of acts of officials that were offences from an international point of view, and of the interpretation of treaties. The second, war and the marine, was to look after the observation of the Geneva Convention [1] and of the general principles of the law of war as recognized by nations; it was to decide questions relating to prizes and violation of neutrality, and claims of private citizens for damages due to the violation of these principles. The third, private international law, was to have charge of conflicts in the civil and the criminal laws of the different coun-

[1] Relating to the treatment of the sick and wounded in armies in the field.

tries and of questions of extradition; it would also have
jurisdiction over political criminals and anarchists. The
fourth and last, social international law, would concern
itself with differences connected with the social purposes of
the nation which have a universal character, such as postal
communications and telegraphs, measures to prevent epi-
demics, the protection of literary, artistic and industrial
property, etc.

The Russian publicist also wanted the Court to cooperate
in the codification and promulgation of international laws,
making itself the intermediary between pure theory and the
conscience of humanity. It seemed to him that the history
of the ancient Germanic and Roman procedure and the development of maritime law in the Middle Ages and of
international law in modern times would authorize the new
institution to crystallize and define equally useful and binding rules.

The tribunal would meet at Brussels, but the various
sections would sit in some neutral country, as near to the
pleaders as possible. Only the French language would be
used, because allowing the use of more than one would produce results very inconvenient in actual practice. The general assembly, in addition to a disciplinary function, would
act as a Court of cassation. A section would have a very
small number of judges, complete strangers to the nations
in the litigation. The Court would be the judge of its own
competence. In case the procedure were dilatory, the
parties could complain to the general assembly, which
would recommend greater activity, if the situation war-
ranted it.

The judgments were to be based on the general principles
of positive international law, accepted in some manner by
the parties to the litigation. As sources of law, the Court
was to follow, in order, (1) treaties, giving preference to
the more recent over the older ones; (2) custom, preferring
a general custom over particular usages; (3) the positive
laws and declarations of the nations; and (4) the opinions
of jurists, who were to be regarded generally as the scientific
authorities. The decisions were made by an absolute ma-

jority vote; appeal might be taken to the general assembly, with the judges who gave the decision excluded.

As to sanctions, Kamarowsky thinks that the international Court should have particular confidence in the sentiment of honor and dignity peculiar to nations, and should allow them a certain period in which to comply with a decision. When that time had expired, the nation in whose favor the decision was given might use all kinds of measures against the recalcitrant, from the breaking off of diplomatic and commercial relations to blockade and the declaration of war. A power that would apply these coercive measures itself, independently of the parties, constitutes, he thinks, the last problem of international organization.

Several of these propositions which are only mentioned here will come up again in the detailed discussion of the organization finally given to the Permanent Court.

21. To any one who knows international life in its two aspects, scientific and practical, the enumeration of these earlier advocates of organized international justice would be altogether incomplete, if an important place among them then were not given to James Brown Scott, founder and President of the American Institute of International Law. At the Second Peace Conference, in various associations, in the magazines of the United States, in the Institute, in a long series of publications listed in the bibliography of this book, and in the Committee of Jurists, where he edited the final draft, and in short, in all the methods within his reach, visible and invisible, he has been an indefatigable propagandist of the idea of international justice, and has tirelessly prepared such formulas for putting it into operation as were adapted to the actual situation at each moment. His name is linked with the success of this innovation, so important in international life, and his work is mentioned more than once in the following pages of this book.[1]

22. Only a few years ago the German professor, Dr. Hans Wehberg, discussed several problems relating to the

[1] James Brown Scott. See the extensive list of his publications in the bibliography at the end of this book.

possible organization of a Permanent Court of International Justice.[1] In a judicious discussion of the personal qualifications of the judges, he is inclined to rule out diplomats and to regard it as necessary that they be jurisconsults. He gives good reasons why it is necessary not to let nationals of the litigating states participate, and why judges should not be specially designated by them in any case. He reviews the different methods hitherto proposed for the nomination of the judges, pointing out the defects in each.

Among the technical advantages of making the Court permanent he mentions the greater swiftness and the reduction of the cost of deciding each case; he studies the possibility of subsidizing the Court, and the desirability of creating a corps of international lawyers whose ordinary and constant occupation would be to represent nations before the Court. The difficult problem of sanctions does not escape his attention; he declares himself a firm believer in the moral authority of the decisions and in the value and force of public opinion for their voluntary execution.

23. In 1918, during the World War, D. G. Nyholm, president of one of the mixed courts of Egypt, prepared and published at Cairo a carefully worked out plan for a Permanent Court, which he considered to be the most obvious and most pressing necessity under the conditions resulting from the peace. Under Article 10 of his plan, the judges were to be chosen by an electoral college organized by the allied powers for that purpose.

The powers were to be divided into seven classes, analogous to the arrangement in Article 38 of the regulations of the Universal Postal Union. A certain number of units, running from 200 to 1, was to be assigned to each class, and each power was to name a corresponding number of representatives, excluding diplomats and members of legislative assemblies. From these lists, which were to be sent to Holland, twenty names were to be chosen by lot, with a reservation that the nationals of any state could never

[1] Dr. Hans Wehberg. Das Problem eines internationalen Staatengerichtshofes. Munich-Leipzig; 1911.

exceed a certain proportionate number; these twenty were to constitute an electoral college, who were to choose eighteen judges and eighteen deputy judges by a simple majority vote.

The judges must be fifty-five years old, must have served as judges for two years, and must know as many languages as possible, French and English being essential. They were to be non-removable, and could retire on a pension at seventy, or sooner if ill, by a unanimous vote of the Assembly.

Of these eighteen judges, a tribunal of nine, chosen in rotation, would have jurisdiction over all disputes of a legal nature that might cause an international conflict; but states at war could not summon their adversaries before it in the time between the declaration of war and its end, nor could it summon them for acts arising directly out of the war.

The Court was to be the judge of its own competence; it was to apply to its judgments the principles of national law and the rules of equity. Compliance with the judgments would be secured through negative measures, fixed by the Court, resulting from temporary or permanent rupture of diplomatic relations.

The author studies in detail and vigorously combats the objections made to the operation of an institution of this nature because of the lack of international legislation, the impossibility of using force for the execution of its decisions, and the question of the election of the judges. He adds that there need be no fear that it will be idle from lack of cases. Diplomatic activity, he believes, would diminish as judicial activity increased, until finally the tribunal had become an indispensable factor in the life of nations.[1]

24. Thus the idea of a judicial power for the world has been explained and made popular by the most authoritative writers for many centuries, with increasing activity in recent times.

From all the regions on the globe, in all languages, from

[1] D. C. Nyholm. Le Tribunal mondial. Cairo, 1918.

all the different schools of philosophy, of law, and of
politics, a unanimous demand for its creation arises. It
is plain that an international court is needed, since such
activity and intelligence have put themselves at the service
of this principle and are fighting for its success.

CHAPTER III

COLLECTIVE PROJECTS

25. Let us consider now the influence on this movement of what may be called social forces, expressed in the collective labors of associations of private citizens, or in the joint action of national governments, or in international conferences. This collective action indicates that the aspiration for a permanent institution of international justice had got beyond the stage where it interested only specialists and experts, and had gradually filtered into public consciousness until it was thought of as a proposal that could be put into operation at once. This chapter shows how these ideas became generally understood and popular.

26. The first manifestations of public interest date back to 1843, when the General Peace Convention held its first meeting at London. The Convention adopted a resolution introduced by Rev. George C. Beckwith and seconded by M. E. Carroll, declaring that it was urgent to demand that the national governments draw up a code of law and establish a supreme international tribunal, as one of the most effective methods for adjusting international disputes peaceably and satisfactorily.

The second congress met at Paris in 1849, with Victor Hugo as chairman. A similar resolution was adopted, after a North American, named Walker, had read a draft plan for a court, in Article 6 of which it was carefully stipulated that the Court's jurisdiction should be limited to the foreign relations of nations and to differences arising between nations, but should under no circumstances extend to domestic regulations or institutions. In other words, the new organ of justice should not and could not be used as a method of intervention.

The third conference, held two years later at Frankfort, adopted a similar resolution, on the motion of Mr. Elihu Burritt, an ardent supporter of the proposal, who pointed out that there had been a strong movement in the United States for the Court ever since 1815, and that in 1844 the Legislature of Massachusetts had adopted a resolution urging the Federal government to make every effort to induce the other Christian nations of the world to establish a high international tribunal.

27. And yet, at the Brussels meeting of the Congress of Friends of Universal Peace, in September, 1848, three years before the meeting just referred to, the following resolution had been adopted:

> "It is of the utmost importance that national governments should adjust the differences that may arise between them, amicably and in accordance with established legal principles, by some form of arbitral procedure, the principles of which should be established by treaty. Special forms of arbitration, or a supreme international court, would give a final judgment."

This resolution deserves to be mentioned, although it indicates an obvious confusion, which at that time was only natural and inevitable, between two very different things: arbitration, the detailed history of which lies outside the scope of this book, and the judicial power between nations, with which this book is concerned. This resolution, although exhibiting this confusion, represents a stage in the transfer of interest from the one to the other method of adjusting disputes.

28. In 1867 another organization, The International League of Peace and Freedom, was founded at Geneva, with the codification of international law and the establishment of an international court as one of its main aims. At its Lausanne meeting in 1889, it adopted a project for organizing the entire continent of Europe into a federation, considering such action essential for the following reasons (among others) : the fundamental and permanent reason for the constant state of war in Europe is that there is no permanent international judicial institution; if the legal decisions of such a tribunal are to be substituted for the solutions which war and diplomacy now try to reach through force or intrigue, it is of primary importance that the court be independent; the judges should be chosen from a wide field; its creation should be due to the will of the peoples; its decisions should be based on international laws enacted by the peoples; and however great its moral authority may be, its decisions, to be effective, must have some coercive force for their sanction.

In 1886, however, this association passed through a moment of weakness and hesitation. The Paris committee, in July, and the assembly, meeting in Geneva in September, in considering a proposal for a council and a high international court drafted by Léon Levy, were of the opinion that the existing political conditions in Europe would turn the creation of an international court of arbitration into a menace rather than a guarantee of peace and justice.

29. The Bar Association of the State of New York, in resolutions adopted at Albany in January 22 and April 16, 1896, asked the President of the United States to prepare a plan for the organization of a Permanent International Court. The court was to have nine judges, one designated by each of nine specified nations, chosen by the Supreme Court of each nation from among the judges of that court, with due regard to their qualities as men of letters and as jurists, their aptitudes, and their personal integrity.

All the nations, whether represented on the bench or not, were to be free to submit their differences to the Court, according to Article 4 of the plan.

30. A North American conference association, called the Lake Mohonk Society because it holds its meetings there, was organized in 1895 for one purpose only: to carry on propaganda for the principle of arbitration and for a court through which it could be applied. It is natural, therefore, that at its 1898 meeting it declared that it was urgent to set up an international court at once; that in 1907 it called upon the Second Hague Conference to establish a permanent legal tribunal; that in 1908, 1909 and 1910 it continued its discussions on this subject; that in 1914 it made a similar recommendation, and that in 1915, in the very middle of the World War, in all good faith and with unshaken conviction, it again asserted that the problems existing between the powers then at war that it had not been possible to solve by diplomatic methods ought to be submitted to a court of justice, for the examination and decision of the most fundamental questions, as well as matters of jurisdiction.

31. The International Law Association, formerly called the Association for the Reformation and Codification of International Law, had this subject under consideration, directly or indirectly, from its London conference in 1893 to its Buenos Aires meeting in 1922. At the Buffalo meeting in 1899, it approved a draft of a statute and rules for a permanent court of international arbitration. The proposals of this draft correspond to that stage in the scientific evolution or practical development of this idea, where the aim was to facilitate arbitration rather than judicial settlement, and where its advocates, confusing the two principles, sometimes without knowing it, tried to engraft a fixed body of judges on to the arbitral procedure.

32. During this time the Interparliamentary Union was keeping this subject alive in political circles in Europe. The Union was founded in 1870, by Baron Walterskirchen, and has had its present form since 1888. Although it began to study the possibility of organizing a permanent court of arbitration as far back as 1891, the most important step it has taken in this connection consists of the report submitted by Lord Wearsdale, at the Hague meeting in 1894, in which the principles on which the new institution should be founded were given as follows: (1) national sovereignty must be maintained inalienable and inviolable; (2) the adhesion of each nation to the permanent international court must be absolutely voluntary; (3) all the nations must enjoy the most complete equality before the court; and (4) the decisions of the court must have the form and character of executory judgments. Since the approval of M. Hauzeau de Lehaie's detailed report at Brussels in 1895, and especially since 1912, the Union has seized every possible occasion for spreading its ideas in political and governmental circles. One illustration of this action is Senator La Fontaine's proposal at the Stockholm Conference in 1914. The work of this association is too well known to need further comment.

33. The Universal Peace Congresses and their general meetings have worked along the same lines, though with a tendency to discuss the need for peace rather than the ways and means of bringing it about. Ever since the meetings at London in 1890, and especially at Milan in 1906, at Munich in 1907, and again at London in 1908, these congresses have been insisting under various forms, more or less detailed, that great moral progress would result from the judicial solution of international disputes by a permanent tribunal.

34. A society formed exclusively for the discussion of this question was organized in the United States in 1910, called the American Society for the Judicial Settlement of International Disputes. It owes its origin to the initiative and persistence of the indefatigable propagandist, Dr. James Brown Scott, to whom reference has already been made in this book. At the first meeting it was expressly stated that the principal object of the new society was the creation of an international court of a permanent nature whose members were judges by profession. This would differentiate it from courts of arbitration, whose members act only for the time, and who may be either actual judges or diplomats or statesmen not always sufficiently versed in matters of law.

Resolutions are not adopted at the meetings of this society; papers are read, and speakers discuss various subjects, after which the meeting is open for general discussion.

The members and speakers, most of them distinguished in professional or political circles, animated by the same idea, afford a striking illustration of the strength and the extent of the demand for the establishment of an international judicial power.

35. The American Society of International Law naturally also gave some attention to this question of general interest. At the 1909 meeting, A. J. Montague proposed that a court of arbitral justice be established, on the same general lines as the United States Supreme Court. At the 1912 meeting James L. Teyron suggested that the judges might be chosen by the president of the Third Hague Conference, and made a well-reasoned argument for dropping the word "arbitral" from the name of the new court. At the 1915 session James Brown Scott advocated the creation of a court, and also suggested, as a method of facilitating its organization, that it follow the general lines of the United States Supreme Court.

36. An association that enjoys such great prestige and that so continuously concerns itself with vital legal matters of international significance as the Institute of International Law could not, of course, ignore the question of a permanent court, nor evade taking a stand on it. It has made various important proposals about arbitration, properly so called, which are outside the scope of this book, and it adopted resolutions at Rome and Grenoble, after the Permanent Court of International Justice was established, which are considered in another chapter of this book (see page   ). Mention should be made here of the action taken at its 1912 session at Christiania. The following resolution, introduced by M. Lammasch, was unanimously adopted:

"While recognizing the great merits of the Court of Arbitration created by The Hague Conference of 1899 for international justice and the maintenance of peace:

"The Institute of International Law:

"With a view to facilitating and hastening the recourse

to arbitration, and to ensuring the adjustment of disputes of a legal character by arbitrators representing the different systems of law and of procedure;

"With a view to increasing the authority of such tribunals before the representatives of the parties to a litigation, by the fact that the members of the tribunals will be known to them in advance, and to increasing the moral force of a judgment by having it given by the largest possible number of arbitrators whose authority is recognized by the nations as a whole;

"With a view to eliminating the doubts that may arise, in a case coming up under a treaty of compulsory arbitration containing a clause to this effect, on the question whether a particular dispute comes within the category of those that are submitted by the said treaty to compulsory arbitration;

"With a view to creating a Court of Appeal from the decisions of arbitral tribunals set up pursuant to The Hague Convention, in cases where the special *compromis* provides for the possibility of revision:

"Considers it highly desirable that Voeu No. 1 of the Second Peace Conference, in favor of the establishment of a Court of Arbitration, be speedily carried out."

Even here the almost classic confusion between arbitration and justice still appears (this will be discussed more fully later) ; but the fundamental conception of a permanent court, organized by the nations for the regulation of their international existence, stands out here with remarkable force and precision.

37. Even more specific and concrete is the action taken by the American Institute of International Law on January 27, 1917; and it gives proof of great courage and profound belief in international justice, as it was taken during the World War. This action is a part of what have been termed "the Havana recommendations," as the meeting was held in that city. The essential clauses of this recommendation are as follows:

"Whereas the principles of law and equity can be most easily determined and applied to international disputes by a Court of Justice open to all the independent powers in the community of civilized nations:

"The Institute recommends:

"That a treaty be negotiated establishing a Judicial Union of Nations, similar to the Universal Postal Union of 1908, composed of all the civilized nations and self-governing dominions, each nation to pledge its good faith to submit all the disputes in which it may become involved that are suitable for judicial settlement or those that involve questions of law and equity, to the Permanent Court of this Union, the decisions of which shall be binding not only upon the nations that are parties to the litigation, but also on all the nations that took part in establishing the Court."

James Brown Scott, President of the Institute, made certain proposals as to the fundamental principles on which the Court should be organized. In order to reach an agreement on these principles as soon as possible, it was decided to submit the following questions to the national American societies of international law:

(1) Is it desirable to create an international court of justice to deal with differences of a legal nature that may arise between nations? If so, should it be an American Court, or a World Court?

(2) Would it be desirable to take, as the basis for organizing this Court, the United States Supreme Court and the draft plans presented at the Second Hague Conference?

38. The Federation of League of Nations Societies met at Brussels in December, 1919, after the Treaty of Versailles had been signed but before it had been ratified. The Federation declared that in organizing an international court of justice, it should be stipulated that there should not be more than one judge of any nationality, that the principle of the legal equality of states should be recognized in electing them, and that each nation should submit a list of candidates composed partly of its nationals and partly of subjects or citizens of other countries, in order to demonstrate that these judges were not to be national representatives, but were to represent justice alone.

39. L'Union Juridique Internationale, organized at Paris in 1919 while the peace treaties were being drafted, worked out another plan for a tribunal the next year. This plan provided that there should be nine judges, elected for a nine year term by a secret vote in the Assembly of the League. It was to be an open election, but the electors were to be provided with a list of eligible persons consisting of persons nominated by the governments, each government to have the right to name a maximum of three, and of members of international legal societies.

No nation could have more than one judge of its nationality; the court, composed of fifteen judges and six deputy judges, would sit with only eleven on the bench. The four that were not to sit were to be designated by the parties, two by each side, or by lot, if no agreement could be reached. The tribunal was to base its judgments on law, justice, and equity.

40. Other resolutions or agreements of minor importance that have been adopted on this subject would fill several volumes. Various associations and persons with official standing in their own lands have expressed opinions or made proposals about an international court, and several nations have also prepared or authorized the preparation of plans for the establishment or for the working of a tribunal. These last plans, drafted at the same time as the Treaty of Versailles or shortly afterward, ought, chronologically, to be studied farther on; they are grouped here, however, for the sake of clarity. The same thing is true of the Hague Conferences of 1899 and 1907, to which a separate chapter of this book—the next—is given, not only because of the importance and value of the statements made there and the votes that were taken, but also because these proposals represent a new form and a new degree of interest in the subject: in that a great number of powers met to deliberate, jointly and officially, on a convention for the solution of this problem.

41. The resolution adopted by the Massachusetts Legislature in 1844, in favor of a permanent court of international justice, has already been mentioned. A little later, in 1852, another state, Vermont, took similar action.[1] In 1867 Lord Stanley, Minister of Foreign Affairs in England, and in 1895 the Duke de Decazes, holding a similar office in France, stated in the legislative assemblies of their countries that it was necessary to establish a court.[2] Gladstone, when Premier, and President Grant and President Taft made similar statements, without reservations of any kind.

42. After the 1919 Paris Conference where the peace treaties were made, three elaborate official plans for a Permanent Court were submitted to the world for its approval. It is not possible to study them carefully here, but they must be mentioned briefly because they represent the first developments of national executive concern in the creation of this institution.

The first, submitted by the Italian government, called the Court the International Court of Justice; it proposed that it be composed of judges, one appointed by each contracting state for a term of six years; they were eligible for reappointment. The Court was to form a panel or section to deal with each case brought before it; the section was to consist of the President, or if he were disqualified, the Vice-President, one judge chosen from the full Court by each party, and four other judges chosen by the judges themselves from their own number by secret ballot.

It was to be competent to hear (a) all cases submitted to it by a regular *compromis* between the parties; and (b) cases submitted by only one of the parties, if the Council of the League was of opinion that, either by reason of its

[1] Wehberg. L'Amerique et la Cour permanente de justice internationale. Brussels, 1923.
[2] Cited by Marcoartu, Internationalism, London and New York, 1876.

intrinsic character or because of existing agreements, it was necessary to solve it according to the principles of international law rather than on grounds of equity or political expediency.

The Court was to establish its own rules for procedure in cases where the *compromis* did not stipulate what rules should be applied; in default of other rules, those laid down in the Hague Convention of October 18, 1907 for the pacific settlement of international disputes were to be observed so far as possible.

It is easy to see that this plan is still very closely bound up with arbitration, and that it shows in a very high degree the influence of its traditions and practices. Nevertheless it proves unmistakably that the question had become the order of the day, and that the Italian government, in taking the initiative in official action, recognized the necessity of attacking and solving the problem.[1]

43. The German delegation for the negotiation of the Treaty of Versailles also presented a draft to the Paris Conference, on May 9, 1919. This plan has a certain analogy to the Italian draft. By Article 14, a Permanent International Tribunal, which was to be in operation for nine years, was to be appointed by a Congress of States. Each state was to propose at least one and at most four persons willing to serve and possessing the necessary qualifications; at least one of those named by a state had to be a national of another country. Each nation was to vote for fifteen of those on the list; the fifteen persons receiving the highest number of votes were declared elected. Vacancies were to be filled by the persons receiving the next highest numbers. Decisions were to be given by a tribunal of three members, each party choosing one and these two selecting the third; if no agreement were reached, the full tribunal was to appoint the President.

The tribunal was to have jurisdiction over disputes be-

[1] Permanent Court of International Justice, Advisory Committee of Jurists. Documents relative to the organization of the Court, p. 120. (Cited hereafter as Documents relative, etc.)

tween states, and also over (a) complaints of private persons against foreign states and governments, where the state tribunals had declared themselves incompetent, and over (b) disputes between subjects of different states that were members of the League, so far as the interpretation of treaties formed the subject of the dispute.

The tribunal was to draft rules of procedure, based on the Hague Convention of October 18, 1907 for the pacific settlement of international disputes, subject to the approval of the Congress of States. Its decisions were to conform with international agreements, the usages of international law, and the general principles of law and equity. The nation against which the decision was given was to be under obligation to comply with it in good faith.[1]

44. The Austrian delegates to the same Peace Conference at Paris presented a note on June 23, 1919, based on suggestions made by Professor Lammasch.[2] It contained a draft for a tribunal composed of fifteen judges and eight deputy judges, elected by the General Assembly of the League, in such a way that no state had more than one member. In a litigation, each party was to eliminate three of the judges; and either party might claim special forms of procedure to decide whether the question involved its vital national interests or whether it were or were not of a legal character.

The principal advantage claimed for this arrangement was that it offered, "so far as is possible in human affairs, an almost absolute guarantee for the impartiality of its verdicts," based on the following rules: (a) the judges would be elected for a term of years and not for a special case, so that their opinion on any given case would not be known in advance; (b) they would not act as judges, but as persons enjoying the full confidence of the majority of states that established the tribunal; (c) the nationals of the parties to the litigation would be excluded; and (d) each party would be entitled to eliminate three judges, with-

[1] Documents relative, etc.. p. 124.
[2] *Ibid.*, p. 130.

out giving reasons, which would make it possible to eliminate nationals of states in alliance with the opposed party.

The governments of the victorious nations, in acknowledging the receipt of these two drafts, stated that they would be given deailed study by the League of Nations when the time came for preparing a plan for the Permanent Court in accordance with Articles 14 of the Treaty of Versailles and the Treaty of Saint-Germain.

45. In 1917 three northern European nations, Sweden, Denmark and Norway, began to work out a plan for the organization of the world, one part of which naturally dealt with the question of international judicial power.[1] This draft based the organization of the Court "as far as possible on the principle of the juridical equality of states;" the national governments were to nominate the candidates for election, and the judges were to be elected from this list by an electoral assembly composed of the persons at the head of the national groups in the Permanent Court of Arbitration.

It is interesting to notice that exactly the opposite arrangement was finally adopted by the League of Nations.

The Court was to have fifteen members chosen without regard to nationality, except that not more than two could be the subjects of one state. The Danish alternative raised the number to twenty-seven, all subjects of different states. They were to be elected for life, or, alternately, for nine years, in which case they were eligible for reëlection. There were to be fifteen deputies, elected for six years. Seven made a quorum. The Court might be divided into two sections, and there was to be a chamber for summary procedure.

It was to take cognizance of all subjects as to which the parties had accepted its jurisdiction, either by general treaties or special agreements, applying whatever principles had been stipulated in the special agreement, or, if no such provision was made, the established rules of international law or general legal principles. It was to deal only with

[1] Documents relative, etc., p. 150.

COLLECTIVE PROJECTS 37

disputes between states, but a state might nevertheless bring
proceedings to establish a claim on behalf of one of its
nationals against another state. The judgment was to
contain a statement of the grounds on which it was based;
it was to be given by a majority vote, any dissenting opinions also being read. The decision was to be without
appeal, but the Court might grant a revision on the ground
of newly discovered evidence. The general expenses of the
Court were to be paid in equal shares by the contracting
states; each party to a trial was to pay its own costs.

46. After the League of Nations was established, each
of these three nations prepared a separate draft for the
Advisory Committee of Jurists which was to prepare a plan
for the Permanent Court. The Swedish plan differs very
little from the joint plan that has just been described. The
principal differences in the Danish plan relate to the number
of judges, the number of candidates each government might
name, the right to challenge a judge or to disqualify a judge,
and the publication of dissenting opinions. The Norwegian
draft made the Assembly of the League the electoral
college, required a majority vote for election, so far as possible, suggested either a life term or a nine year term, with
partial elections every three years, and insisted on the
necessity for giving the Court the widest possible power.[1]

47. An advisory committee appointed by the Swiss Federal Council drafted another plan in the latter part of 1918
and the first part of 1919; it made the Permanent Court
of International Justice one of the organs of the League
of Nations. It was to be established by a Conference of
States, for nine years. Each nation was to propose from
one to four candidates, and was to vote for fifteen on the
list so formed; the fifteen receiving the greatest number
of votes were to be declared elected, and vacancies were to
be filled, in order, by the persons receiving the next highest
number of votes. The seven judges receiving the highest
number of votes were to constitute the Bureau of the Court;

[1] Documents relative, etc., p. 202 et seq.

they were to elect a president and two vice-presidents from among their number. In ordinary cases only five judges were to sit, who were to be chosen as follows: each party was to challenge five judges; if they did not do so, the ten were to be eliminated by lot, and the remaining five were to sit. A judge who was a subject of one of the parties was disqualified *ex officio*.

International disputes suitable for judicial settlement were to be decided by the judge chosen by the parties; but if within two months the parties could not agree on the special agreement or *compromis,* the plaintiff might submit the dispute to the International Court, which would decide whether it had jurisdiction, and would give judgment by default if the defendant did not appear. Sanctions depended on the Permanent Delegation of the League, which would submit them to a council of mediation for decision.[1]

48. Another plan [2] was drafted by the Netherlands, also toward the end of 1919; it set up a Court with seven judges and five deputy judges. The Secretariat of the League of Nations was to ask the law faculties and the highest legal bodies of each nation to name qualified persons; the list of names so obtained was to be sent to the national governments, each of which could add two names or could endorse the nomination of any two already on it. This new list was to be submitted to an administrative council, consisting of certain members of the League (not specified) and the Minister of Foreign Affairs in the nation where the Court had its seat. Only those persons nominated or endorsed by at least three states could be voted for; the *scrutin de liste* would determine who were elected and in what order (the seven with the highest numbers were to be elected as judges, and the five with the next highest as deputy judges).

A distinguishing feature of this draft was that it extended the competence of the Court, not merely to disputes between states that are members of the League, but also to disputes between their nationals, and also between a national and

---

[1] Documents relative, etc., p. 252.
[2] *Ibid.*, p. 278.

another state, and for any kind of judicial dispute. The Court was to formulate its own rules of procedure for cases before the full Court and for those before a special chamber for summary procedure. It is worth noting that under this plan the nationals of any state in the League had the right to benefit by the free legal assistance any state gave to its own nationals in the national courts, in countries where, contrary to the situation in many democracies, justice is not free.

49. The five neutral powers whose drafts have just been discussed—Denmark, the Netherlands, Norway, Sweden and Switzerland—appointed a joint committee, at the suggestion of the Netherlands, to draft another plan, based on those just considered.[1] This joint plan was completed at The Hague on February 27, 1920. Its most important provisions are those opening the Court to all nations, whether members of the League or not (Article 20), and giving it power to try members of the League, without their previous consent, in all matters relating to (a) the interpretation of a treaty, (b) any question of international law, (c) the existence of any fact which, if established, would constitute a breach of an international obligation, (d) the extent and nature of the reparation to be made for a breach of an international obligation, and (e) the interpretation of a judgment given by the Court (Article 21). Article 52 binds each nation to carry out as quickly as possible any sentence given against it, and to notify the Registry of the manner in which it has done so. The next article, however, places the performance of all sentences under the guarantee of the League of Nations, within the limits laid down in the Covenant.

50. All these plans proposed by these various nations, to some of the provisions of which reference will be made later, would not have been possible if it had not been for the joint labors outlined in this chapter, nor if this collective effort had not won the degree of practical success that was

[1] Documents relative, etc., p. 300.

realized by the two Hague Peace Conferences of 1899 and
1907, and especially by the second. For this reason a detailed account of the deliberations of these two conferences
is given in the following chapter.

CHAPTER IV

THE HAGUE PEACE CONFERENCES

51. The First Hague Conference was not a world-wide assembly, and the original purpose in calling it was not for strictly legal ends. Only twenty European, four Asiatic, and two American nations were represented. The New World, always inclined to welcome lofty and progressive ideas, could not lend its support or its initiative to the Conference, because by far the greatest part of it was not invited to attend it.

The first circular sent out by Count Mouravieff, the Russian Minister of Foreign Affairs, in August, 1898, referred only to the reduction of armaments in Europe, as a political method of ensuring peace.

The governments that were asked to the Conference soon realized that it would not be possible to disarm without first removing the fundamental reasons for armaments, and that it would be utopian, and even very dangerous, to begin by attacking the results while leaving the causes untouched; under such conditions, to discuss certain subjects connected with disarmament might lead toward war instead of ensuring peace. And so the Russian minister—either to keep his Conference from being a failure, or else because his second thoughts were more inspired than his first—sent out a second circular four months later which opened the way for the consideration of the rules and principles of law that offered another basis for peace, namely, justice. Thus it came about that the 1899 Conference could organize itself immediately into three committees, one to study disarmament, the second to consider the laws and customs of naval warfare, and the third, the one of particular interest here, to study the peaceful methods of adjusting international disputes,—good offices, mediation, and arbitration.[1]

The chairman of this Third Committee was M. Léon Bourgeois, an eminent statesman, of great mental capacity and extraordinary lucidity, with a gift of logical clarity of expression that was not less notable. The name of M. Bourgeois will always be associated with the history of the Permanent Court; and he had a great deal to do with the beginnings of international justice in the limited form in which it could be realized at this Conference.

At the meeting on May 26 the English delegate, Sir Julian Pauncefote, maintained that new codes and rules for arbitration, whatever merit they might have, did not "greatly advance the grand cause" for which they had met, and that in his opinion it was absolutely indispensable to organize a permanent international court that could meet whenever nations in a dispute called upon it. M. Descamps, secretary of the Committee, observed, on the other hand that a court of this kind would not meet any unsurmountable obstacles provided it were organized on the principle that the international community is one of coordination, not of subordination, and provided it was thus given the character of a free tribunal in the midst of independent states.

By this alternation, which deprived the new conception of justice of every suggestion of compulsion and cut it down to merely one more method for providing by treaty for arbitration, Sir Julian Pauncefote's idea was very greatly weakened. It was only within these narrow limits that the Committee discussed the various proposals; and the decisions that were reached on them weakened and restricted them still more.

52. The plan submitted by the Russian delegates was as follows: the Conference was to designate five nations, who in their turn were to appoint five judges to constitute a court of arbitration, which was to adjust any disputes that

---

[1] See, on the work of the First Hague Conference: Conférence internationale de la Paix, The Hague, 1899; on the work of the Second Hague Conference; de Bustamante, La segunda Conferencia de la Paz, Madrid, 1908.

might be presented to it before another Peace Conference should meet. In case a litigation arose between powers not represented on this court, these powers would have the right to appoint a judge, who might be their own national or not, and who would have all the functions and powers of the other judges. The five powers were to organize a permanent bureau of arbitration at The Hague, to which the contending parties might send notice of their agreement to submit a difference to the court, whereupon the bureau would send immediate notice of the request to the court, and the court would meet at once. Its jurisdiction would include all the cases of compulsory arbitration mentioned in the plan, unless the parties preferred to set up special tribunals.

53. The plan presented by the United States delegation proposed a court composed of persons of great authority and high moral consideration, chosen one from each nation by a majority vote of the judges of the highest court in that country. As soon as nine of the signatory powers had ratified the convention, it was to go into effect. The court was to be permanent, and was to be open to all nations, whether they had ratified the convention or not. Parties could appear before the full court, or before a smaller uneven number of judges. The number, however, could never be less than three; and when there were only three none of them could be a citizen or a national of one of the parties to the litigation. The judgment was to be subject to revision, before the same judges as handed it down, in case any material circumstances not known at the time of the decision subsequently came to light.

54. The English plan, the general lines of which were accepted by the Conference, was less daring. It proposed to set up a court, or to prepare a list of distinguished persons for a court, two to be designated by each nation. In case of a litigation, the number of judges specified in the agreement to arbitrate were to be chosen from this list. An administration bureau was to take charge of all matters of detail and was to serve as the active organ of the proposed institution.

55. The French delegation did not wish to present a separate plan; it agreed that it would acquiesce in the creation of a court, under the double guarantee of entire liberty in having recourse to the court, and freedom in choosing arbitrators. They went one step farther, suggesting that a mandate should be given to the central bureau authorizing it, when it learned of some grave difficulty or crisis, to communicate with the interested powers and offer to them all possible facilities for the work of the court. Several of the smaller European nations were afraid that this mandate could be turned by the great powers, in connection with arbitration, into a new form of intervention; M. Bourgeois made the following eloquent answer:

"International institutions like this court will safeguard the weak as against the strong. In the conflicts of force, when it is a question of mobilizing soldiers and armaments, some nations may be large and some small, some powerful and some weak. When it is a question of throwing the sword into the scales of the balance, one may be heavier and the other lighter. But when it is ideas and rights that are being cast into the balance, the inequality ends, and the rights of the smallest and weakest weigh as much as the rights of the largest and most powerful. This is the feeling on which our work has been based; it was of the weak that we were thinking when we carried it out. May they be able to understand our motives, and to realize our hopes by joining in this effort to make justice more and more the ruling power over the future of humanity."

56. The great powers also made difficulties, and raised objections that could not be answered in the same terms. Dr. Zorn, one of the representatives of Germany, suggested that the whole project was premature, and that its consideration would take the Conference too far away from the work it had begun; he also made formal reservations against the immediate organization of the court. He was not convinced by Asser's proof that arbitration had been used successfully for centuries, nor by Count Nigra's assertion that the entire world wanted to see the court established and would hold the conference responsible if it did not create it, nor by Odier's summary of the universal and unmistakable desire for a court. The Austro-Hungarian delegate, M. Lammasch, came to his support; and the result was that the British plan was adopted as the basis for the Committee's deliberations.

57. Thus the aspiration for permanent and compulsory justice did not survive the First Hague Conference, except in the following phrases in the preamble of the convention for the pacific settlement of international disputes, signed on July 29, 1899:

"The permanent institution of a Court of Arbitration, accessible to all, in the midst of the independent powers, will contribute effectively to this result" (*i.e.* to extend the empire of law and to strengthen the appreciation of international justice).

The convention says, platonically, in Article 19, that the powers reserve to themselves the right to conclude new agreements, general or private, with a view to extending obligatory arbitration to all cases which they may consider it possible to submit to it. And what they gave the name of "The Permanent Court of Arbitration" to, the provisions for which are given in Chapter II of this convention, has never been anything more than a list of candidates for the judicial function, from which nations in a dispute may choose the particular ones they need for each case, by means of a special agreement *(compromis)*.

In spite of its defects, and although it covered so little ground, this convention aroused illusions and hopes all over the world. It at least made the peoples of the world familiar with the name—if not with the reality—of a permanent court; in this sense it made a definite contribution to the desire, and even to the possibility, that the reality would overtake the name and that the court would come to deserve its title. It also did obviously encourage the use of arbitration, by the moral and material facilities it provided for carrying it out; and the rules of procedure contained in it are useful and practical, and will be serviceable for a long time. It also encouraged national and international peace societies to persevere and to redouble their efforts for the triumph of the cause. It was a beacon on the road that was to lead to the situation existing today; and it deserves an honorable place on what may be called the family tree of the Permanent Court of International Justice.

58. Thanks to the initiative of the United States and Russia, the Second Hague Conference met in 1907; it was more significant than the First Conference, because nearly all the nations in the world were represented, and because its program was much more extensive, including the entire law of war. As to the particular subject, however, that is of interest for this book, the Russian circular of 1906, calling the Conference, did not seem to consider it of any special importance or interest. "Improvements need to be' made," it said, "in the convention for the pacific settlement of international disputes. As the result of recent arbitrations, the jurists on the tribunals have raised certain questions of detail for which provision should be made by the necessary development of the convention. It would seem especially desirable that fixed rules be laid down as to the languages to be used in the proceedings, in view of the difficulties that may arise in the future when cases are brought more frequently before its arbitral jurisdiction."

These anæmic aspirations were not made any more robust by the reference to the subject made by the chief Russian delegate in the opening session.

59. Luckily the instructions to the delegates of the United States, signed by Mr. Elihu Root, then Secretary of State, went farther, in the letter and the spirit. He first observed that two general lines of advance in the field of arbitration were clearly indicated, one providing for obligatory arbitration as broad in scope as then seemed practicable, and the other increasing the effectiveness of the system so that nations would be more ready to have recourse to it voluntarily. The delegates were instructed to try to bring about the development of the existing court into a permanent tribunal composed of judges who were judicial officers and nothing else, who were paid adequate salaries, who had no other occupation, and who were to devote their entire time to the trial and decision of international causes. The judges were to be so chosen from different nations that the different systems of law and procedure and the principal languages would be represented. The court should have such dignity, consideration and rank that the best and ablest jurists would accept appointment to it, and that the whole world would have absolute confidence in its judgments. Here at last a new road was opened; and the deliberations on the question of an international court entered on a new and extremely important phase.

60. The Second Conference tried to improve in two ways on the work done in 1899. The first was that it wanted to change voluntary arbitration into compulsory arbitration, thus making judicial settlement inevitable and unescapable for certain kinds of international disputes. The second consisted of substituting for the existing list of arbitrators a veritable court, always ready to carry out its functions, and equipped with everything necessary for its work. These two reforms, which really complete and develop each other, were discussed and voted on, and in the end had much the same fate. The method used at the conference, of considering them one by one, will be followed here, taking compulsory obligation first.

61. As in 1899, Germany was the principal enemy of compulsory arbitration in 1907. The German Empire had somewhat modified its position, however; it no longer directly opposed this relative form of international justice, but confined its objection now to the establishment of it by means of a joint treaty; the result was the same, but the choice of means used showed that Germany had come to recognize the force of public opinion on the subject. The principle had won; but the battle was still going on over matters of procedure. It was all in vain that Mr. Choate pointed out, with great sense, that he could not understand the legal reasoning by which it was possible for nations to make arbitration agreements with each other, two by two, but impossible to do it when they were all together in a Conference. It is always easier to fight against a sincere belief than against a pretext used to hide the fact that there is no reason for refusing.

By a vote of 35 to 5, with 4 not voting, the First Committee adopted the following Article:

"Differences of a legal nature, and particularly those relating to the interpretation of treaties between two or more of the contracting powers which may arise hereafter and which have not been adjusted by diplomatic means, shall be submitted to arbitration, provided they do not affect the vital interests, independence or honor of one or more of the contracting states, and do not affect the interests of other states not parties to the litigation."

62. In a subcommittee that considered this point, the North American and the English delegations maintained that some of the disputes included in the provisions of this Article might well be submitted either to compulsory arbitration or to judicial settlement, without the stipulated reservations. Various propositions were made by the United States of America, Great Britain, Portugal, Serbia, Sweden and Switzerland. The vote of the eighteen nations represented on this subcommittee on each of these propositions is given—*i.e.,* on the proposal that the nations should agree that questions arising under treaties on the subjects listed below should be submitted, without the above reservations, to arbitral or judicial settlement:

(a) Free reciprocal aid to indigent sick persons: 12 to 4, the four being Austria, Belgium, Germany and Greece; with two abstentions, Russia and Switzerland.

(b) International protection for workingmen: same vote as above.

(c) Means of preventing collisions at sea: same as above.

(d) Weights and measures: same as above.

(e) Gauging of ships: same as above.

(f) Wages and estates of deceased sailors: same as above.

(g) Governmental claims for pecuniary damages, when liability is admitted by the parties concerned: 12 to 5, Russia joining the majority and Brazil the minority, and Switzerland abstaining.

(h) Protection of literary and artistic works: 10 to 4, the negative votes the same as in (a), but with Italy and Sweden joining those that abstained from voting.

(i) Regulation of commercial and industrial associations: 9 to 5, the Argentine joining the minority, and 4 abstentions, Brazil, Italy, Mexico and Switzerland.

(j) Pecuniary claims from military operations, civil war, the arrest of aliens and the seizure of their goods: 9 to 5, with 4 abstentions, Brazil, Russia, Sweden, and the United States of America.

(k) Sanitary regulations: 9 to 6, the 6 being the Argentine, Austria-Hungary, Belgium, Germany, Greece, and Italy, with 3 abstentions, Great Britain, Russia and Switzerland.

(l) Equality of treatment of nationals and aliens, in taxation and imposts: same vote as on (k), except that Brazil voted against and Italy for, and that the United States abstained and Great Britain voted.

(m) Customs tariffs: same vote as for (l).

(n) Regulation of epizootics, phyloxera and similar plagues: 9 to 7, with two abstentions, Mexico and Russia.

(o) Monetary systems: 8 to 3, with 2 abstentions.

(p) Acquisition and ownership of property by aliens: same vote as in (o).

(q) Civil and commercial procedure: 8 to 5, with 5 abstentions.

(r) The application or interpretation of treaties of any nature, as to pecuniary claims arising under them: 8 to 6, with 4 abstentions.

(s) Repatriation: same vote as in (r).

(t) Postal, telegraph and telephone regulations: 8 to 5, with 5 abstentions.

(u) Dues levied on ships, for wharfage, lighthouse service, pilotage, salvage dues, in case of damage or shipwreck: 7 to 7, with 4 abstentions.

(v) Private international law: same vote as in (u).

Two things attract attention at once; one is that already the number of international questions which some of the nations believe should be normally and continuously adjusted by judicial methods is extraordinarily large. The other is that the objection or the fear of such a method of solution was so strong that even in the simplest and easiest subjects there was always some nation that voted no or that did not vote.

63. The subcommittee reported to the Committee only the eight conventions that had received a majority vote —listed above from (a) to (h). When they were voted on by the Committee, 35 nations voted for them and 8 against. The 35 were the United States of America, the Argentine Republic, Bolivia, Brazil, Chile, China, Colombia, Cuba, Denmark, the Dominican Republic, Ecuador, Spain, France, Great Britain, Guatemala, Haiti, Mexico, Nicaragua, Norway, Panama, Paraguay, The Netherlands, Peru, Persia, Portugal, Russia, Salvador, Serbia, Sweden, Uruguay and Venezuela.

The 8 voting against them were Germany, Austro-Hungary, Belgium, Bulgaria, Greece, Rumania, Switzerland and Turkey. Five nations did not vote—Italy, Japan, Luxemburg, Montenegro and Siam.

It is interesting to analyze this vote from a geographical point of view. Ten European nations voted for it, eight against it, and three did not vote; and this minority of ten, it should be remembered, was arguing merely for compulsory arbitration within rather narrow limits. The Asiatic vote was equally divided, two favorable and two not voting. The whole American hemisphere, from north to south, without a single exception, supported resolutely and decisively the principle of compulsory judicial settlement. As the author of this book has pointed out elsewhere,[1] America remembered that it had made a practice of arbitration during the nineteenth century on a far more extensive scale than the other continents, and that one of the greatest successes ever obtained in arbitration—the Alabama affair, justly commemorated by a marble tablet in the Municipal Building of Geneva—was a part of the history of the New World.

64. The minority made such obstinate resistance to allowing compulsory arbitration to figure in the resolutions or even to be mentioned in the Final Act, that Count Tornielli, one of the Italian delegates, proposed a soothing resolution that was unanimously adopted at the October 16 meeting, with three not voting. It read as follows:

"The Conference, actuated by the spirit of mutual agreement and concession characterizing its deliberations, has agreed upon the following Declaration, which, while reserving to each of the Powers represented full liberty of action as regards voting, enables them to affirm the principles which they regard as unanimously admitted:—

"It is unanimous

1. In admitting the principle of compulsory arbitration.
2. In declaring that certain disputes, in particular those relating to the interpretation and application of the provisions of international agreements, may be submitted to compulsory arbitration without any restriction."

This was little enough; but even this would have been utterly impossible at the First Hague Conference. In 1907 the delegates could discuss and adopt proposals that no one had even dared to propose in 1899. National governments, spurred on by the force of public opinion, decided to make

[1] de Bustamante.—The Permanent Court of International Justice: Conference at the Academy of International Law at the Hague, August 1, 1923.

use of the new impulse, and began to drown it out with formulas and phrases. It naturally seemed to the public that the time was approaching when the governments would yield obedience to it,—in spite of the fact that the principle of compulsory arbitration had not advanced a single step at the Second Hague Conference.

65. The other direction in which, as has been pointed out, the Second Conference desired to complete and develop the initial work of the First, by establishing a genuine Permanent Court of Arbitration, took concrete form in two plans, one proposed by Russia and the other by the United States of America. The Russian plan was extremely modest and timid; it was based on the proposal that the tribunal then in existence, i. e., the candidates for the judicial functions on The Hague list, should meet once a year at The Hague to elect by secret ballot three persons from that list who should hold themselves ready during the ensuing year to meet at any time as the Permanent Court.

66. The plan submitted by the United States was much more detailed and complete. James Brown Scott, one of the American experts, took an active part in its preparation and discussion. The plan had six articles, as follows:

"I. A permanent court of arbitration shall be established, composed of fifteen judges of the highest moral consideration and of recognized competence in international law; they and their successors shall be chosen in the manner determined by this Conference, but they shall be so chosen in the different countries that the different systems of law and procedure and the principal languages shall be properly represented in the personnnel of the Court; they shall be appointed for.... years, or until their successors have been appointed and have accepted.

"II. The Permanent Court shall convene annually at The Hague on a specified date and shall remain in session as long as may be necessary; it shall choose its own officers, and, except as otherwise provided in the Statute, shall establish its own rules of procedure; every decision shall be made by a majority vote, and nine members shall constitute a quorum. The judges will be of equal rank, shall enjoy diplomatic immunity, and shall receive a salary that will permit them to devote themselves to the consideration of the cases that are brought before them.

"III. In no case (unless the parties thereto expressly consent) may a judge take part in the consideration or decision of a case before the Court in which his own state is a party.

"IV. The Permanent Court shall have jurisdiction to hear and determine all cases involving disputes of an international character between sovereign states that it has not been possible to settle by diplomatic means, which are submitted to it according to an agreement between the parties, either at their origin or for revision or appeal, or to determine relative rights, duties or obligations following upon judgments, decisions or sentences of commissions of inquiry or of special arbitral tribunals.

"V. The judges of the Permanent Court shall be competent to act as judges on any commission of inquiry or special arbitral tribunal that may be formed by any power for the consideration of any subject that may be specially referred to it and that is to be determined by it.

"VI. The present Permanent Court of Arbitration shall, as far as possible, constitute the basis of the Court, regard being had to the representation upon it of the powers that recently adhered to the convention of 1899."

67. It is impossible for a nation to agree to submit its causes to a Court the composition of which has not been determined. International justice is greatly to be desired, but it must be justice, not a caricature of it, and not a masquerade. This was the reason why several nations, officially or privately, went on record as being against the Court until some method for electing the judges had been adopted that recognized the fundamental legal equality of nations and that could not be converted into a new and secret tool for political domination. This was the motive

that prompted certain publicists to oppose the proposal
to organize the Court in the manner suggested at the Second
Hague Conference; these writers were not opposed to the
establishment of a court, as M. Hans Wehberg has wrongly
stated.[1]

According to this proposal, the number of judges was to
be based on the population of the world; there was to be
one judge for a certain number of inhabitants. The nations
in which the population was greater than this number were
to have only the one judge, but the states whose population
was smaller than the number were to be grouped together
to name a judge. To put it more crudely, all the great
powers were to be represented separately, and the
small powers only collectively. The writer of this book
can only repeat today what he wrote about this point
sixteen years ago, after having thought about all these
years.

Taking the population of the world as the basis for electing the members of a court of justice would obviously result
in grave errors, legal and material. The population of the
international community is the number of the states that
compose it; at the time of the Second Hague Conference,
it consisted of 44 or 45 nations. To try to divide up a state
into its component elements and to give to one of these
elements, population or territory—and even commerce was
suggested—separate functions, and an international representation, is equivalent to introducing a new element, utterly
foreign to the situation, which would inevitably lead to
equivocal decisions.

If a permanent and individual judge were given to one
nation with extensive territory, numerous inhabitants, or
extensive commercial relations, while two, four, six or even
eight other nations were grouped together to name one
judge, a most evident inequality would be established.
Moreover, it would be practically impossible for these joint
electors to agree. Suppose neighboring states were grouped
together, or those using the same language, or those having

---

[1] Hans Wehberg—The Problem of an International Court of Justice,
Translated by C. G. Fenwick, Oxford, 1918, p. 241.

similar legal systems, or the same religion, or well developed relations: it is precisely these nations that are arrayed
against each other on political, legal and economic questions; these are the very states that would most frequently
have questions to be arbitrated between themselves, and
therefore the election of one joint judge might well be a
new source of discord.   States might even go to war over
the election of a judge for a court of peace.

A very curious argument was put forward, based on the
extent of the material interests of a nation, the theory being
that the use of the new court would be in proportion to
these material interests.   If any one were to propose, in any
given nation where social classes are well differentiated,
that the control of the nomination of all the judges of the
national courts, or the direct appointment of a majority
of them, should be given to the class or classes that would
bring the most law suits, no one would take the suggestion
seriously.   Imagine a country where the millionaires, on
account of the land they own, or their industries, or the
extent of their commerce, could tell the rest of the inhabitants that they would appoint two-thirds of the judges of
the Supreme Court, and that their possible adversaries
might name the other third!

68. This proposal was abandoned very quickly; another
proposition was substituted for it which really was worse.
A twelve year term was taken, as a base; eight nations were
each to have a permanent judge, for the entire term; these
nations were Austria-Hungary, France, Germany, Great
Britain, Italy, Japan, Russia, and the United States.   For
all the other nations a varying system of rotation was proposed.   Three other states, different in history, population,
territory and commerce, namely, The Netherlands, Spain
and Turkey, were to have a judge for ten years out of the
twelve; so that these three would have the same continuity
n judicial functions as the eight great powers, Spain was
not to have any judge the fourth year and the tenth; the
Netherlands and Turkey were not to have any in the sixth
vear and the twelfth.   Thirteen other states would have

a judge only four years out of the twelve; four others, Belgium, Persia, Serbia and Siam, were to have them only two years out of the twelve; and the remaining eighteen nations, sixteen of which were American republics, were to have a judge only one year out of the twelve.

M. Ruy Barbosa, speaking for the Brazilian delegates in the subcommittee, opposed this plan with great firmness and determination; most of the delegates of the American nations supported him, and several European nations. He presented the reasons for his position in a notable document quoted here in full:

"Whereas to begin by fixing an arbitrary number for the judges of the Permanent Court of Arbitration according to *a priori* idea of the number there should be, and then to try to make the representation of all the nations fit into that number, is to reverse the necessary and inevitable terms of the problem;

"Whereas this inversion of terms is all the more unjustifiable because the number of states to be represented on the Court is perfectly well known, and a smaller number of judges than of states has been adopted;

"Whereas inverting the inalterable terms of the problem in this fashion is to arrogate into oneself the right to assign to the various states unequal representation in this International Court;

"Whereas in the convention for the pacific settlement of international disputes adopted at The Hague on July 29, 1899, the signatory powers, among which were all the nations of Europe and the United States, Mexico, China and Japan, admitted that each one of the contracting states, without regard to their importance, was to have equal representation on the Permanent Court of Arbitration;

"Whereas they adopted this basis of representation, not as a voluntary act of grace, but in admission of a principle that could not be evaded in the formation of an international body set up for the purpose of adjudicating differences between independent sovereign states;

"Whereas the obligation to respect this principle, inevitable in any organization of this kind, becomes all the more imperative when the organization to be formed is the definitive institution in which nations are to place their supreme trust for the judicial settlement of their disputes;

"Whereas, therefore, it is impossible to depart in the proposed Court from the principle of the equality of all the signatory states, which can be recognized only by granting to each state the right of complete and permanent representation;

"Whereas no government could, even if it would, renounce this right, which involves the sovereignty and consequently the independence of states in their mutual relations;

"Whereas this principle is not observed if the member of the Court that each nation is allowed to name may sit for only a certain number of years, different terms to be allotted to the different states according to their importance, which has no relation whatever to the subject, and which, clearly partial to certain European states, does not correspond to the obvious realities;

"Whereas it is sheer sophistry to pretend that the equality of states as sovereign units of public international law, can be satisfied in this manner, and that this sovereign right is not impaired by being submitted to simple conditions under which it may be exercised;

"Whereas it cannot be said that a right equal in all who possess it is merely being submitted to simple conditions for its exercise when some of those who possess it are to be limited to periods more or less limited, while others are to have the privilege of exercising it continually;

"Whereas, therefore, it is necessary to retain in the proposed Court the same principle of continual equality in the representation of nations that was pledged in the convention of 1899;

"Whereas when the nations excluded from the First Hague Conference were invited to the Second Conference, it was not for the purpose of obtaining their solemn signatures to an act of diminution of their sovereignty, in reducing it according to a scale of classification which the more powerful nations would like to establish;

"Whereas the cause of peace would not be advanced by creating between the nations, by means of binding stipulations, categories of sovereignty, humiliating some for the benefit of others, and undermining the foundations of all by proclaiming, by a curious fallacy, the legal superiority of force over right;

"Whereas if the intention is to base the new Court on such foundations, it would be better not to create it at all, particularly since the nations may have recourse to the existing Court for the pacific settlement of international disputes, and also possess the right, which this Conference has admitted and which it cannot deny to them, to have recourse freely to other forms of arbitration;

"Whereas, once this is admitted, there is no advantage in having two Courts, one beside the other, both considered permanent;

"Whereas if the chief fault of the existing Court is that it is not really permanent, it would be much more practical and efficient to make it permanent, by remedying this easily correctible defect, than to undertake this duplication of the arbitral Court;

"Whereas it would not be impossible to reach the desired end, using the elements of the existing Court, but changing the Court so as to give it a different substance and genuine permanence;

"Whereas it is in no sense essential, to make the existing Court permanent, that all its members should live at its seat, because a minimum quorum could be established for the full sessions, consisting, for ex-

ample, of one quarter of its members, stipulating that
this many of its members, by turn, should live in some
part of Europe from which they could reach The
Hague within twenty-four hours after being summoned;

"Whereas on this basis the number of judges could
be set at fifteen, or even less, which would be better,
if the total number of judges was less than the number of signatory states;

"Whereas, in accordance with the rules established
by the First Hague Conference, it should be admitted
that signatory powers have the right to agree on the
joint designation of one or more judges, and it should
also be admitted that a judge already named by one
nation may be adopted by others;

"Whereas, since the right to name judges is optional,
like all other rights, some nations will probably refrain from exercising it, and since, moreover, in order
to exercise it, a nation must guarantee to discharge
its duty of paying the salary of the judges it names;

"Whereas for this reason it may be possible to set
an even smaller number for the full sessions of the
Court than would result from the combination proposed in the Anglo-German-American plan;

"Whereas the Court would function more easily and
speedily, and with greater stability and increased capacity, with this reduction in the minimum quorum, because of the irritating tendency the members of large
judicial bodies show to depend on each other to do the
work, which in the end reduces to a very small minority those who actually work, study, and do their
duty by the cases;

"Whereas furthermore even this quorum would not
have to act except in certain cases, when the parties
request it, or when certain difficulties had to be solved,
because the very essence of arbitration, which must be
safeguarded, is that the parties to the litigation must
be assured of their right to choose from among the
members of the Court the judge or the judges to

whom they are willing to submit the settlement of their disputes:

"The delegation of Brazil, acting under specific instructions from its government, therefore cannot possibly agree to the proposition under discussion, and takes the liberty of suggesting the following principles as the foundation on which a new proposal may be built:

"1. The new Permanent Court of Arbitration shall be composed as follows:

"Each power shall designate, in accordance with the conditions stipulated in the 1899 convention, one person capable of discharging the functions of arbitrator, as a member of this institution.

"Each power shall also have the right to appoint one substitute.

"Two or more powers may agree to designate jointly their representatives in the Court.

"The same person may be named by different powers.

"The signatory powers shall, so far as possible, choose their representatives in the new Court from those in the present Court.

"II. The present Court shall go out of existence as soon as the new Court is established.

"III. The persons appointed shall serve for nine years, during which term they may not be removed except in cases where, in accordance with the laws of their country, judges with life tenure lose their office.

"IV. No power may exercise its right of nomination without engaging itself to pay the salary of the judge it wishes to appoint, and without depositing that amount each year in advance, in accordance with regulations to be drawn up by the convention.

"V. In order that the Court may sit in full session, the presence of at least one-fourth of the members named is necessary.

"In order to ensure that the requisite number is present, the members shall be divided into three groups, according to the alphabetical order of the signatory states.

"The judges in each of these groups will sit by terms for three years, during which time they will be required to live in a place from which they could reach The Hague in twenty-four hours after the first telegraphic notice is sent out.

"All the members of the Court shall have the right to sit at all sessions of the full Court, if they desire, even though they do not belong to the group specially called for that period.

"VI. The parties to a dispute are free to choose whether they will submit the controversy to the full Court or will choose from the members of the Court as many judges as they may agree upon.

"VII. The Court shall meet in full session whenever it is called upon to decide a dispute the settlement of which has been referred to it by the parties, or in cases submitted by the parties to a smaller number of arbitrators when the latter appeal to the full Court for a decision on a question that has arisen during the proceedings in the case.

"VIII. In order to complete the organization of the Court on these basic principles, any suitable provisions of the Anglo-German-American project that are not inconsistent with these principles may be adopted."

The destructive effect of this document was immediate and surprising. The scheme of rotating the judges, by which some nations would have had a judge for only eight years in an entire century, while others would have had one for the whole hundred years, was abandoned by its defenders. The subcommittee to which it had been referred, composed of eight powers, seven of whom would have had permanent judges and one a temporary one, gave it the *coup de grâce*. Their action did honor to justice.

The constructive part of the plan proposed by the distinguished Brazilian, who was elected not long after as one of the first members of the Permanent Court of International Justice, was less effective; but three other suggestions were made, that came rather close to his idea and in part followed it.

69. One of these three suggestions was to the effect that the members of the 1899 Court should choose from their number fifteen or seventeen judges to organize the new Court. Some one objected on the ground that as these electors were not experienced jurists, they would not be qualified to execute this trust; for this reason, among others, the subcommittee did not adopt this proposal.

At this point an attempt was made to combine the two principles, of nomination and election, and the possibility was discussed of having each government nominate four candidates, from whom the members of the existing Court should elect the judges of the new Court. This combination had as little luck as the previous proposal, and the question came back unsolved to the committee d'examen. This proposal, in a different form, came to the surface again later on.

70. The United States delegation, making every possible effort to induce the Conference to take one forward step, then presented a new proposition:

"I. Each signatory power shall have the right to designate one judge and one substitute judge, qualified and willing to accept the posts, and shall send their names to an international bureau.

"II. The bureau shall make an alphabetical list of all nominations for judge and for substitute judge, stating the nation that nominated them, and shall send the list to all the signatory powers.

"III. Each signatory power shall notify the bureau which of the judges and substitutes it chooses, voting for fifteen judges and substitutes at the same time.

"IV. When the bureau has received the lists of persons chosen, it shall ascertain the fifteen persons that have received the greatest number of votes.

"V. In case of a tie vote, involving the reëlection of the fifteen judges and the fifteen substitutes, the choice between them shall be made, by lot, by the bureau.

"VI. A vacancy in the post of judge or substitute judge

shall be filled by the nation that nominated the person whose seat has become vacant."

Five nations voted in the committee meeting for this proposal, and nine against it. It was lost by a majority that almost amounted to two-thirds.

71. Under these conditions, all that the Conference could do was to adopt a resolution recommending that the powers adopt the plan of establishing a Permanent Court of Arbitral Justice, and that they add to it as soon as possible a convention containing its statute and providing a method of electing the judges.

There certainly was nothing very significant about this resolution, and yet six nations would not vote on it; they were Belgium, Denmark, Greece, Rumania, Sweden and Uruguay. Fifteen nations made specific reservations as to the method of electing the judges, insisting upon the principle of the legal equality of nations. These states, whose action should never be forgotten, were Bolivia, Brazil, China, Colombia, the Dominican Republic, Ecuador, Guatemala, Haiti, Mexico, Nicaragua, Panama, Paraguay, Persia, Salvador and Venezuela.

72. The draft for the organization of the Court on which this vote was taken contains two relatively important articles, one on the composition of the Court, and the other on its jurisdiction and procedure.

According to the first of these two articles, the creation of the New Court was not to involve the suppression of the existing Court; its principal purpose was to provide a Court of free and easy access, composed of judges representing the various juridical systems of the world, and capable of ensuring continuity in jurisprudence. It was to be composed of judges and deputy judges, chosen from persons of the highest moral reputation, and fulfilling conditions qualifying them, in their respective countries, to occupy high legal posts, or else jurists of recognized competence in international law. They were to be appointed, as far as possible, from the members of the Permanent Court of Arbitration, for a period of twelve years, which might be renewed. In the exercise of their functions outside of their own country they were to enjoy diplomatic privileges and immunities.

Each year the Court was to nominate three judges, to form a special delegation, and three more to replace them, should necessity arise. A member of the delegation might not exercise his duties when the power which appointed him, or of which he was a national, was one of the parties. The members of the delegation were to conclude all matters submitted to them, even if the period for which they have been appointed judges had expired.

A judge might not exercise his judicial functions in any case in which he had acted, in any way whatever, in the decision of a national tribunal, a tribunal of arbitration, or a commission of inquiry, or if he had figured in the suit as counsel or advocate for one of the parties. A judge might not act as agent or advocate before the tribunals or commissions, nor act for one of the parties in any capacity whatsoever so long as his appointment lasted.

The judges were to receive an annual salary of 6,000 Dutch florins, payable semi-annually. In the exercise of their duties and in certain special cases, they were to receive in addition 100 florins per day. They were also entitled to receive a traveling allowance, fixed in accordance with the regulations existing in their own country. They might not accept from their own government or from that of any other power remuneration for services connected with their duties as members of the Court.

The Court was to have its seat at The Hague, and could not change it except when absolutely obliged by circumstances (force majeure). The delegation, with the assent of the parties, might choose another site for its meetings, if special circumstances rendered it necessary. The Court was to meet in session once a year, beginning on the third Wednesday of June and lasting till all the business on the calendar had been transacted. This session was not to take place if the delegation considered the meeting unnecessary; but a power that was a party to a case actually pending before the Court in which the pleadings were closed or were about to be closed might insist that the session be held.   When necessary, the delegation might summon the Court in extraordinary session.

As to the Court's competence: it was provided that it should be competent to deal with all cases submitted to it, in virtue either of a general undertaking to have recourse to arbitration, or of a special agreement. The delegation, on its part, was to be competent:

1.   To decide the arbitrations referred to in the preceding paragraph, if the parties were agreed that the summary procedure laid down in Part IV, Chapter IV of the convention for the pacific settlement of international disputes was to be followed;

2.   To hold an inquiry in accordance with Part III of the same convention, if the parties by an agreement submitted it to the delegation;

3.   To settle the *compromis* (special agreement) referred to in Article 52 of the same convention, if the parties agreed to leave it to the Court;

4.   To settle the *compromis* in disputes covered by a general treaty of arbitration concluded or renewed after the convention now under discussion went into force, providing for a *compromis* in all disputes and not expressly or by implication excluding the settlement of the *compromis* from the competence of the delegation.   Recourse could not, however, be had to the Court if the other party declared that in its opinion the dispute did not belong to the category of questions to be submitted to compulsory arbitration, unless the treaty of arbitration conferred on the Court the power to decide this preliminary question; and

5.   To settle the *compromis* in disputes arising from contract debts claimed from one power by another power as due to its nationals, and for the settlement of which the offer of arbitration has been accepted.   This arrangement was not applicable if acceptance were subject to the condition that the *compromis* was to be settled in some other way.

Only the contracting powers might have access to the Court. The Court was to decide what its usual language was to be and what languages might be used before it; its decisions were to be considered in private, and the reasons on which they were based must be given; the names of the judges taking part must be given. Each party was to pay its own costs and a share of the costs of the trial, unless costs were awarded against one party. The general expenses of the Court were to be borne by the contracting powers.

The convention was to be in force for twelve years, and was to be tacitly renewed for periods of twelve years, unless denounced.

The above statement of the principal proposals of this plan, with some details, is given here, in order to indicate the intentions and tendencies of the world on this subject during the 1907 Conference, and also that they may be kept in mind as a precedent and subject of comparison with the Statute in force today. When the present Statute is studied in detail, farther on in this book, the analogies and differences between the two will be referred to.

73. Except for making certain useful practical changes in the 1899 Court, and other improvements in matters of detail, no immediate and apparent progress was made at the 1907 Conference with relation to the creation of a Permanent Court. There was a manifest desire to transform optional arbitration into compulsory arbitration, in as many classes of disputes as possible, and to endow the world with an institution that would always be ready to investigate and adjust international differences; but neither of these desires was realized.

It must be admitted, however, that great progress was made toward the achievement of these aims. The day was past when a Permanent Court was of interest only to isolated writers, living at different times and in different lands, sometimes read and sometimes forgotten, dreaming, in their libraries or in their more or less official positions, of helping to make the world's future brighter by their proposals.

It was no longer a question of the more or less spectacular and transcendental associations and peace congresses with no responsibility and without the connections necessary for carrying out their resolutions. Now it was the nations themselves, acting through their diplomatic representatives and meeting in a sort of universal parliament, that had brought the question up for discussion, that had considered it and had voted on it, and, in the very midst of their conflict of opinions as to how it should be organized, had gone on record as being convinced that the time for solving this question had come.

It was no longer theories, but realities, that were being discussed; an important group of nations, significant both for their number and for the future they possessed, had registered their votes and the forces they controlled for the realization of this principle. Public opinion had won the first battle, and would continue to wage war until the final triumph. On the fundamental consideration that there should be a court, all the nations were in accord, and it was becoming more and more possible to get them on to common ground for the realization of the plan.

74. While the Conference was in session, a North American philanthropist, Andrew Carnegie, was passing through The Hague; he gave a large sum for the construction of the Palace of Peace.

The 1899 Court of Arbitration was to have its seat in this building, and when it was finally established the Court of Justice was to sit there too. Thus a shelter and a roof were provided for it before it was born. One of its practical needs was met in advance. International justice owes to Mr. Carnegie a debt it never can pay.

CHAPTER V

THE CENTRAL AMERICAN COURT OF JUSTICE

75. On December 20, 1907, two months after the Second Hague Conference had ended its work, five American republics, Costa Rica, Guatemala, Honduras, Nicaragua and Salvador, signed a special convention establishing a Court of Justice, for the purpose of efficaciously guaranteeing their rights and maintaining peace and harmony unalterably in their relations.

They called it the Central American Court of Justice; and they gave it the following jurisdiction: over (a) all controversies or questions which might arise among them, of whatsoever nature and no matter what their origin might be, in case their respective Departments of Foreign Affairs had not been able to reach an understanding; (b) the questions which individuals of one Central American country might raise against any of the other contracting governments, because of the violation of treaties or conventions, and other cases of an international character, no matter whether their own government supported their claim or not, provided, however, that the remedies which the laws of the respective country afforded for such a violation had been exhausted or that a denial of justice had been shown; (c) cases between two or more governments or between one government and one individual, when submitted by a common accord; and (d) international questions which any one of the five governments and a foreign government might submit to it by a special agreement.

By an annexed article, included in the treaty so that the legislatures of the five nations might include it in their ratification if they desired, the Court's jurisdiction was amplified so as to include conflicts that might arise between the legislative, executive and judicial powers, and when as a matter of fact the judicial decisions and the resolutions of a national congress were not respected.

The Court was to sit in Cartago, in the republic of Costa Rica, but it might temporarily transfer its seat to another point in Central America when it deemed it expedient for reasons of health, or in order to ensure the exercise of its functions or the personal safety of its members.

It was to consist of five justices, one appointed by each republic, and selected from among the jurists who possessed the qualifications which the laws of each country prescribed for the exercise of high judicial office, and who enjoyed the highest consideration both because of their moral character and their professional ability.   The five judges were MM. José Artúa Aguilar, for Costa Rica; Angel Maria Boca-negra, for Guatemala; Alberto Uclés, for Honduras; José Madriz, for Nicaragua; and Salvador Gallegos, for Salvador.

Vacancies were to be filled by substitute justices, named at the same time and in the same manner as the regular justices, and possessing the same qualifications.   The legislative power of each of the contracting nations was to appoint one regular and two substitute justices.   The attendance of the five justices was declared indispensable to constitute a legal quorum for the decisions of the Court.

The salary of each justice was 8,000 pesos a year, in American gold, paid by the Treasury of the Court, except that the salary of the justice of the country where the Court had its seat was to be fixed by its government.   Each nation was also to contribute 2,000 pesos a year toward the ordinary and extraordinary expenses of the Court.   The contracting republics bound themselves to include their respective contributions in their budgets and to remit quarterly in advance to the Treasury of the Court the share they might have to bear of the cost of its services.

The regular and substitute justices were to be appointed for a term of five years, to be counted from the day on which they assumed the duties of their office.   They were eligible for re-election.   In case of death, resignation or permanent incapacity of any of them, the vacancy so caused was to be filled by the respective legislature, and the judge so appointed was to complete his predecessor's term.

As long as they remained in the country of their appointment, the regular and substitute justices were to enjoy the personal immunity which its laws granted to the magistrates of its Supreme Court of Justice, and in the other contracting republics they were to have the privileges and immunities of diplomatic agents. The office of justice was declared incompatible with the exercise of a profession and with the holding of public office.

Article 13 declared that the Central American Court of Justice represented the national conscience of Central America, and that therefore the justices who compose the tribunal were not to consider themselves barred from the discharge of their duties because of the interest which the republics to which they owed their appointment might have in any case or question. As to allegations of disqualification for personal interest, the rules of procedure which the Court would adopt would make proper provisions.

At its first annual session the Court was to elect a President and a Vice-President from among its members, and was to organize the personnel of its office by designating a registrar, a treasurer and such other subordinate employees as it might deem necessary, and to draw up an estimate of its expenses.

When differences or questions subject to the jurisdiction of the tribunal arose, the interested party was to present a complaint comprising all the points of fact and of law relative to the matter, and all pertinent evidence. The tribunal was to transmit a copy of the complaint without loss of time to the governments or individuals interested, asking them to furnish their replies and evidence within a designated term, which might in no case exceed sixty days from the date of notice of the complaint.

If the designated term expired without an answer to the complaint having been received, the Court was to require the defendant or defendants to reply within a further term of not over twenty days; if that term expired without a reply having been received, the Court, in view of the evidence presented, and of such evidence as it might have seen fit to obtain, was to render its decision, which was to be final.

If the defendant government or individuals appeared before the Court within the time set, and presented their replies and evidence, the Court was to decide the matter within thirty days without further process or proceedings; if a new term for the presentation of evidence was requested, the Court was to decide whether or not it should be granted; if it decided to grant it, it must fix a reasonable time for it. After the end of this extension of time, the Court must give its final judgment within thirty days.

Each one of the governments or individuals directly concerned in the questions to be considered by the Court had the right to be represented before it by a trustworthy person or persons, who was to present evidence, formulate arguments, and do everything else beneficial, in their judgment, to the defense of the rights they represented, within the terms fixed by the treaty and the rulers of the Court. From the moment at which any suit was instituted against any one or more governments, up to the day of the final judgment, the Court might, at the request of any one of the parties, fix the situation in which the contending parties must remain, so that the difficulty should not be aggravated and matters might be kept in *statu quo* pending the final decision.

For all the effects of this treaty, the Central American Court of Justice was to address itself to the governments or tribunals of justice of the contracting states, through the Ministry of Foreign Relations or the registrar of the Supreme Court of the respective country, according to the proceedings necessary to ensure the execution of the measures taken within the scope of their functions. The Court might also appoint special commissioners to carry out these formalities, calling on the local government for its coöperation and assistance to the commissioner in the discharge of his mission. The contracting governments bound themselves formally to obey and to enforce the orders of the

Court, by furnishing all the assistance that might be necessary for their most complete and expeditious execution.

In deciding points of fact that might be raised before it, the Court was to be governed by its free judgment; on points of law it was to be governed by the principles of international law. The Court was given power to determine its own competence in any case, by interpreting the appropriate treaties and conventions in force, and applying the principles of international law.

Every final or interlocutory judgment required the concurrence of at least three of the justices. In case of a disagreement, one of the substitute justices was to be chosen by lot; if a majority of three still was not reached, other justices were to be chosen in succession by lot until a majority of three for some decision was obtained. The judgments were to be in writing, and had to contain a statement of the reasons on which they were based. They were signed by all the justices, and countersigned by the registrar. At the request of any one of the parties, the Court would interpret the judgment.

The judgments of the Court were to be communicated to the governments of the contracting republics. The interested parties solemnly bound themselves to submit to the judgments, and all agreed to lend all moral support necessary for their proper fulfillment, thereby, as the treaty states, "constituting a real and positive guarantee of respect for this convention and for the Central American Court of Justice." The High Contracting Parties solemnly bound themselves that on no ground and in no case would they consider the treaty as void, and that they would therefore consider it as being always in force during a period of ten years counting from the last ratification. In case of a change or alteration in the political status of one or more of the contracting republics, the functions of the Court were to be suspended *ipso facto,* and a conference was to be convoked forthwith by the respective governments to adjust the constitution of the Court to the new order of things. In case the governments did not agree unanimously, the convention was to be considered rescinded.

76. This covenant deserves unqualified praise. It constitutes a victory for international law, won just after a similar project had been practically defeated by all the nations in the world. It is easy to see from reading it that the men that drafted it were wise, intelligent and practical, inspired with good will and of undeniable patriotism. It has its defects; later on, in speaking of the reasons why it was not renewed, these mistakes will appear, but most of them, perhaps, could not have been foretold, or else were accentuated by a change in history that it would have been difficult to foresee.

The Court was successfully established very soon after the convention was signed; the five republics that signed it ratified it with remarkable promptness, and on May 25, 1908, the Court was solemnly installed at Cartago, where Andrew Carnegie had had a palace built for its seat. This palace was destroyed soon afterward by an earthquake.

A brief statement is given below of the cases decided by this Court and of the general sentiment in which its work was carried on.

77. The first case of which the Court took cognizance, soon after its institution, was brought by the government of Honduras against Guatemala and Salvador. The complainant maintained that a revolution stirred up on its territory in July, 1908, by citizens of the other two republics had been fomented and encouraged by the two governments, and that at the very least they contributed to make it possible by not exercising the due diligence to which they were bound under a treaty between the nations. The decision, handed down on December 19, 1908, found the two defendant republics guiltless of the offenses charged, after an examination of the questions of law and fact involved in the matter; numerous scientific authorities were cited, including a resolution of the Institute of International Law. The decision was received with respect, and friendly relations were reëstablished between the contracting parties.

In the session of June 22, 1911, a debate arose, which cannot really be called a litigation, over the fact that Nica-

ragua had recalled one of its justices on the Court in order
to substitute another person; but the Court admitted that
its powers did not extend to judging the action of a government, even in reference to the actual membership of the
Court. It subsequently applied this standard of its
powers.

The five cases that followed were all brought by individuals against various governments, more or less at the
instigation of political groups or national interests. One
of these persons, Salvador Cerdá, brought an action against
the republic of Costa Rica for illegal detention; it was
decided, on October 14, 1911, that the Court did not have
authority to investigate the complaint under the conditions
in which it was presented. Another was an action brought
by Pedro Fornos Diaz against the government of the
republic of Guatemala for injuries to person and property
which he claimed had been caused by the arbitrary acts
of that government; the complaint was declared to be non-
receivable because the complainant had not first exhausted
all the legal remedies available to him in Guatemala; it
was held that no nation is under any international liability
toward a citizen of another state, so long as he has not
made use of all the means of defense possible under local
laws.

Somewhat later Felipe Molina Lavios, a citizen of Guatemala, brought suit against the government of Honduras
because he had been arrested there and then expelled from
the country. On December 10, 1913, the Court declared
that the demand was not receivable, because the Court had
no jurisdiction to take cognizance of it in the form in which
it had been presented. A citizen of Nicaragua, Alejandro
Bermúdez y Nuñez, also sued the government of Costa
Rica on the ground of expulsion. On April 7, 1914, the
Court held that this complaint was also non-receivable from
every point of view.

A number of citizens of Central America made a joint
demand upon the Court, in the proper form, asking it to
declare null and void a recent election by the constitutional
Congress of Costa Rica of M. Alfredo González Flores

as premier; he was afterward made the chief executive. In its decision of July 3, 1914, the Court declared that the complaint was non-receivable, because the persons who presented it were lacking in international juridical capacity and because the Court had no jurisdiction in matters of this kind.

A much more serious question, from an international point of view, came up some time afterward. It was caused by the Bryan-Chamorro treaty between the United States of America and Nicaragua; in it Nicaragua granted concessions to the United States for the construction of an interoceanic canal and for the establishment of a naval base in the Gulf of Fonseca, with long leases of two islands in the Atlantic Ocean called Great and Little Corn. This treaty gave rise to two suits. One was brought by Costa Rica, on March 24, 1916; Costa Rica stated that the Bryan-Chamorro treaty violated its rights which had been recognized in the Cañas-Jerez treaty of 1858, in the arbitral decision of President Cleveland in 1888, and in the general treaty of peace and amity between the Central American republics signed at Washington in 1907. The other suit was brought by the government of Salvador on August 28 of the same year; it maintained that the concession obtained from Nicaragua for a naval base in the Gulf of Fonseca was injurious to its vital interests, because it was a menace to its peace and safety, because it violated its rights as co-owner of the Gulf of Fonseca, and because it was opposed to Costa Rica's future aspirations as a Central American republic.

These two cases affected the interests of a third nation, not subject to the jurisdiction of the Court and not a party to the suits. So far as was possible, the Court avoided deciding anything that concerned this third party; aside from this, however, it upheld these two claims on September 30, 1916, and March 9, 1917. In the second decision the Court held, among other things, that the Bryan-Chamorra treaty, by the provision for the concession for a naval base on the Gulf of Fonseca, did menace the national security of Salvador and did violate its rights as co-proprietor of the Gulf, as well as its rights under Articles 2 and 11 of the treaty of peace and amity of Washington; it held that the government of Nicaragua was under obligations to use every means possible under international law to reëstablish and to maintain the legal situation existing between the republics before the Bryan-Chamorro treaty, so far as the matters in litigation were concerned. Nicaragua refused to comply with these two decisions, claiming that the Court did not have jurisdiction to render them.

78. The American Institute of International Law was in session at Havana from January 22 to January 27, 1917. The well known internationalist Luis Anderson, one of the founders of the Institute, was present; he represented Costa Rica in the negotiation of the 1907 treaty creating the Central American Court of Justice, giving his advice then on many important discussions and agreements. He and the learned Guatemalan publicist, Professor José Matos, proposed the following resolution, which summed up the legal opinion of the whole of America:

> "A vote of sympathy with the Central American Court of Justice, the first Permanent Court of arbitral justice, established by the convention signed in December 20, 1907, by the Republics of Costa Rica, Guatemala, Honduras, Nicaragua and Salvador, with the recommendation that it be continued, as it is a guarantee of peace between the republics of Central America."

The resolution was passed unanimously.

The recommendation in the last part of the resolution—and the most important part of it—which was inserted in the final act of the session, refers to the fact previously mentioned in this chapter: that the convention was made for ten years only, with no provision for renewal, and without any provision that it should continue in effect without being renewed. Similar requests and expressions of opinion came from many parts of America, and the Court was authorized to work out and propose the changes in the treaty establishing it which seemed desirable in view of the experience of the Court. Nevertheless no new treaty was made, and the Court was allowed to die at the end of the term originally set for it. There are certain causes to which this result may be attributed.

79. In the first place, the Court was set up for five nations only, and it could not do its work without having a judge from each one. However just its judgments were, they necessarily had unpleasant results for one nation or another, and thus friends and enemies developed; the Court was thus placed between the victors and the vanquished.

If it had had an unlimited term, like national courts, this difficulty would have reached a balance in the end, and the general advantageousness of order and justice would have silenced complaints and insincere or exaggerated grievances. In so short a period, however, it was not easy to maintain perfect serenity in discussing the circumstances that had to be met, nor to find formulas that would satisfy every one for its defects or changes.

Another source of difficulty was the right given to private citizens to sue their governments. Sometimes the individual standard may put private interest above the public interest; sometimes the determining motives of governmental action are inspired by political reasons that do not fit into the mould of law; sometimes national parties, in struggles that are not always moderate, want to make a tool of justice, and try to use it, by means of individual law suits, as a weapon against the party in power; for all these reasons, this system tends to discredit any Court, and makes some persons fear it and others regard it as a veritable danger.

Add to this the special political situation of the Central American republics in relation to another great nation on the same continent, that is not regarded in the same light by all, which makes what one nation regards as a necessity or an advantage seem like a danger to others: and the onlooker sees immediately another rock on which the Court could not help dashing in the last part of its life.

Add also to this, and to other suppositions or realities which will easily suggest themselves, the fact that the Court's life ended, by the treaty that gave it birth, at the moment when the European war, after becoming almost a world-wide war, had had so changed the atmosphere of the whole world that pacific solutions seemed less possible and appropriate, and before the new aspirations which the coming end of the war was soon to turn into international realities had had time to become clear in the general consciousness. It was this combination of unfavorable circumstances that prevented the Central American Court of Justice from going on.

Nevertheless, in its short life, it demonstrated clearly how useful the existence of a judiciary power between sovereign and independent states really is. It was the first actual historical example of such a judiciary power, and it will always have the place of honor in the history of the development and life of international justice. The New World may well be proud that the first permanent international court ever known was a Latin-American institution.[1]

[1] Anales de la Corte de justicia Centro-Americana, t. 1 et suiv., 1911-1917 (the official reports of the Court).

CHAPTER VI

THE PARIS CONFERENCE AND THE TREATY OF VERSAILLES

80. Public opinion in the neutral countries and in the belligerent countries opposed to the Central Powers viewed the events of the war of 1914-1918 in the light of certain great international principles of peace and justice, which they believed should have been applied for the protection of the world. The ultimatum to Serbia denied the rights of small nations as against the great nations, and disregarded the necessity that the fate and the dignity of weak nations should not be dependent on the will of the strong. The invasion of Belgium violated a solemn treaty and an admitted neutrality, under the plea of necessity, invoked by the nation that made itself the judge of the necessity. The military success of an apparently invincible army involved the peril of the domination of the whole world, in violation of its age-long and necessary organization in independent peoples. The difficulty and the danger to commerce on all the seas on the planet threw into sharp relief the principle of the freedom of the seas, without which modern life would be impossible. All these factors, with others of less importance, led strength to the desire born of the calamities of war to obtain victory at any cost and then to use the victory in a manner more in conformity with the ideal of humanity, by making it a means for finding and applying all possible and effective guarantees against the recurrence of the frightful convulsions of war.

The dawn of the triumph of the allied armies—though on the far horizon—revived the pacifist aspirations and proposals for a juridical organization of the world, which had necessarily been suppressed by the vital importance of the conflict of arms. And as the United States of North America had entered the war, and as that country is a

79

democracy, it was essential that its President should state
and re-state to the whole world, in his messages to Congress
and in his public addresses, what the nation was doing and
what ends it had in mind.   President Woodrow Wilson
was a man of great intellectual ability, deeply versed in
matters of public law; not content with being an idealist
in theory, he insisted on the realization of his ideals.   He
raised the tone of the conflict, and endowed the world with
a new institution for its guidance, to save the world from
the repetition of disaster, and to guarantee justice and
security in the future.   Under the impulse of his Word, the
world is now witnessing the rebirth of aspirations, not
toward a new international law, but toward new guarantees
for the observance and the development of existing law.
Official government circles are now beginning to work out
the means for its realization.

Almost all the great wars of the last few centuries, especially those of the nineteenth century, were followed by the
recognition or declaration in the peace treaties of some
important principles or rules of international life.   The
Napoleonic wars even brought about a concentration of
political forces, dating back beyond 1815, for the reorgani-
zation of the world.   Then, during the first quarter of the
nineteenth century, a degree of unity of action was developed, through congresses of an essentially diplomatic and
political nature; they amounted only to an intermittent
force, and made themselves the tool of monarchical interests
by recommending intervention in the affairs of other nations.   This new stage, after the World War, was to witness the conception of a great international organization, as
democratic as possible, where the small nations were to
have the same voice and vote as the great, and which would
act directly between the nations, in a collective form and
without separate interests, for the common weal and not
for the profit of certain states.

Such is the genesis of the projects for the League of
Nations, which were becoming frequent by the beginning
of 1918.   One phase of these plans developed into the Permanent Court of International Justice.

It is not necessary to discuss here the plan proposed by Italy and submitted to the Peace Conference at Paris, because it has already been discussed.[1]

81. The statement had already been made, in a report prepared by S. E. Mejes, David Hunter Miller, and Walter Lippman, and submitted to President Wilson by the *American Inquiry* in January, 1918, that out of the determination to resist the effort of the Germans to dominate the world a league of peoples had arisen, dedicated, among other things, to the peaceful solution of international disputes. The Fourteen Points were submitted at about this time to Congress by President Wilson; the fourteenth read as follows:

> "A general association of nations must be formed under specific covenants for the purpose of affording mutual guarantees of political independence and territorial integrity to great and small states alike."

In the fourth part of his address at Mount Vernon on July 4, 1918, President Wilson went still farther in this direction, in calling for the creation of a political organization to assure that the combined force of the free nations will prevent aggression and will guarantee peace and justice, through the means of a final and conclusive tribunal of opinion to which all will submit and which will sanction international agreements which cannot be obtained amicably by the interested nations. These words deserve special attention, for President Wilson's attitude during the Paris Conference and the proposals he made did not always indicate that he had any faith in a world-wide judiciary power, nor that he was particularly inclined to praise or defend it.

82. After the signature of the armistice had made a peace conference possible and essential, the government of France began to prepare for it and to make plans for its organization. In a preliminary plan transmitted by M. Jusserand, the French Ambassador at Washington, to Mr.

[1] See page 33.

Lansing, Secretary of State, on November 29, 1918, "the international arbitral organization of The Hague" is mentioned as one of the purposes of the League of Nations that was to be formed.

83. The British Cabinet had appointed a League of Nations Committee, with Lord Phillimore, eminently qualified and capable, as its chairman. This Committee submitted its plan on March 20, 1918; in Article 3, 1° it provided as follows:

"If in the future a conflict arises between any of the Allied powers, concerning the interpretation of a treaty, any question of international law, the existence of any fact which, if established, would constitute a breach of an international obligation, or the nature and extent of the reparation to be made for the breach of an international obligation, which diplomacy has failed to settle, the Allied powers recognize that arbitration is the most effective and at the same time the most equitable means of settling it."

This proposal is not altogether plausible; it is, as the Committee admitted, merely an adaptation of Article 38 of the 1907 Hague Convention for the pacific settlement of international disputes. It was hardly a generous proposal, as it was limited to the Allied governments, excluding not only the enemy nations whose admission was not then in question, but also, and with much less justification, the neutral states; and it was not courageous, because it proposed merely a vague platonic adhesion to the principle of arbitration, with no reference to making it compulsory, and without raising it to world-wide power by establishing a permanent court.

84. Colonel House, who was President Wilson's personal representative in Europe, was also asked by the President to prepare a draft for the organization of the League of Nations. In his plan, sent to the President on July 16, 1918, Colonel House admitted that in the past he had been opposed to the idea of a court, but that on working the matter out, the Court had come to seem to be a necessary part of the machinery, and, perhaps, in time, even the strongest part of it. He therefore included in his plan the following articles:

"X. An International Court composed of not more than fifteen members shall be constituted, which shall have jurisdiction to determine any difference between nations which has not been settled by diplomacy, arbitration, or otherwise, and which relates to the existence, interpretation, or effect of a treaty, or which may be submitted by consent, or which relates to matters of commerce, including, in such matter, the validity or effect internationally of a statute, regulation or practice. The Delegates may, at their discretion, submit to the Court such other questions as may seem to them advisable.

"The judges of the International Court shall, both originally and from time to time as vacancies occur, be chosen by the Delegates. A judge of the International Court shall retire from office when he shall have reached the age of seventy-two years, and may be so retired at any time by a vote of two-thirds of the Delegates, but in case of retirement of a judge from office, the salary paid to him shall be continued to be so paid during his natural life.

"XI. Any difference between nations relating to matters of commerce and which involves the validity or effect internationally of a statute, regulation or practice, shall, if the Powers having adopted such statute, regulation or practice so request, be submitted to its highest national court for decision, before submission to the International Court.

"XII. The highest national court of each Contracting Power shall have jurisdiction to hear and finally determine any international dispute which may be submitted by consent for its decision.

"XIV. Any Power which the Delegates determine shall have failed to submit to the International Court any dispute of which the Court has jurisdiction as of course, or failed or neglected to carry out any decision of that Court, or of a national court to which a dispute has been submitted by consent for decision, or failed to submit to arbitration any dispute pursuant to Article 13 hereof, or failed to carry out any decision of the arbitrators, shall thereupon lose and be deprived of all rights of commerce and intercourse with the Contracting Powers.

"XV. If any Power shall declare war or begin hostilities before submitting a dispute with another Power as the case may be, either to the International Court or to arbitration, as herein provided, or shall declare war or begin hostilities in regard to any dispute which has been decided adversely to it by said Court or by the Arbitrators or pursuant to Article 12 hereof, as the case may be, the Contracting Powers shall not only cease all commerce and intercourse with that Power as in Article 14 provided, but shall also arrange to blockade and close the frontiers of that Power to commerce and intercourse with the world."

There is a certain salutary radicalism about this proposal, so far as its provision for compulsory jurisdiction is concerned, and in the relatively limited hypotheses it proposes, although it includes in these hypotheses certain commercial rules and practices that do not relate directly to affairs between nations, at least not in the terms that are used. Moreover, the jurisdiction of national courts ought not to be fixed or extended by an international convention, nor is it wise as a rule to give national courts such functions. The plan deserves praise for the courage with which it attacks the question of sanctions, although, if it had been accepted, the execution of this positive and concrete order would have encountered grave difficulties.

85. President Wilson did not pay much attention to this part of his trusted counsellor's plan. When he edited the first plan, which was not made public during the Conference, it was arbitration, not the Court, that was in his mind; Article 5 makes certain rules about the choice of arbitrators, and possibly the reference to a different institution in Article 9 is merely due to inadvertence in copying. It was worded as follows:

"In the event of a dispute arising between one of the Contracting Powers and a Power not a party to this Covenant, the Contracting Power involved hereby binds itself to endeavor to obtain the submission of the dispute to judicial decision or to arbitration."

President Wilson's second plan, however, the first one printed for the Conference, distributed on January 10, 1919, makes no direct reference to the Court. Neither does the third and final draft.

86. The same thing is true of General Smuts' plan, dated December 16, 1918. General Smuts has said that before he drafted his plan he knew of the plan of the British committee alluded to above. He speaks of a court of arbitration and of conciliation, using the first phrase for questions arising between members of the League concerning the interpretation of a treaty and questions of international law and of international obligations.

87. The British draft of a Covenant for the League of Nations, which was approved in general terms by the British government, has more scope, but less hardihood. It was sent to President Wilson by Lord Robert Cecil, who seems to have been its main sponsor, according to a confidential letter of January 20, 1919. In Chapter II, "Avoidance of War," the following provisions occur:

"1. Each one of the States members of the League agrees that it will not, except in accordance with Article 12, go to war with another state member of the League:

"(a) without submitting the matter in dispute to a Court of International Law or to the Conference or to the Council of the League; and

"(b) until the Court or the Conference or the Council of the League has had reasonable time to render its decision or report on the matter, provided that in the case of the Conference or the Council the time shall not exceed . . . months; and

"(c) within a period of three months after the rendering of the decision or the report, including for this purpose a majority report, or after the expiration of the reasonable period referred to in (b); and also that it will not go to war with another State member of the League which complies with the decision of the Court, or, subject to Article 9, with the recommendation of the Conference or of the Council of the League.

"2. If there should arise between two States members of the League any dispute likely to lead to a rupture, which both parties agree to refer to the decision of a court of international law, or which under some convention between them either party is entitled to claim as of right should be referred to the decision of a court of international law, the parties or party, as the case may be, shall inform the Chancellor of the League, who shall forthwith make all necessary measures for bringing the dispute before the Court accordingly. All questions of procedure shall, if not settled by agreement between the parties, be decided by the Court, and pending the assembly of the Court, may be decided by the Chancellor.

"3. Pending the creation of a Permanent Court of International Justice, the Court of International Law to which the case is referred under the preceding article shall be the court agreed on by the parties or stipulated in the convention existing between them.

"7. When the Conference or the Council finds that the dispute can with advantage be submitted to a court of international law, or that any particular question involved in the dispute can with advantage be referred to a court of international law, it may submit the dispute or the particular question accordingly and may formulate the question for decision and may give such directions as to procedure as it may think desirable. In such case the decision of the Court shall have no force or effect unless it is confirmed by the report of the Conference or the Council.

"Pending the creation of a Permanent Court of International Justice, the Court of International Law referred to in this article shall be a tribunal of arbitration nominated by the Conference or the Council from among the members of the Permanent Court created by the Convention for the pacific settlement of international disputes."

This plan represents a real advance; the repeated references to a permanent court, and the assumption that a Court is to be established, give it a sense of genuine reality and distinguish it from arbitration for separate cases, though this is also more or less recommended.

From this plan, as will soon be clear, was to spring a very important decision of the Peace Conference; it was incorporated in the Treaty of Versailles and in the later peace treaties that also contain the Covenant of the League of Nations.

88. On January 25, 1919, in a plenary session of the Peace Conference, it was decided that it was essential, for the preservation of the organization of the world that the associated nations proposed, to create a League of Nations, in order to provide international coöperation, ensure the fulfillment of international obligations and create methods for preventing war. These propositions imply international justice, implicitly if not explicitly.

The Conference decided to appoint a committee representing the associated governments to prepare a plan for the organization and the working of the League. This Committee, appointed two days later, was composed of the following persons (the representatives of the four states given last were not appointed till February 6, 1919): for the United States of America, President Wilson and Colonel Edward M. House; for the British Empire, Lord Robert Cecil and Lieutenant-General Jan C. Smuts; for France, M. Léon Bourgeois and M. Fernand Larnaude; for Italy, MM. Orlando and Scialoja; for Japan, Baron Makino and Viscount Chinda; for Belgium, M. Hymans; for Brazil, M. E. Pessoa; for China, Dr. Wellington Koo; for Portugal, M. Jaime Batalla Rey; for Serbia, M. Vesnitch; for Greece, M. E. Venizelos; for Poland, M. R. Dmowsky; for Rumania, M. Diamandy, and for Czechoslovakia, M. C. Kramar.

89. Before the first meeting of the committee was to be held, at the Hotel Crillon on February 3, 1919, the technical experts of the United States of America and of Great Britain, MM. Miller and Hurst, prepared for the discussions a joint compromise plan, in which the idea of arbitration predominated, but which nevertheless upheld the idea of establishing a permanent judiciary institution. This is shown in Articles X to XII of this plan, which are as follows:

"Article X. The High Contracting Powers agree that should disputes arise between them which cannot be adjusted by the ordinary processes of diplomacy, they will in no case resort to armed force without previously submitting the question and matters involved either to arbitration or to inquiry by the Executive Council, and until three months after the award by the arbitrators or a recommendation by the Executive Council, and that they will not even then resort to armed force as against a member of the League which complies with the award of the arbitrators or the recommendation of the Executive Council.

"Article XI. The High Contracting Powers agree that whenever any dispute or difference shall rise between them which they recognize to be suitable for submission to arbitration and which cannot be satisfactorily settled by diplomacy, they will submit the whole subject matter to arbitration and will carry out in full good faith any award or decision that may be rendered.

"Article XII. The Executive Council will formulate plans for the establishment of a Permanent Court of International Justice, and this Court will be competent to hear and determine any matter which the parties recognize as suitable for submission to it for arbitration under the foregoing article."

90. This committee met ten times, between February 3 and February 13. On February 14 a joint official draft of a Covenant for the League of Nations was submitted to the Peace Conference in general assembly. In general it relates, so far as international conflicts are concerned, to inquiry, conciliation, and arbitration; but Article 14, taken almost literally from the Hurst-Miller draft, is a sort of safety valve, an uncertain step toward judiciary power. In order that the reader may judge for himself, three articles are quoted below from this plan, which was approved by the Conference on the day it was submitted:

"Article XII. The High Contracting Parties agree that should disputes arise between them which cannot be adjusted by the ordinary processes of diplomacy, they will in no case resort to war without previously submitting the questions and matters involved either to arbitration or to inquiry by the Executive Council, and until three months after the award by the arbitrators or a recommendation by the Executive Council, and that they will not even then resort to war as against a member of the League which complies with the award of the arbitrators or the recommendation of the Executive Council.

"In any case under this article, the award of the arbitrators shall be made within a reasonable time, and the recommendation of the Executive Council shall be made within six months after the submission of the dispute.

"Article XIII. The High Contracting Parties agree that whenever any dispute or difficulty shall arise between them which they recognize to be suitable for submission to arbitration and which cannot be successfully settled by diplomacy, they will submit the entire matter to arbitration. For this purpose the Court of Arbitration to which the case is referred shall be the court agreed on by the parties or stipulated in any convention existing between them. The High Contracting Parties agree that they will carry out in full good faith any award that may be rendered. In the event of any failure to carry out the award the Executive Council shall propose what steps can best be taken to give effect thereto.

"Article XIV. The Executive Council shall formulate plans for the establishment of a Permanent Court of International Justice, and this Court shall, when established, be competent to hear and determine any matter which the parties recognize as suitable for submission to it for arbitration under the foregoing article."

91. The general plan of the Covenant, and its various clauses and conditions, known to all the world since that

day, were studied and criticized in every detail by the national governments and in the press. As it was necessary to accept these observations and, where they were admissible or practicable, to apply them, the committee met five times between March 22 and April 11. The result of its labors was the new version submitted to the Conference in plenary session on April 28. The final form of these three articles is given below:

"Article 12. The members of the League agree that, if there should arise between them any dispute likely to lead to a rupture, they will submit the matter either to arbitration or judicial settlement or to enquiry by the Council, and they agree in no case to resort to war until three months after the award by the arbitrators or the judicial decision or the report by the Council.

"In any case under this Article, the award of the arbitrators or the judicial decisions shall be made within a reasonable time, and the report of the Council shall be made within six months after the submission of the dispute.

"Article 13. The members of the League agree that whenever any dispute shall arise between them which they recognize to be suitable for submission to arbitration or judicial settlement, and which cannot be settled satisfactorily by diplomacy, they will submit the whole subject matter to arbitration or judicial settlement.

"Disputes as to the interpretation of a treaty, as to any question of international law, as to the existence of any fact which, if established, would constitute a breach of any international obligation, or as to the extent and nature of the reparation to be made for any such breach, are declared to be among those which are generally suitable for submission to arbitration or judicial settlement.

"For the consideration of any such dispute, the court to which the case is referred shall be the Permanent Court of International Justice, established in accordance with Article 14, or any tribunal agreed upon by the parties to the dispute or stipulated in any convention existing between them.

"The members of the League agree that they will carry out in full good faith any award or decision that may be rendered, and that they will not resort to war against a member of the League which complies therewith. In the event of any failure to carry out such an award or decision, the Council shall propose what steps shall be taken to give effect thereto.

"Article 14. The Council shall formulate and submit to the members of the League for adoption plans for the establishment of a Permanent Court of International Justice. The Court shall be competent to hear and determine any dispute of an international character which the parties thereto submit to it. The Court may also give an advisory opinion upon any dispute or question referred to it by the Council or by the Assembly."

92. A comparison of this second version of Article 14 with the earlier version approved in the plenary session of the Conference immediately discloses certain important changes that deserve consideration. The disappearance of the word arbitration is not the least important of these; its first result is that the Court is no longer considered as a mere element of a system of arbitration, but is connected with a world-wide judiciary power. It ceases to be a mere opportunity for arbitration, and aspires to become something of a different nature, which Article 14 neither defines nor states. The second result—this one is lamentable—is that, as similar changes were not made in the revision of other articles of the Covenant, its rules, and especially its sanctions, may be considered as applicable to the arbitral procedure alone, which leaves the Court that the Council was to create somewhat deprived of collective protection and of sanctions. It should also be noted that the draft now to be made was to require a new convention freely and expressly accepted by the states in the League.

93. Although the version approved on February 14 contained a compulsory arbitration covenant, in Article 13, and although the Court to be created was to have compulsory jurisdiction of cases arising under it, in the new version

of April 28 this obligatory form of arbitration was somewhat abbreviated, and the new court seemed to have only
voluntary jurisdiction, completely in the power of the parties.   It is clear that in the international community, precisely as in a national community, sovereignty resides in
the persons that compose it, and that all the public powers
have their source in these persons; it is clear, as a consequence, that no world wide judiciary power can obtain
legitimate title to exercise its functions except through the
consent of the separate states: it is equally clear that this
consent can be given, either as to particular isolated cases,
or for classes or groups of disputes, or that it may be a
general and absolute consent, and that in the future the new
institution may be converted into the supreme dispenser of.
international justice; but it is none the less accurate to say
that in Article 14 of the Treaty of Versailles and in the
subsequent treaties, the opportunity was lost for strengthen-
ing the prestige and authority of the tribunal announced in
it by giving it compulsory jurisdiction from the very start,
at least in certain cases.   In subsequent agreements connected with these treaties, discussed in a later chapter, this
obvious omission was partially corrected.

94. The last part of Article 14 gives the Court an advisory, and not jurisdictional, function which did not appear
at all in the first version of February 14, 1919.   There was,
perhaps, a feeling that the new organs of the League of
Nations, the Council and the Assembly, would need an advisory body of unquestioned technical ability, independent
in station, with great prestige and dignity, whose members
in their special province as jurists could supply whatever
diplomats and statesmen might lack on certain occasions,
and which would also act as guide and counsellor.   In this
way a nation could not only escape from the peril of certain
mistakes, but could also avoid international complications,
and even conflicts, by yielding beforehand to the authority
of an opinion from a highly respectable source, thus avoiding the necessity—sometimes wrongly felt to be humiliating—of yielding later to its decision.

The entire question of this advisory function will be discussed later on, in the detailed analysis of the powers given to the Court. It is sufficient merely to point out here that these opinions may concern only international questions, for, as President Wilson pointed out in his address on February 14, when he presented and defended the Covenant in the plenary Conference, the unlimited right of discussion and inquiry given to the Council and the Assembly of the League is as to such matters only.

95. In addition to this task, which brings the Permanent Court into direct and almost continuous contact with the League of Nations, outside, of course, of its judiciary function, a third mission was suggested for it, this a very special mission. Acting under instructions from the French government, one of the French members of the committee that drafted the Covenant, M. Fernand Larnaude, dean of the faculty of law at Paris, submitted a proposal or amendment giving to the Court the special function of passing on all questions of interpretation of the Covenant of the League. Two other members of the committee, Lord Robert Cecil, representing the British government, and M. Vittorio Orlando, representing the Italian government, suggested that it would be better to leave any difficulties of interpretation of the Covenant to the Council, since it was charged with carrying out the Covenant: the majority agreed with them. This does not mean that these questions of construction cannot be submitted to the Court for an opinion, or as litigated matters; it was simply a matter of preventing the Court from being turned into an auxiliary of the League, which would have been obliged to wait constantly for the Court's opinion before carrying out its work. Both needed to be, and became, separate organisms; they do not respond to the same impulse or to the same necessity; they can, and should, complete each other, without blending into each other.

96. In other parts of the Treaty of Versailles and the subsequent treaties, the Paris Conference had occasion to establish the obligatory jurisdiction of the new Court, and frequently did so. For questions connected with ports, waterways, and railroads, and with the regulation of labor, it applied completely the principle of compulsory jurisdiction. This principle was equally victorious in other special treaties, beginning with the treaty for the protection of minorities in Poland, signed at the same time as the Treaty of Versailles. The idea of justice had such influence with those who drafted it that they provided, so frequently as to have caused comment, for the organization of special tribunals for reclamations between the former belligerents. They even went so far in the Treaty of Versailles as to organize a jurisdiction for penal offenses, which was less successful; they also provided other forms which will be discussed later.

97. In trying to form an impartial judgment of these 1919 treaties, the place of honor in the list of their unquestionable merits—which ought to make up for some of their mistakes—must be given to the fact that they gave official and definitive recognition to the enlightened public opinion of the world, and established as a reality the project that failed at the Hague Conference of 1907. No one was afraid of the idea by this time, and it no longer stirred up the old storms. The flight of time is not in vain; the human conscience cannot be in contact with progress and justice without responding to their influence and assimilating itself to what they require. In the past the conquerors were always able to impose their will upon the conquered, because their weight was heavier in the scales of force to which M. Bourgeois referred in a phrase quoted in an earlier chapter of this book. Now, for the first time in history, the victorious peoples, in writing out the conditions of peace, instead of leaving the future interpretation of these conditions to the will of the conquerors, invited the conquered to appear with them before a Court of Justice to discuss their meaning on equal terms.

CHAPTER VII

THE ADVISORY COMMITTEE OF JURISTS AND THE COUNCIL AND ASSEMBLY OF THE LEAGUE OF NATIONS

98. The first ratifications of the Treaty of Versailles, Article 14 of which directed the Council to formulate and submit to the members of the League plans for the establishment of a Permanent Court of International Justice, were deposited at Paris on January 10, 1920. The Council met at London on February 12; it adopted the suggestion of appointing an Advisory Committee of Jurists to prepare a plan, and made a preliminary list of persons to be asked to serve on the Committee.

Some of these persons were unable or unwilling to serve; the Committee was finally composed of the following jurists, named here in alphabetical order: MM. Mineichiro Adatci, Envoy Extraordinary and Minister Plenipotentiary of Japan at Brussels; Rafael Altamira, Senator and Professor of law at the University of Madrid; Clovis Bevilaqua, Legal Adviser to the Ministry of Foreign Affairs of Brazil, represented at first by Raóul Fernandes, former Brazilian delegate to the Paris Conference, who later was appointed a member of the Committee because M. Bevilaqua was unable to be present; Baron Descamps, Senator and Belgian Minister of State; Francis Hagerup, Envoy Extraordinary and Minister Plenipotentiary of Norway at Stockholm; Albert de Lapradelle, Professor of Law at the University of Paris; Dr. Loder, Member of the Supreme Court of the Netherlands; Lord Phillimore, Member of the Privy Council of England; Arturo Ricci-Busatti, Minister Plenipotentiary of Italy and Legal Adviser to the Ministry of Foreign Affairs of Italy; and Elihu Root, former Secretary of State of the United States of America. Dr. James Brown Scott was present at the meetings of the Committee as legal adviser to Mr. Root. The Secretary

General of the League of Nations appointed Commander
Anzilotti, Under-Secretary General of the League, as Secretary General of the Committee, with M. Ake Hammarskjöld, Secretary of Legation and a member of the Permanent Secretariat of the League, to replace him when he
could not be present.

99. The Committee met at The Hague on June 16,
1920; Baron Descamps was elected President, and Dr.
Loder Vice-President. It held its first public meeting on the
same day; the Jonkheer H. A. van Karnebeek, Minister of
Foreign Affairs for the Netherlands, made a short speech
expressing the cordial welcome and good wishes of the
Dutch government, and M. Léon Bourgeois, delegated by
the Council of the League to inaugurate the work of the
Committee, welcomed its members, and then made a very
important statement on the subject of the establishment of
the Permanent Court. Referring to a report he had made
on this question to the Council at the London meeting, he
stated the principal questions which the Committee would
have to solve as follows:

How should the Permanent Court be organized?
How should its members be appointed?
What will be their number and status?
In what country and in what town will the seat of the
Court be fixed?
What will be its rules of procedure, both in the matter
of preliminary pleadings and of judgments?
What, finally, will be the limits of its competence?

M. Bourgeois stated that the Court must be a true
Permanent Court, with a mandate that would ensure the
establishment of a real jurisprudence, by its duration. The
judges, he pointed out, chosen not by reason of the state
of which they are citizens, but by reason of their personal
authority, their past career, and the respect attached to their
names over the entire world, would represent a truly international spirit which was by no means, as had been pretended, a negation of the legitimate interests of each nation,

but was, on the contrary, the safeguard of these interests, within their legitimate limits.

These declarations, made by the representative of a great European power, are notable for their nobility and significance.

In analyzing the relation between the various organizations that grew out of the peace of Versailles, M. Bourgeois came to the question of sanctions for the decisions of the Court, and pointed out that the Covenant foresees several degrees of sanctions, juridical, diplomatic, economic, and, as a last resort, and within limits very closely confined, military sanctions as well. He closed his speech with these words:

"Gentlemen, you are about to give life to the judicial power of humanity. Philosophers and historians have told us the laws of the growth and decadence of Empires. We look to you, gentlemen, for the laws that will assure the perpetuity of the only empire that never can decay, the empire of justice, which is the expression of eternal truth."

A speech by the President, Baron Descamps, to which reference will be made later, closed the first public session, and the deliberations of the Committee began. This chapter relates only to certain questions discussed by the Committee, and principally to the most important ones that were changed subsequently by the Council and Assembly. The Committee's action on the other subjects will be commented on in subsequent chapters.

100. The Committee adopted as the basis of its work the acts and resolutions of the Second Hague Conference and the drafts submitted by Sweden, Denmark, Hungary, the Netherlands, Switzerland, Germany and Austria, which were discussed in the preceding chapters of this book. On Mr. Root's suggestion, the Committee published these documents.[1]

---

[1] Documents, etc., pp. 348-372. The official reports of the action of the Advisory Committee of Jurists, the Council, and the Assembly, in connection with the organization of the Permanent Court, are given in the following publications: (1) Minutes (Procès-verbaux) of the Proceedings of the Advisory Committee of Jurists, cited in this book as *Minutes, etc.;* (2) Documents Presented to the Committee Relating to Existing Plans for the Estab-

One of the members of the Committee, the Brazilian jurisconsult, M. Clovis Bevilaqua, who was not able to be present at the Committee meetings, sent in a draft which proposed that the Permanent Court of International Justice should be composed of nine judges, with life tenure, living at the seat of the Court, which should be at the seat of the League.

101. The Committee of Jurists was in session from June 16, 1924 to July 24; in this brief period, hardly over a month, the Committee, in thirty-five sessions, prepared, revised and unanimously approved the draft it had been asked to prepare and sent it to the Council, with an explanation of the reasons for its provisions prepared by M. de Lapradelle.

This preliminary draft, as it is officially termed, is substantially the statute in force today. Its first Article, of a general nature, was as follows:

"A Permanent Court of International Justice, to which parties shall have direct access, is hereby established, in accordance with Article 14 of the Covenant of the League of Nations. This Court shall be in addition to the Court of Arbitration organized by the Hague Conventions of 1899 and 1907, and to the special Tribunals of Arbitration to which States are always at liberty to submit their disputes for settlement." In the sub-committee of the Assembly the British government suggested that the phrase "to which parties shall have direct access" be deleted, on the ground that it was connected with compulsory jurisdiction; the representative of France was of the same opinion. MM. Fernandes, speaking for Brazil, Ricci-Bussatti, for Italy, and Huber, for Switzerland, maintained, correctly, that the phrase had no relation to the question of obligatory jurisdiction, but simply aimed to dispense with any intermediary between the parties and the Court, and to indicate

lishment of a Permanent Court of International Justice, cited here as *Documents, etc.;* (3) Documents Relative to the Measures taken by the Council of the League of Nations under Article 14 of the Covenant and the Adoption by the Assembly, cited here as *Documents relative, etc.;* and (4) Acts and Documents Concerning the Organization of the Court, Series D, No. 2, cited here as *Acts and Documents.*

that the Court would always be open and ready. The phrase was struck out, by a vote of 8 to 2, on the ground that it did not serve any useful purpose, although not involving any difficulties. This Article, without this phrase, was then approved by the sub-committee and by the Assembly.[1]

The rest of the Advisory Committee's draft, which contains 72 articles, is divided into three chapters, on the organization of the Court, its competence, and its procedure.

102. The first chapter will not be discussed until later, because it is not the most important, and because it will be more convenient to discuss its final form, as changes have been made in it. One Article in the second chapter, however, caused great difficulty in the Council and in the committee and sub-committee of the Assembly, on account of its extreme importance. This was Article 33, which was as follows:

"When a dispute has arisen between states, and it has been found impossible to settle it by diplomatic means, and no agreement has been made to choose another jurisdiction, the party complaining may bring the case before the Court. The Court shall, first of all, decide whether the preceding conditions have been complied with; if so, it shall hear and determine the dispute according to the terms and within the limits of the next Article."

This next Article 34, which must also be quoted in order that the force of Article 33 may be understood, is as follows:

"Between states which are members of the League of Nations, the Court shall have jurisdiction (and this without any special convention giving it jurisdiction) to hear and determine cases of a legal nature concerning:

(a) The interpretation of a treaty;

(b) Any question of international law;

(c) The existence of any fact, which if established, would constitute a breach of an international obligation;

(d) The nature or extent of reparation to be made for the breach of an international obligation;

[1] Documents relative, p. 114.

(e) The interpretation of a sentence passed by the Court."

Baron Descamps, President of the Advisory Committee, indicated in a note he read at the second meeting that he was not altogether in sympathy with compulsory jurisdiction:

"With regard to competence, either potential, or made efficiently obligatory, the variety of internal differences,—some of which are of a legal order while the others are political,—the difficulty of finding a clear line of demarcation between those two classes, the mixed character of certain differences which are considered as proceeding at the same time from law and from politics, and, above all, the fear of various states that a limitation might be imposed on their sovereignty, that they might have to submit to obligatory jurisdiction, and sacrifice beforehand and altogether certain rights considered as inalienable, were as many reasons capable of preventing practical men from accepting rules which implied a common obligation, identical for all." [1]

At the third meeting Lord Phillimore, with much more hardihood and decision, said incidentally that in his opinion the Committee's task was to prepare plans for the establishment of a Permanent Court of Justice which should be a Court of Justice in the true sense of the word, a Court before which it should be possible to call states that had broken the law of nations, without having to obtain their consent in advance.

These two positions were somewhat modified during the discussions; in fact, at one time the President went even farther than the English jurist in supporting compulsory jurisdiction. The difference in opinion was due to the different meanings given by the two groups to Article 14 of the Covenant, which, strictly speaking, did not exclude the compulsory conception; and the general condition of European politics and Mr. Root's indications of the feeling in the United States also had their effect. M. Loder took

---

[1] Minutes, p. 45.

the most radical position on one side, maintaining the importance of giving the Court jurisdiction over all the disputes between nations that it has not been possible to adjust by other means. M. Adatci was the most pronounced opponent of this position; he went so far as to make an express reservation on this subject, when the other members of the Committee finally voted to give the Court compulsory jurisdiction over certain classes of disputes. The final form of this Article, by which the Court's compulsory jurisdiction was limited to five specified groups of cases of a legal nature, consequently represents concessions made by both sides. It was nevertheless a rational compromise; and it was a great advance over anything that had ever been favorably considered before, and really constituted a great triumph for international justice. But the difficulty of getting this principle adopted in the Advisory Committee of Jurists should have indicated that it would meet almost decisive opposition in the Council and the Assembly.[1]

103. In the Council, which is a political rather than a juridical body, the idea of compulsory juridiction and of unilateral arraignment seemed at first thought incomprehensible, useless, and unacceptable. The draft of the Committee of Jurists had been sent first to the governments of the nations in the League; the first attacks came from them. For example, the Council for Diplomatic Litigation attached to the Italian Ministry of Foreign Affairs stated that it did not think it advisable in the present condition of international relations to retain Articles 33 and 34; if retained, they should be modified so as not to imply any obligation to submit certain disputes to the Court. And Mr. Balfour, in a note submitted at the October, 1920 meeting of the Council, maintained that the draft "goes considerably beyond the Covenant."

M. Bourgeois, in a preliminary report to the Council on the Advisory Committee's draft, also insisted that the pro-

[1] Minutes, etc. Pages 45, 104, 224-232, 233, 244, 286, 308-311, 314, 582-3, 615-6, 619 and 651.

vision for compulsory jurisdiction in the draft constituted
a modification of Article 12 of the Covenant; there should
be no question at that time, he thought, of modifying the
Covenant, but only of applying it as it stood; he therefore
proposed an amendment, which the Council accepted, that
practically suppressed the compulsory jurisdiction. Faithful, however, to his general position and to his lofty juridical and political ideas, he added that in adopting his proposal the Council did not wish to declare itself opposed to
the actual idea of the compulsory jurisdiction of the Court
in questions of a judicial nature, and would have no objection to the consideration of the problem at some future
time.

The result of his observations was that the Council substituted for Article 33 of the Committee's draft an altogether different wording which entirely destroyed it; their
wording is as follows: "The jurisdiction of the Court is
defined by Articles 12, 13 and 14 of the Covenant." The
Council also amended Article 34 to read as follows: "Without prejudice to the right of the parties according to Article
12 of the Covenant to submit disputes between them either
to judicial settlement or arbitration or to enquiry by the
Council, the Court shall have jurisdiction (and this without
any special agreement giving it jurisdiction) to hear and
determine disputes, the settlement of which is by treaties
in force entrusted to it or to the tribunal instituted by the
League of Nations." Thus the proposal to make any general provision in the statute for compulsory jurisdiction
was rejected.[1]

104. In the Assembly the Advisory Committee's draft
was referred to a committee for consideration, which in
its turn referred it to a subcommittee, composed of five
persons who were members of the Advisory Committee—
MM. Adatci, Fernandes, Hagerup, Loder and Ricci-
Busatti, and five others, MM. Doherty of Canada,
Fromageot of France, Huber of Switzerland, Sir Cecil
Hurst of Great Britain, and Politis of Greece.

[1] Documents relative, etc. Pages 26, 29, 38, 46 and 47.

Several nations offered amendments to the form of the Statute as changed by the Council. The delegations of Panama and of Colombia offered amendments reinserting the Advisory Committee's provision word for word. Italy proposed the insertion in Article 33 of the phrase "if the parties have agreed to settle the dispute by judicial means," and the suppression in Article 34 of the words "and this without any special convention giving it jurisdiction;" in other words, Italy completely refused to accept any degree of compulsory jurisdiction. The Argentine Republic took exactly the opposite point of view; it insisted that these two Articles be comprehensively and definitively amended, to read as follows:

"33. When a dispute has arisen between States, and it has been found impossible to settle it by diplomatic means and no agreement has been made to choose another jurisdiction, the party complaining may bring the case before the Court. With regard to claims founded upon private rights which a state has adopted in favor of its nationals against another state, recourse shall be had to diplomatic means only in the specific case of a refusal of justice on the part of the local tribunals, which must first be resorted to. The Court shall first of all decide whether the preceding conditions have been complied with; if so it shall hear and determine the dispute according to the terms and within the conditions of the next Article.

"34. Between states which are members of the League of Nations, the Court shall have jurisdiction (and this without any special convention giving it jurisdiction) to hear and determine cases of any nature whatever, except questions which affect constitutional laws of the contesting states. The Court may not in any case pronounce upon the validity or nullity of the awards made by the tribunals of the signatory states within the limits of their jurisdiction. The Court shall also take cognizance of breaches of the rules and usages of war; it shall then apply sanctions established by the convention—general or particular—between the parties, or by the Assembly of the League of Nations, or by international custom."

Although there was a manifest desire in the Assembly to reach a unanimous and agreeable decision on this subject as speedily as possible, the debate on it would have endangered the whole project if it had not been for a happy proposal made by M. Fernandes, the Brazilian delegate, which by adding the so-called optional clause, made it possible for any nation to accept the Court without compulsory jurisdiction, while allowing the supporters of compulsory jurisdiction to accept it then and there so far as they were concerned. The two contested Articles 33 and 34 were combined in one Article numbered 36 in the Statute in force. By its provisions,

"The jurisdiction of the Court comprises all cases which the parties refer to it and all matters specially provided for in treaties and conventions in force.

"The members of the League of Nations and the states mentioned in the Annex to the Covenant may, either when signing or ratifying the protocol, or at a later moment, declare that they recognize as compulsory *ipso facto* and without special agreement, in relation to any other members or states accepting the same obligation, the jurisdiction of the Court in all or any of the classes of legal disputes concerning:

(a) The interpretation of a treaty.

(b) Any question of international law.

(c) The existence of any fact which, if established, would constitute a breach of an international obligation.

(d) The nature or extent of the reparation to be made for the breach of an international obligation.

"The declaration referred to above may be made unconditionally or on condition of reciprocity on the part of several or certain members or states, or for a given time.

"In the event of a dispute as to whether the Court has jurisdiction, the matter shall be settled by the decision of the Court."

In the two meetings of the Assembly held on December 13, 1920, a great many of the delegates, especially those from Latin-American countries, lamented bitterly that any such compromise was necessary, and expressed the hope that by an increasing number of treaties and conventions the compulsory jurisdiction of the Court would be extended, until at last the whole world would regard it as natural and indispensable. The list of such treaties in Chapter XI shows that this hope is already in large measure realized.[1]

105. Article 14 of the Covenant, as has already been said, authorizes the Court to give an advisory opinion upon any dispute or question referred to it by the Council or by the Assembly. The Advisory Committee of Jurists drafted an article on this point, providing that when the Court was giving such an opinion on a question of an international nature that did not refer to a dispute that had already arisen, it should appoint a special commission with from three to five members to give the opinion, but that when the question was the subject of an existing dispute, the Court should act under the same conditions as when a litigated case is submitted to it by the parties. The report submitted with the draft statute by the Advisory Committee, which was prepared by M. de Lapradelle, says that in the first case (of an opinion not referring to an existing dispute), since the question may subsequently be brought before the Court in its judicial capacity, either on account of its character or because the parties make a special agreement to that effect, the Court must be so constituted that the giving of the opinion in the abstract does not restrict the Court's power to deal with it when it comes up as a concrete situation: hence the special commissions. The second case, M. de Lapradelle thought, seemed different, though perhaps not really so.[2]

Italy proposed an amendment authorizing the Court to appoint special commissions to give an advisory opinion in both of these kinds of cases; the subcommittee adopted

---

[1] Documents relative, etc. Pages 87, 89, 90, 91, 93-5, 100, 170, 228-253.
[2] Minutes, pages 730-2. See also, on another point, the dialogue between Mr. Root and M. de Lapradelle, pages 584-5.

this amendment on December 1, 1920, but four days later
it agreed unanimously to strike out this article altogether,
because, as M. Fromageot pointed out, Article 14 of the
Covenant establishes the fact that these opinions are to be
given; and the work then before the subcommittee was
only the organization of the Court, not the conditions under
which it should give its judgments. The Statute is therefore utterly silent on the advisory function of the Court,
though it is mentioned expressly in Article 14 of the
Covenant.[1]

106. Another question on which a serious difference of
opinion was manifested was the question of the official
language of the Court. The Advisory Committee of
Jurists decided without hesitation on French, which had
been the international language for centuries, down to the
Peace Conference that prepared the Treaty of Versailles.
The report of the Committee, adopted by the Committee
without discussion, pointed out that it would be absurd
to allow each of fifteen or twenty judges to express himself in a different language, and to allow the parties to
use languages the judges did not understand; it added that
French had been used at the Hague Conferences in 1899 and
1907, and that it was the official language of the Permanent Court of Arbitration except when all the parties spoke
English; this Court may also authorize the use of another
language when the parties demand it and the Court deems
it advisable.

When the Council began to consider the Advisory Committee's draft, Mr. Balfour said immediately that the provision making French the official language of the Court
ought not to be accepted until the United States had joined
the League and had had the opportunity of expressing
its opinion. He must have forgotten that Mr. Root was
on the Advisory Committee, and he did not foresee that
the entry of the United States was so far distant. He
added that the Treaty of Versailles had put the two languages on an equality, that in every instrument issuing out

[1] Documents relative, etc., pages 146 and 156.

of the League the equality was maintained, and that if the Permanent Court were made an exception to this arrangement his government would regard it with the greatest disfavor. He said later that English and French corresponded with two great legal traditions, one of which was founded on Roman law and the other on English common law. It is not altogether obvious, however, and Mr. Balfour did not explain this point, why French, and not Italian or Spanish, is the language that corresponds to the juridical traditions of the Roman law.

The Japanese delegate, M. Ishii, stated that he was completely in accord with Mr. Balfour. M. Bourgeois, after pointing out that the French language had been chosen by a Committee on which both English and American lawyers were serving, made the sensible observation that unity of language was an essential principle in the judgments delivered by a Court of Justice; it was indispensable that there should always be a single authentic text. Mr. Hymans called attention to the practical inconveniences caused in Belgium by the bi-lingual system, the judgments being pronounced in two languages. M. Quiñones de León, speaking for Spain, suggested that states using the Spanish language might well ask that it be used, in case of a dispute between them. Dr. da Cunha insisted that whatever language was used in the pleadings, the judgments should always be given in French, in order to ensure continuity in the legal traditions that would be based on the decisions of the Court. Finally M. Caclamanos, of Greece, was authorized to draft a resolution on the subject. This resolution was adopted, M. Bourgeois refraining from voting on it. By this resolution French and English were made the official languages of the Court. If the parties agreed that the case should be conducted in French, the judgment was to be delivered in French, with a similar provision as to English. If the parties made no agreement which to use, each might use the language it preferred in the pleadings, in which case the decision would be given in both languages, the Court indicating which text was to be considered authoritative. The Court might also, at the request of the parties, authorize the use of another language.

In the subcommittee of the Assembly, an amendment offered by Spain was considered and rejected, which would have made it obligatory, instead of permissive, for the Court to authorize the use of another language if the parties requested it; M. Ricci-Busatti pointed out that the field for the election of judges would be greatly narrowed if they were required to know more than two languages, and that interpreters could be used to meet the inconvenience caused to the parties by the limitation to two languages. The Spanish delegate, M. Palacio, introduced his amendment again before the full committee, where it was again defeated; and it met the same fate in the Assembly, in spite of the efforts of M. Palacio, M. Aguero of Cuba and M. Garay of Panama.[1]

107. M. Huber of Switzerland was the first to raise the point of the form for the adoption of the Statute of the Court. There were two possibilities: a unanimous resolution by the Assembly, and an international convention ratified by the different states. The first method would have made the Court merely an annex of the League of Nations; by the second it would be limited to the states that accepted and ratified it. Several delegates considered that in the second case it was a useless formality to have the Assembly vote on it, if it had to be followed by the preparation of an international convention.

Some doubt as to the meaning of Article 14 of the Covenant, which directed the Council to "formulate and submit to the members of the League for adoption" plans for a Court, was the cause of much of the discussion on this subject of the method of adopting the Statute. One delegate stated that in an official letter sent by President Wilson to the Swedish delegates, he had said that the words "members of the League" in this Article were to be understood as referring to the Assembly.

The real difficulty was commented on by several persons;

[1] Documents relative, etc. Pages 39, 42, 43, 51, 102, 134 and 255.

it is that the Court, on the one hand, is supported by quotas of the contributions of the several nations to the League, which are voted for the Court by the deliberative body of the League; and yet on the other hand, whatever Article 14 may say, above it stand the political constitutions of the different nations, on which the Covenant has not had, and has not desired to have, any effect. The majority of these constitutions require, for a convention by which an organism of such importance and significance as the Permanent Court is created, the action and approval of one, or of two, of the powers of the nation.

This was the view that in the end was accepted, as the final convention, adopted on December 13, 1920, shows:

"1. The Assembly unanimously declares its approval of the draft Statute of the Permanent Court of International Justice—as amended by the Assembly—which was prepared for the Council under Article 14 of the Covenant and submitted to the Assembly for its approval.

"2. In view of the special wording of Article 14, the Statute of the Court shall be submitted within the shortest possible time to the members of the League of Nations for adoption in the form of a Protocol duly ratified and declaring their recognition of this Statute. It shall be the duty of the Council to submit the Statute to the members.

"3. As soon as this Protocol has been ratified by the majority of the members of the League, the Statute of the Court shall come into force and the Court shall be called upon to sit in conformity with the said Statute in all disputes between the members or states which have ratified, as well as between the other states to which the Court is open under Article 35, paragraph 2, of the said Statute.

"4. The said Protocol shall likewise remain open for signature by the states mentioned in the Annex to the Covenant." [1]

108. The other changes made by the Council and the Assembly in the draft-scheme of the Advisory Committee of

---

[1] Documents relative, etc. Pages 87, 97-99, 108-9, 131-2, 148, 157, 166-8, 178, 198-202, 224, 241, 256 and 257.

Jurists, as well as the vote takcn in the Committee on the
question of criminal jurisdiction for the Court and the
decisions on the salary of the judges will be discussed in
another place.   The acts of these three bodies—Advisory
Committee of Jurists, Council and Assembly—deserve high
recognition, not only for the swiftness with which they
worked and for the lofty attitude with which they discussed and decided the questions involved, but also for the
desire they manifested to reach a solution, and for their
willingness to yield on matters of personal opinion and on
certain interests of their nations, in order to establish the
new institution by unanimous action, essential to success.
Thanks to them, the world has been endowed with international justice, so long sought and desired.

109. On December 16, 1920, three days after the Assembly had approved the Statute, the Protocol containing it
was ready for signature.   Forty-six nations signed it within
a short time.   When the next Assembly met, the following
year, twenty-eight states had deposited their ratifications,
and the Statute consequently went into effect.   It was then
possible to proceed with the election of the first judges.
This the Council and the Assembly did, from the 14th to
the 18th of the same month—September, 1921; this election is described in detail in the following chapter.   The
jurists who were elected accepted the office at once, so that
the Court was able to meet at The Hague in January, 1922,
to choose its officers and to adopt rules for its procedure.
   The official inauguration took place on February 15,
1922.   The Queen of Holland was one of the spectators of
the impressive proceedings.   The League of Nations was
officially represented by M. da Cunha, who laid stress on
the part played by Brazil and by America as a whole in the
development of international law, and on the hope placed
by America in this new institution, and by Sir Eric Drum-
mond, appointed Secretary General of the League in the
Treaty of Versailles, who, with all his personal and official
authority, stated with exactness the relation between the
two organisms: "At last an international judicial organ has

been established which is entirely free of political influences and absolutely independent of any political assembly in its deliberations." The addresses of welcome by the representatives of the Netherlands were equally impressive and affecting; and the courteous response of the President of the Court was full of encouragement for the future.

The Permanent Court was installed in the Palace of Peace, the construction of which was made possible by the gift of the American philanthropist, Andrew Carnegie. The name of the building it occupies symbolizes its mission and its future. May it realize and surpass the hopes with which it was conceived, and the good wishes with which the world received it.

CHAPTER VIII

THE JUDGES—THEIR ELECTION, QUALIFICATIONS, RIGHTS AND DUTIES

110. What qualifications must the judges of this Court, the highest Court in the world today, possess? The provisions on this point in the Statute are very brief. Article 2, on the organization of the Court, provides that they shall be independent, and shall be elected regardless of their nationality from amongst persons of high moral character who possess the qualifications required in their respective countries for appointment to the highest judicial offices, or who are jurisconsults of recognized competence in international law.

One of these qualifications, high moral character, would be very difficult to establish affirmatively; it will always have to be left to the good judgment of those who make the nominations and cast the votes. If, by any chance, it should happen that one of the persons elected did not possess high moral character, and if this defect were to be established by judgments against him, for example, the full Court itself would be the only body that could take action; it, as will be pointed out later, could, by a unanimous vote, exclude him.

The next qualification implies that a professional title is necessary, of the kind generally required for the highest judicial functions of any country, and an essential qualification of a jurist under the candidate's national laws. As to the recognized competence in matters of international laws,—this is another vague and indefinite qualification which must be regarded as a recommendation to the electors, which they are to take into account in casting their vote.

One noteworthy phrase in this Article is the one declar-

112

ing that the judges are to be elected regardless of their
nationality. This is a decisive step toward what may be
called the internationalization of the Court. It also
amounts to an open break with the tendency to allow certain
countries to have, permanently and *ipso facto,* preëstab-
lished representation in international judicial institutions,
because of their military power, their population, the extent of their territory, commerce or industry, or because
of their political interests. Today it is possible to consider
the vote of a majority of the nations at each election as
their voluntary act; but this conception of equality was not
accepted as a right at the Hague Conference of 1907;
they only pretended to accept it, and actually disregarded
and violated it.

The idea of the priority of great nations came to light
again, as was natural, in the Advisory Committee of Jurists.
M. Adatci was the first to insist on it; he maintained it
tenaciously, and claimed that it was founded on sociological
doctrines of the predominance of the strongest in the social
organism; he also cited as a precedent the Commission of
Transit named by the League—a precedent both unjust and
out of place. He went so far as to say that if Japan did
not have a representative on the Court, he feared that the
Japanese people would never accept its jurisdiction. Lord
Phillimore, with equal vehemence, insisted that the ordinary
Englishman would not be satisfied with a Court on which
his country was not represented and that the Court could
not live unless all the great powers were represented on it,
using the phrase "great powers" in its common and narrow
meaning of states with large territory and great population.

This last phrase would in the long run have allowed
certain nations to monopolize the Court. Take the five
that called themselves great powers then—the United
States, Great Britain, France, Italy and Japan, and add to
them at least Germany and Russia, in Europe; in Asia,
China and the British Dominion of India, which is an
independent member of the League; in America add the
Argentine, Brazil, and Chile, to use Lord Phillimore's suggestion: this makes twelve nations already, for a Court of

eleven judges. The other nations, called the small nations, would have to content themselves forever with admiring the Court from the outside, because they would always see over its door, *"Lasciate ogni speranza."* Shut out from being judges, they would never have appeared before it to be judged, and therefore this aristocratic Court would have had no authority, no power, and no prestige.

Other jurists belonging to great powers, however, including M. de Lapradelle, the French professor and publicist, submitted arguments against this position that it was impossible to refute. They pointed out that without equality there is no justice, and that it would be impossible for nations to hope for the last from an institution that disregarded the first. The insistence by the great powers on a judge of their own nationality makes the small nations refuse to accept this humiliation, and the Court is stranded. This was what killed the Court in 1907, and it will kill it in any new attempt, no matter what it may be. If the great powers demand judges of their own nationality to try their cases, they are trying to connect justice with national interests; if they insist on national judges in cases with other nations, they are bringing into the Court a political interest of domination or intervention, utterly without foundation and alien to the nature and to the purposes of the judiciary power.

Common sense won in the end, and the draft contained no national qualification for the judges. The method of electing the judges, and another rule which will be discussed a little farther on, contributed to bring about this fortunate result, on which the Committee is to be congratulated. The draft was accepted in the form in which it has been discussed above; it is, with some unimportant changes, the provision adopted, on motion of Louis Renault, at the 1907 Hague Conference.[1]

111. Article 9 of the Statute provides that at every election the electors shall bear in mind that not only should

[1] Minutes, pp. 102-111, 115, 118-137, 158-166, 446-450, 611-12, 623, 645, 698-9.

all the persons appointed as members of the Court possess
the required qualifications, but also that the whole body
should represent the main forms of civilization and the
principal legal systems of the world. There is nothing to
take exception to in this rule, which tends to internation-
alize the Court, if one may use that phrase, so that it
may be assumed that its decisions are based on a world-
wide comprehension of the problems and the applicable
principles of law. This is not, as has been suggested, another method of ensuring that the great powers will have
judges, because very nearly all of the nations from which
judges would be likely to come have the same form of
civilization and the same legal system as other nations
of slighter political importance.

It is not at all clear, however, how this rule can be effectively carried out, except by the good will of the electors,
as the extent of its application is rather vague and uncertain, although there is an element of certainty in it. Modern civilization has not destroyed differences of civilization
nor variations in legal systems; but it has greatly modified
them. In any case, the Statute does not make any provision
for enforcing this recommendation, nor set up any power
with authority to declare that it has been disregarded.

112. Indirectly, by designating French and English as
the official languages of the Court, the Statute requires
the judges to know these two languages. It would be
absurd, especially in the oral pleadings, if the judges could
not understand what counsel, witnesses, and experts were
saying except as they gathered it from translations more
or less authentic. This ends the personal qualifications
imposed by the Statute; no minimum or maximum age
limit is set; nothing is said about judicial services or about
the active practice of law, nor about the other elements
or circumstances that are usually stipulated for similar
functions in national affairs. If the reference in Article
2 to the qualifications required in their respective countries
for appointment to the highest judicial offices implies the
adoption of these conditions imposed by the national laws,

the result would be illogical and inequitable. In one nation, A, only persons who have served twenty years as a judge may be appointed to its Supreme Court: then a judge who had served only eighteen years could not become a judge of the Permanent Court; but in another country, B, where only ten years of service may be required, a person who had been a judge for eleven years would be eligible. This is a point which was not considered by the drafters of this Article, except at the beginning, in the plans that preceded the Statute.

113. One of the most successful points of the Advisory Committee's work is the election procedure—a very difficult and contentious subject. The League of Nations, a new element in the situation since the failure of previous attempts to agree on a procedure, made it possible to find the arrangement which had been sought for so long. Nevertheless the majority of the governments represented on the Committee of Jurists, as well as of its individual members, would not have gone beyond a more or less restricted and regulated vote by the Assembly. It chanced to be two jurists of the United States, Elihu Root, the eminent lawyer and statesman, and Professor James Brown Scott, versed in international affairs, an indefatigable worker for the conception of the Permanent Court of International Justice, who deserve the credit for having thought out and proposed a method of electing the judges which so far at least, has proved an unqualified success.

The electoral procedure is divided into two stages, one that may be called social, consisting of the nomination of candidates, and another that may be called political or diplomatic, consisting of the final election of the judges from the persons nominated. The first stage is entrusted to the national groups in the Court of Arbitration established under the two Hague Conventions of 1899 and 1907 for the pacific settlement of international disputes. Each of the adhering nations appoints four representatives, as a maximum, for a term first set in the 1899 convention at four years but extended in 1907 to six years, as members of the list of arbitrators from which governments that desire to set up an arbitration tribunal may choose their representatives.

These four persons in each national group are to make the nominations for their nation of judges for the new Permanent Court. Theoretically, this applies to the nations that have been members of the League from the beginning, to the nations mentioned in the Annex to the Covenant, and to the nations that subsequently entered the League. The other nations—and as a matter of fact there are several others—do not have this right to nominate, under Article 4 of the Statute, although, as will be seen later, they may nevertheless be obliged to accept the Court's jurisdiction in certain cases, and although they have the privilege of accepting its jurisdiction for any or all classes of disputes that may arise between them and the other nations. To put it differently: according to Article 4 of the Statute, some nations that may, and some that must, appear before the Court as parties have no right to nominate candidates through their national groups on the Permanent Court of Arbitration, this privilege being reserved to the nations in the League, or mentioned in the Annex.

On the other hand, this privilege was given to the national groups of nations that have not ratified the Treaty of Versailles and have not accepted the Statute of the Court. At the time of the first election, the four United States members of the Court of Arbitration issued a statement saying that they would make no nominations because they did not consider themselves legally qualified to do so, because their country had not ratified the Treaty of Versailles. They thus renounced on this occasion a right which had been conferred on them. But nations that have not ratified the Statute may nominate candidates. This situation, anomalous though it is, is not objectionable. The Court will not lose anything, and in fact, it will gain in prestige and authority, from the fact that among those who share in forming it there are some that do not need it and that for the time do not want to join it. They would be all the more impartial and disinterested in their nomi-

nations, should the case occur. And the longer the list
is from which the Council and the Assembly make their
choice, the more names it will include of competent and
authoritative persons.

Since it may happen that a nation may belong to the
League of Nations but not to the Permanent Court of
Arbitration, the second paragraph of Article 4 of the
Statute now provides, thanks to a very important amendment made by the Assembly, that such a nation is to make
its nominations for judges through a national group to
be appointed by its government under the same conditions
as apply to the appointment of the national groups in the
Court of Arbitration. In this particular instance, this arrangement does not imply the same guarantees of qualification for making the nominations, for here the four in the
national group are appointed by the national government
only for the one purpose of making the nominations, and
thus the government has an indirect method of making
these nominations itself; but it was the best arrangement
that could be devised under the circumstances.

At least three months before the date of the election,
the Secretary General of the League of Nations is required, by Article 5, to send a written request to the members of the Court of Arbitration belonging to the states
that are members of the League of Nations or that are
mentioned in the Annex to the Covenant or to the states
which joined the League subsequently, and to the national
groups appointed as provided in the preceding paragraph,
inviting them to undertake, within a given time, by national groups, the nomination of persons in a position to
accept the duties of a member of the Court.

No group may nominate more than four persons, not
more than two of whom may be of their own nationality;
and none of them may be of its nationality, if there already
is a judge or a deputy judge of that nationality in the
Court. In no case may the number of candidates nominated by a group be more than double the number of seats
to be filled—*e.g.*, when one vacancy is to be filled, a group
may nominate only two persons.

As to one of these provisions: each country knows its own men of worth and capacity, and its national group can bring them to the attention of the other states by nominating them. But the matter of international reputation, by which the two candidates not of the group's own nationality must be chosen, is a more difficult affair, because any general knowledge of the qualities on which it should depend is hindered by the obstacles of race, differences of language, and differences of legal systems. Requiring each national group to include strangers in its nominations means that each candidate must have not only authority at home, but also a reputation abroad, which increases the probabilities of a satisfactory choice. There is no reason, however, for exaggerating this point by requiring, as was proposed during the preliminary work on the Statute, that only those candidates proposed by the national groups of three or more nations could be voted for; this arrangement would either limit the field of election, or else force or inspire political or diplomatic understandings, the result of which would be objectionable. More than once already the Council and the Assembly have elected a candidate nominated by a single national group, and there is nothing dangerous or inconvenient in the present procedure.

114. The national groups of the Permanent Court of Arbitration are not absolutely independent morally in making the nominations. Article 6 of the Statute recommends that before making its nominations a national group consult its highest court of justice, its legal faculties and schools of law, and its national societies and national sections of international societies devoted to the study of law. The national group therefore obtains, or asks for, the collaboration of the judiciary and of the institutions, official or unofficial, for teaching law, and the individual initiative of associations devoted to studying law: thus obtaining the benefit of a point of view generally in opposition to that of a national government. This gives a sort of juridical plebiscite, official and unusual, which tends to remove any possibility of direct governmental influence on the nominations, and guarantees impartiality and competence.

The Statute does not lay down any regulations to control the action of the national group and of these various official and private organizations in carrying out this mission. Such regulations would not be in order, as it is a question of providing for the execution of an international convention within the domestic or internal life. The assumption is that each nation will provide its own regulations, if cases of election become more frequent and difficulties arise.

115. In the session of February and March, 1921, the Council of the League authorized the Secretary General to take all the necessary steps for the first and so far the only general election. The first step was to ask the governments concerned to complete their national groups in the Court of Arbitration, or to appoint national groups, if they were not members of that Court. This done, the members of these national groups were invited, in March, to send in their nominations by August 15.

89 candidates were presented. They are listed below; the nationality of each candidate is given in the parenthesis after each name, and then the nationality of the group or groups that nominated him is given, if it is different from his own: Gustave Ador (Switzerland), candidate of France; Sir P. S. Sivaswami Aiyar, K.C.S.C.J.E. (India); Ricardo J. Alfaro (Panama); Amir Ali (India); Rafael Altamira (Spain), candidate of Spain, Venezuela and Colombia; Alejandro Alvarez (Chile), candidate of Brazil, Chile and Uruguay; Paul André (France); Dionisio Anzilotti (Italy); Ruy Barbosa (Brazil), candidate of Bolivia, Brazil, Chile, Uruguay, Venezuela, Cuba and Colombia; Jose Batle y Ordonez (Uruguay), candidate of Chile and Uruguay; Frederick V. N. Beichmann (Norway), candidate of Denmark and Norway; Clovis Bevilaqua (Brazil), candidate of Portugal; Antonio S. de Bustamante (Cuba); Francisco Bustillos (Venezuela); Auguste Bonamy (Haiti); Louis Borno (Haiti); Eugène Borel (Switzerland); Sir Robert Laird Borden, G.C.M.G.

(Canada); Simon Bossa (Colombia); Léon Bourgeois
(France), candidate of Bolivia; Stoyan Daneff (Bulgaria);
S. R. Das (India); Baron Descamps (Belgium), candidate
of Belgium, Greece, and Japan; Charles Doherty
(Canada); Charles Dupuis (France), candidate of Poland; Rafael Erich (Finland); Joseph Fadenheht (Bul-
garia); Paul Fauchille (France), candidate of Belgium;
Vicomte Robert B. Finlay, G.C.M.G. (Great Britain),
candidate of Great Britain, Chile, Greece and Australia;
M. P. Friis (Denmark), candidate of Siam; Henri Froma-
geot (France), candidate of the Netherlands; Arthur
Goddyn (Belgium); J. V. Gonzalez (Argentine), candi-
date of Brazil; C. Gram (Norway), candidate of Sweden;
Alfred Halban (Poland); K. H. L. Hammarskjöld (Swe-
den), candidate of Sweden, China and Italy; Michel
Hansson (Norway); Son Altesse Hassan Khan Mochirod
Dovler (Persia); Charles Herrmann Otavsky (Czechoslo-
vakia); Manuel Gonzales Hontoria (Spain); Max Huber
(Switzerland), candidate of Switzerland and Austria;
Paul Hymans (Belgium), candidate of China; Karel Kad-
letz (Czechoslovakia), candidate of Bulgaria; Albert de
Lapradelle (France), candidate of Finland; F. Larnaude
(France), candidate of Persia; Chi-Chao-Liang (China);
B. C. J. Loder (the Netherlands), candidate of Finland,
The Netherlands, Poland and Switzerland; Croneliu
Manolesco Romniceano (Rumania); Baron Erick Marks
de Wurtemberg (Sweden), candidate of Denmark, Nor-
way and Sweden; Vojteck Mastny (Czechoslovakia);
Mohamed Ali Khan Zokaol Molk (Persia); John Bassett
Moore (United States of America), candidate of Italy;
Eusebio Morales (Panama); Démètre Negulesco (Ruma-
nia); Phya Kritika Nukornkitch (Siam); Didrik G. C.
Nyholm (Denmark), candidate of Denmark, Norway
and Sweden; Rodrigo Octavio (Brazil), candidate of
Panama; Yorazu Oda (Japan); Lord Walter G. Philli-
more, D. C. L. (Great Britain), candidate of Belgium,
the Netherlands and Switzerland; Edoardo Piola Caselli
(Italy); Phya Chinda Pirom (Siam); Raymond Poincaré
(France), candidate of Portugal; Nicolas Politis (Greece),

candidate of Czechoslovakia; Roscoe Pound (United States of America), candidate of Siam; Arturo Roderiguez Ribeiro (Portugal); Sir Henry E. Richards (Great Britain), candidate of Japan; Elihu Root (United States of America), candidate of Bolivia, Brazil, France, Uruguay and Venezuela; Michel Rostworowsky (Poland); Antoine Rougier (France), candidate of the Kingdom of the Serbs, Croats and Slovenes; Karl Schlyter (Sweden), candidate of Austria; James Brown Scott (United States of America), candidate of Haiti; Augusto L. Vieira Soares (Portugal); Georges Streit (Greece); A. A. H. Struycken (the Netherlands); Erland Tybjerg (Denmark); Fernando Velez (Colombia); Eliodoro Villazon (Bolivia); William Wallach (India); Wang-Chung-Hui (China); André Weiss (France), candidate of France, Greece, Japan and Persia; Sir Johannes W. Wessels (South Africa); Baron R. A. Wrède (Finland); Michel Yovanovitch (Kingdom of the Serbs, Croats and Slovenes), candidate of Czechoslovakia; Estanislao Zeballos (Argentine), candidate of Panama; Ivan Zolger (Kingdom of the Serbs, Croats and Slovenes).

Ten of these declined the nomination before the election was held; these were MM. Ador, Bourgeois, Doherty, Fromageot, Gonzalez Hontoria, Hymans, Lange, Marks de Wurtemburg, Poincaré, and Wessels. This left 79 candidates from whom eleven judges and four deputy judges were to be chosen.[1]

116. The lamentable death of M. Ruy Barbosa, who was never well enough to take his seat as one of the Judges of the Court, was the cause of the first vacancy in the Court. Early in 1923 the Secretary General of the League invited the national groups to designate candidates for the vacant post. By September 3, 1913, the time limit for the submission of nominations, thirty-three candidates had been nominated, as follows: Alejandro Alvarez (Chile), candidate of Guatemala and Switzerland; Amir Ali (India);

---

[1] Léon Bourgeois. L'Oeuvre de la Société des Nations (1920-1922), Paris, 1923, Vol. I, p. 209. Cosmo de la Torriente. La Liga de las Naciones. Trabajos de la 2e Asamblea. Habana, 1922. Vol. 1, pp. 56-59.

Frank A. Anglin (Canada); Ernest Arendt (Luxembourg); P. L. de la Barra (Mexico), candidate of Bulgaria and Hungary; F. V. N. Beichmann (Norway), candidate of Denmark; Auguste Bonamy (Haiti); Baltasar Brum (Uruguay), candidate of Salvador; José A. Buero (Uruguay), candidate of Cuba; Jacob W. Chydenius (Finland); Baron Descamps (Belgium), candidate of Kingdom of the Serbs, Croats and Slovenes; Joaquin V. Gonzalez (Argentine), candidate of Uruguay; J. Gustavo-Guerrero (Salvador); Knut H. L. Hammarskjöld (Sweden), candidate of China; E. Lafleur (Canada); Gezà de Magyary (Hungary); Phya Kritika Nukornkitch (Siam); Manuel M. de Oca (Argentine), candidate of Bolivia; Rodrigo Octavio (Brazil) candidate of Guatemala and Panama; Karl Hermann Otavsky (Czechoslovakia), candidate of his own country and of the Kingdom of the Serbs, Croats and Slovenes; Theodor Papazoff (Bulgaria); Epitacio da Silva Pessoa (Brazil), candidate of his own country and of Belgium, Chile, Colombia, Cuba, Denmark, British Empire, Spain, United States of America, Finland, France, Haiti, Italy, Japan, Panama, Peru, Poland, Portugal, Sweden, Switzerland, Uruguay and Venezuela; Nicolas Politis (Greece); Miguel Cruchaga Tacornal (Chile), candidate of his own country and Brazil; Michel Rostworowsky (Poland); Joseph Schey (Australia); Eliodoro Villazon (Bolivia); Wang-Chung-Hui (China); Juan G. Wessels (South Africa); Michel Yovanovitch (Kingdom of the Serbs, Croats and Slovenes), candidate of Czechoslovakia; and Estanislao S. Zeballos (Argentine), candidate of The Netherlands.

Two of the persons nominated, MM. Nicolas Politis and Alejandro Alvarez, declined the nomination. This left twenty-nine candidates for the vacant place.

117. These two lists of candidates for the two elections show that the national groups take a genuine interest in the matter; they also indicate the wide variety of the names proposed to the Council and Assembly. It ought to be easy to make a good choice from such a long list of candidates. The procedure worked out by the Advisory Committee of Jurists has been successful; its character is not altered by the fact that in the 1923 election one candidate was nominated by twenty-two nations; this will not happen often. Moreover, it does no real harm if the opinion of the Court of Arbitration is thus shown before the election; the electors are perfectly free to heed this opinion or to disregard it.

118. As has already been indicated, various systems for the final election of the judges were proposed before the Advisory Committee of Jurists and elsewhere, all more or less influenced by the fundamental principle of the equality of nations. The theoretical and scientific projects made at various times have already been discussed, as has also the work of the Hague Peace Conferences; no further mention need be made of them here, particularly as they made no acceptable or accepted contribution of a practical nature. Only the discussions and agreements that resulted in the establishment of the Permanent Court are stated here.

As always happens when a question of this kind is being considered, some persons wanted to recognize the supremacy of the great powers because of their force, while others wished to acknowledge the predominance of the small nations because of their number; in the long run both groups realized that it would not do to run aground on either shoal, if the Court was to be accepted by all nations and if its decisions were to have the authority and prestige essential for their being obeyed. The position taken by the first group, according to which no judicial power could endure unless its existence were guaranteed by the permanent representation of each great power by a judge of its own nationality, was represented in the Advisory Committee of Jurists by the proposals of MM. Ricci-Busatti and Adatci. The former introduced a resolution,[1] stating that "it seems necessary that the fundamental principle of the legal equality of states should be made to agree with

[1] Minutes, p. 183.

certain considerations due to the powers who play a pre-
dominant part within the League of Nations;" he therefore proposed a Court of fifteen members, chosen as follows: each nation in the League was to nominate one
person, but the persons named by the nations permanently
on the Council—*i.e.*, France, Great Britain, Italy and
Japan—were to be judges, automatically and *ipso facto*,
as were also all persons named by at least three states.
The others, if there were any others, were to be elected
by the Assembly, the electoral function of which would
thus be made a mere nullity. It is probable that too many
judges would have been elected under this scheme, because
many groups of three nations would have been formed in
order to obtain possession of a seat; the plan does not
provide which judges would have priority if this happened.

M. Adatci's plan was as follows:

"The Court shall be composed of judges, one named
by each of the members of the League of Nations represented permanently on the Council, and eight other judges
designated by the Assembly."

Less arbitrary than the Italian proposal, it allowed the
Assembly, where each of the associated nations has a vote,
to elect the majority of the judges; but none the less it
struck the same rock that wrecked the Second Hague Conference plan and made it impossible to create a court at
that time. M. Adatci realized this, no doubt, for he withdrew his amendment when the Committee was about to vote
on it; this saved it from the fate of the Italian plan, which
was defeated by a vote of six to two.[1]

One of the jurists made another attempt to ensure that
the great powers, who then seemed destined to have a majority in the Council, would be sure to have a preponderating, though disguised, influence on the election; he
proposed that two lists of candidates be made, one by
members of the Permanent Court of Arbitration, the other
by the Council after it had seen the first list.[2] The Council

[1] Minutes, p. 392 and 394.
[2] *Ibid.*, p. 374.

was thus to act as mentor to the Assembly, to guide its action, or to correct its mistakes. Its proposed recommendation could have been used as a means of influencing the election for the benefit and advantage of the great powers. Luckily this proposal was equally unsuccessful; it would have made it very difficult to get the Statute accepted.

119. Several members of the Advisory Committee supported a proposal that had appeared in several drafts sent in by governments and individuals, to have the judges elected by the Assembly alone. The objection of the great powers and their friends to this proposal could not be overcome; they were afraid that the small states would outvote them in the Assembly and that they would not be represented on the Court. The struggle between superiority in numbers and superiority in power, which has kept political life all over the world upset ever since the French Revolution and will continue to keep it upset until the two coincide, came to the surface here in international life; it seemed almost certain that it would result in preventing the establishment of the Court. If the Court was to be established, the supporters of the opposed principles had to change their objective points. No progress could possibly have been made if the nations, all distrusting each other, cared only about getting the advantage over each other—the great powers trying to dominate judicially the small, and the small powers trying to prevail judicially over the great. It was indispensable to find another really simpler solution: that the Court could not be established either by the will of the great powers alone, or by the will of the small powers alone, but that it was essential that both groups of nations must acquiesce and concur in the election of each and of all of the judges.

120. The skill and talent of Elihu Root and James Brown Scott, to which attention has already been called, brought harmony into a situation that had begun to seem irreconcilable. They proved their skill by not launching their plan until the other proposals had been rejected, so that both victors and vanquished might regard it as the only way of avoiding utter shipwreck for the Court and bitter failure for the Advisory Committee of Jurists. They were also skilful enough to present and explain it gradually, not stating the complete plan all at once, so that the Committee could get used to the idea and could finally accept it as a familiar arrangement. And when once their plan is explained and understood, the genius of these two men needs no further proof.

The plan consists simply of submitting the list of candidates, prepared from the nominations of the national groups on the Court of Arbitration, to a double, but separate vote, in the Council, where the great powers are permanently represented as well as small ones, and in the Assembly, where all the members are represented with absolutely equal votes, and in not considering any candidate elected who does not obtain a majority of the votes in each of these two bodies. Under this plan the great powers, who dominate the Council morally and who then dominated it materially as well, cannot impose their will upon the majority of the small nations which control the Assembly; and the majority of the small nations, controlling the Assembly, cannot overcome the will of the great powers, controlling the Council. This gave a balance of power, like that which rules public affairs for the general good, in almost all really democratic nations.

An attempt was made to defeat this fortunate solution by creating an apparently insoluble difficulty; one proposal was that the Assembly should vote first, so that the subsequent vote by the Council would amount to a sort of veto; another was to the effect that the Council should be the Assembly's moral guide; neither suggestion was adopted, and the two bodies were left free to regulate the details of their procedure. This they did with great dignity and concord, arranging to meet at the same time to cast their votes.

121. The provisions of the Statute on this point are clear and simple; the Council and Assembly accepted them

with only slight changes in the wording which need no comment. According to Article 8, the Assembly and the Council proceed independently of one another to elect first the
judges, then the deputy judges. According to Article 10,
those candidates who obtain an absolute majority of votes
in the Assembly and Council shall be considered as elected.
In case two persons of the same nationality happen to
receive a majority of votes in both bodies, the older of the
two is considered elected. According to Article 11 and 12,
if one or more seats remain to be filled after the first meeting, a second meeting, and if necessary a third, shall be
held; if one or more seats remain unfilled after the third
meeting, a joint conference may be formed at any time,
at the request of either the Assembly or the Council, consisting of six members, three appointed by the Assembly
and three by the Council, who are to choose one name
for each seat still vacant and submit it to the Assembly
and Council. The person or persons so designated need
not be one of those nominated by the national groups, provided the recommendation of the joint conference is unanimous. In case the joint conference is satisfied it will not
be successful in procuring an election, the other members
of the Court are to fill the vacant seats, within a period
fixed by the Council from among the candidates that
received votes in the Assembly or in the Council. If
there is a tie vote here, the eldest judge has the casting
vote.

122. Before passing any judgment on these provisions,
it may be well to see first how they have worked out so far.
The first election of judges began on September 14, 1921;
the Council and the Assembly met at the same time, but in
separate sessions. As the result of this election, the Court
would be definitely set in motion; eleven judges and four
deputy judges were to be chosen out of the list of seventy-
nine candidates mentioned before (in No. 113).
On the first ballot taken in the Assembly, nine persons
obtained a majority vote; forty-two nations were represented, which made it necessary for a candidate to receive

twenty-two votes to be elected. The following persons received more than the necessary majority:

> Altamira (Spain), 23 votes.
> Alvarez (Chile), 24 votes.
> Anzilotti (Italy), 24 votes.
> Ruy Barbosa (Brazil), 38 votes.
> Bustamante (Cuba), 26 votes.
> Finlay (Great Britain), 29 votes.
> Loder (Holland), 24 votes.
> Oda (Japan), 29 votes.
> Weiss (France), 30 votes.

On the second ballot John Bassett Moore (United States) was elected, with 22 votes. No candidate received a majority on either the third or fourth ballot, but on the fifth ballot M. Huber (Switzerland) also received the necessary 22 votes. This completed the Assembly's list of nine judges.

The Council notified the Assembly that it had elected the following:

> MM. Altamira (Spain).[1]
> Anzilotti (Italy).
> Ruy Barbosa (Brazil).
> Bustamante (Cuba).
> Descamps (Belgium).
> Finlay (Great Britain).
> Loder (Holland).
> Moore (United States).
> Nyholm (Denmark).
> Oda (Japan).
> Weiss (France).

Nine names appeared on both lists—MM. Altamira, Anzilotti, Ruy Barbosa, Bustamante, Finlay, Loder, Moore, Oda, and Weiss; two vacancies remained, for which four persons—Alvarez, Descamps, Nyholm and

---

[1] The number of votes each of these candidates received in the Council is not stated; as the Council then had eight members, however, each person elected must have had at least five votes.

Huber—had been chosen by one or the other of the two electoral bodies. Additional ballots for these two places were taken on the same day; the Assembly gave 22 votes to M. Huber, as before, and 27 to M. Nyholm, who had been on the Council's list. The Council also elected these two candidates, thus completing the full bench of eleven judges.

The election of the four deputy judges was held in the evening. The Assembly elected M. Alvarez (Chile), with 27 votes, and M. Negulesco (Rumania), with 23 votes, on the first ballot; no one received a majority on the second ballot; but on the third M. Wang (China) was elected, with 26 votes, and M. Yovanovitch (Kingdom of the Serbs, Croats, and Slovenes) with 22 votes. The Council elected three of these—MM. Negulesco, Wang, and Yovanovitch; its fourth nominee was M. Descamps (Belgium). Each chamber took two more ballots without result, as the Assembly insisted on M. Alvarez and the Council on M. Descamps. Resort was then taken to the provision made in the Court Statute (Article 12) for such a contingency, according to which a joint conference of six members, three appointed by the Council and three by the Assembly, may be appointed whenever three meetings have been fruitless; this joint conference is authorized to choose one name for each vacant seat, and submit it to the Assembly and Council for their acceptance. The Assembly appointed representatives of Denmark, Switzerland, and Holland, and the Council named representatives of Belgium, Spain, and China. This joint conference decided on M. Beichmann (Norway), who was accepted unanimously by the Council and by a majority vote in the Assembly.

123. The first Permanent Court of International Justice thus had the following members:

Judges:

MM. Rafael Altamira (Spain).
    Dionisio Anzilotti (Italy).
    Ruy Barbosa (Brazil).

Antonio S. de Bustamante (Cuba).
Lord R. B. Finlay (Great Britain).
Max Huber (Switzerland).
B. C. J. Loder (Holland).
John Bassett Moore (United States).
D. G. C. Nyholm (Denmark).
Yorozu Oda (Japan).
André Weiss (France).

Deputy Judges:
F. V. N. Beichmann (Norway).
D. Negulesco (Rumania).
Wang-Chung-Hui (China).
M. Yovanovitch (Kingdom of the Serbs,
    Croats and Slovenes).

From the continental point of view, three of the judges
are American—one North American, one Central American, and one South American; seven are European; and
one is Asiatic. Three of the deputy judges are European
and one Asiatic. Each of the nations ranked as a great
power at the end of the World War had a judge of its
nationality, although one of them had not joined the
League of Nations or adhered to the Court. The six other
judges, and all the four deputy judges, belong to the small
nations.

124. The election procedure of the Statute was tested
a second time on the death of M. Ruy Barbosa, the distinguished Brazilian statesman and jurisconsult. This
election was held on September 10, 1923. This time there
were twenty-nine candidates. Forty-six nations were represented in the Assembly meeting, thus making twenty-four
votes necessary to elect. M. Epitacio da Silva Pessoa
(Brazil) received thirty-five votes on the first ballot.
A moment later the Council notified the Assembly that it
had elected the same candidate.

125. Twice, therefore, the method of electing the
judges proposed by the representative of the United States

on the Advisory Committee of Jurists and accepted by the others has undeniably proved successful. The Assembly did not overpower the Council, nor the Council dominate the Assembly. The two bodies acted separately, but simultaneously, thus preventing the vote of either body from being influenced by the vote of the other. And on the one occasion when the two were not in accord, the joint conference proposed a different candidate, whom both accepted.

The primary and decisive test of any new organization, public or private, *i.e.*, whether it works satisfactorily, was met by this new institution with such complete success that no room is left for anything but rejoicing. Various theoretical criticisms which might be made of the system are overwhelmed by the reality of its effectiveness.

126. Certain anomalies in this election procedure should, nevertheless, be mentioned; they could easily be corrected without any essential changes. Two of these, for example, are relatively important. One is that the League of Nations is regulated, as to its original Covenant, by the Treaty of Versailles of June 28, 1919, while the fundamental charter of the Permanent Court of International Justice, the Statute, was approved by the Assembly on December 13, 1920. The contracting parties in these two documents are not the same international legal entities, and several states are in the curious position of being members of the League of Nations and of not having signed or ratified the Statute of the Permanent Court. And since this Statute (in Article 8) confides the election of the judges to the Assembly and the Council, it follows that the states not members of the Court take part in electing its judges, though they have never accepted its jurisdiction in any way.

Perhaps there is no great harm in this, although it seems illogical. Justice does not suffer because some of those who determine the judges have no need of it; and there obviously can be no suspicion that these non-member states are influenced by any personal considerations in voting. Nevertheless it does not seem altogether natural that a nation should assume a right, not conferred on it by any agreement to which it is a party, of voting to choose the judges, while holding back from joining the group bound by the Protocol establishing and organizing the Court. Such a nation shows either little faith or little confidence in the consequences of the vote it casts or in the position it takes.

The other matter is perhaps more significant. According to Article 35 of the Statute, the Court is open, not only to the States mentioned in the Annex of the Covenant, but also to other states not mentioned there. All that these last states need to do, as will be explained later in detail, is to file with the registrar of the Court a declaration, which may be either general or particular,[1] to the effect that they accept its jurisdiction and agree to carry out its decisions in good faith and not to go to war against another nation that respects the decision; such a state may also accept the optional clause, thus submitting itself to the compulsory jurisdiction of the Court. In spite of these obligations, no provision has been made for the participation of such states in the election of the judges, if they have not been willing, or have not been permitted, to join the League of Nations. Sometimes, under treaties made before or since the Court was established, a nation may be authorized to appear before the Court as plaintiff, or may be obliged to appear as defendant, without having had any opportunity to participate in the election of the judges. Germany has been in this position more than once.

127. Once elected, what rights do the judges possess? The first is that they are not removable during the term for which they are chosen, which is nine years (Article 13). The Advisory Committee of Jurists was unanimous on this point,[2] and the Council and the Assembly accepted their recommendation.

This question has been a subject of controversy a long time; the most divergent points of view have been shown.

---

[1] See page 199.
[2] Minutes, p. 442.

Kamarowsky, for example, thought that the judges should
not be removable, but that very severe personal qualifications should be imposed.[1]   Wehberg, for different reasons, was of the same opinion.[2]   Morellet maintained that
national and international courts function under different
conditions, because the international judge should be acceptable to the nations that submit their cause to his judgment, and therefore a court whose personnel changes at
certain periods ought to be able to count steadily on the
confidence of the nations.[3]   The writer of this book, in
statements of his own, insisted on the advantages of non-
removability, although discussing then a court where each
nation had its national judge.[4]

At the Second Hague Conference MM. Bourgeois,
Scott, Merey and others championed life tenure for the
judges; but the plan for a permanent court approved at
that time provided a definite term of office, of twelve years
—a little longer than in the statute now in operation.   The
Brazilian plan, curiously enough, made the term nine years.
The same diversity appeared in the other proposals considered by the Advisory Committee of Jurists.   Sweden,
two members of the Norwegian committee, and M. Lafontaine were in favor of non-removability; the Netherlands
stood by the twelve-year term of the 1907 draft; Denmark,
the other members of the Norwegian committee, Switzerland and Germany proposed nine years; and Italy and M.
Gram suggested seven.   In the Central American Court of
Justice a term of only five years had been set.   Every shade
of opinion was represented.

The members of the Advisory Committee did not agree
at first on the length of the term, for various reasons; none
of them was in favor of non-removability.   Lord Phillimore, supported by M. Altamira, proposed ten years.
M. Loder agreed with them.   The President, M. Des-

---

[1] Kamarowsky, Comte de—Le Tribunal International, p. 502.
[2] Wehberg, Hans—Das Problem eines internationalen Staatengerichtshofes,
p. 85.
[3] Morellet, J.—L'Organization de la Cour Permanente de Justice International, p. 66.
[4] de Bustamante—La 2a Conferencia de la Paz, T. I, p. 182.

camps, preferred six years, at least during the first years
of the Court.   M. Hagerup suggested a longer term (not
life tenure), its length to have some connection with the
amount of the pensions provided for the judges. The Committee finally agreed on nine years.   In the reference to this
point in the Committee report, sent with Council with the
Committee's draft statute, M. de Lapradelle, who prepared
the report, says that this period was chosen in order to
ensure a certain continuity of jurisprudence, but also to
make it possible to replace judges who no longer justified
the confidence placed in them by the nations.[1]

128. What one would like to see, for the sake of the
success and prestige of a Court of this kind, is that the
judges should have life tenure.   It would free the judges
from all personal ambitions for the future, and would
allow them to devote the rest of their lives to carrying
out their functions, free from preoccupation over material
considerations.   This continuity in office would result in
a natural continuity of jurisprudence, which would tend to
lessen the number of cases and contended questions, by
making the law certain and ascertainable.   It would thus
have, in an international court, all the advantages which
make it advisable and indispensable in national courts.

Nevertheless, the question is a complicated one, because
it is closely bound up with other questions that cannot be
dealt with in international life from a purely abstract point
of view.   If there were as many judges as there are nations
in the Court, and if each nation designated its own judge,
the question of life tenure would be much simpler.   But
since there are only about one-fifth as many judges as nations in the Court, and since the judges are elected by a
majority vote, it may easily happen that some nations
would be gratified by being represented on the bench for
a long time, while others would never be so honored.
While the world remains as it is, it would be difficult for
the latter nations to reconcile themselves to being excluded.

On the other hand, the life tenure might prevent the

[1] Minutes, p. 190, 194, 195, 197, 714.

representation on the Court of all the principal judicial systems which the Statute calls for.   And it might be that by consecrating his whole life to one task—perhaps living always in one place—a judge would imperceptibly develop a sort of second nature in judicial matters, and his feelings and judgments might be influenced by the atmosphere about him.   The judges would practically become de-nationalized in their mental reactions, which would detract from the efficacy and collective authority of their decisions.

In the Advisory Committee of Jurists, one of the members maintained, on this point, that a nine-year term would be equivalent to life tenure, because the persons elected as judges would no doubt be of mature age.   This argument is hardly convincing, for there was a difference of twenty-seven years in the ages of the judges chosen at the first election in 1921, the oldest having been born in 1842 and the youngest in 1869.   Certainly a nine-year term is not equivalent to life tenure for the latter?

That the judges are expressly made eligible for re-election, by Article 13 of the Statute, may seem to offset the disadvantages of the temporary appointment.   Too much reliance should not be placed on this provision, however; the strongest reasons for continuing a judge in office may have to yield to the conditions that may arise in any large electoral body, or to the fact that some of the electors will have appeared in cases before the Court and will have been defeated or disappointed,—or to the practical necessity for rotating the judges among the various nations. Experience alone can solve this problem; and we may rely on the impartiality, the good judgment, and the high moral standards of that great human organization, the League of Nations.

129. In case it should happen from some unforeseen situation, such as a general state of war, that the electors could not meet at the proper time or could not decide upon judges, Article 13 of the Statute makes the wise provision that the judges shall continue in office till their successors are appointed.   And as a judge's term may end during the proceedings in a case in which he is sitting, the same Article properly provides that he shall continue to sit in such a case until it is completed.

130. In one case only is the term of office less than nine years. In case a seat becomes vacant, it is filled at a special election, and the person chosen is elected only for the unexpired portion of his predecessor's term. This provision (in Article 14 of the Statute) was made for reasons connected with the election, rather than for any fundamental difference in functions. Moreover, under the system now in operation, it is not an important point; so far there has been only one vacancy, and in that case another citizen of the same country as his predecessor was chosen, so that that seat in the Court will remain with that nation for the entire term of nine years.

131. It was necessary to provide the procedure by which a judge no longer qualified might be removed, and the Statute provides an apparently satisfactory solution of this difficult question. The situation is not referred to the judgment of the electors, nor to any other bodies or governments, who may not have the necessary information or the requisite impartiality for doing full justice. It is the Court itself which, by Article 18, is to declare the place vacant; this may be done only if the incumbent has ceased to fulfill the required conditions. This provision contains one new and exceedingly important guarantee of justice: the decision must be unanimous.

The Rules of Court adopted by the Court on March 24, 1922, for the regulation of its internal affairs provides in Article 6 that if this case arises the President, or if necessary the Vice-President, is to convene the judges and deputy judges; the member affected is to be allowed to furnish explanations, after which he is to withdraw; the other judges discuss the question, and then take a vote.

132. Article 19 of the Statute says that "the members of the Court, when engaged on the business of the Court, shall enjoy diplomatic privileges and immunities." The French and English texts are slightly different, but they certainly mean the same thing.[1] This prerogative is clearly justifiable; it was proposed long ago in plans for a court already commented on in this book. The Court needs, more than any other person, to be absolutely independent of the governments or nations between which it is to deal out justice; it is necessary that its judges should be beyond any administrative or judicial action on the part of the nations through which they pass or in which they sit. Although M. Ricci-Busatti, with a rather exacting standard, insisted in the Advisory Committee that he wanted it clearly understood that diplomatic privileges would be given to judges only during the actual performance of their duties,[2] the Committee, after some discussion, agreed that the judges should enjoy these rights not only during their residence in the Netherlands, but also in the countries through which they would have to travel on their way to and from the Court.

"Outside of their country," the Root-Phillimore plan proposed to add (Article 20), and this phrase was retained by the Committee of Jurists. In the Assembly, however, on the motion of the British delegation, it was suppressed, and it does not appear in the final Statute. This final result is the logical one; the mission of a judge has the same character and calls for the same guarantees in reference to his own nation as with reference to foreign nations. His situation is the opposite to that of diplomatic representatives; they act in one nation in the name of the other, belong to this other one, and are its officials and members, whereas these international judges are to deal justice to their own countries as to the others, and it is therefore necessary for them to be free of any restraint or any influence so far as the whole world is concerned.

One distinct problem, not settled in the Statute and not yet regulated, is the question of the rank or precedence

---

[1] The French text is: "Les membres de la Cour jouissent dans l'exercice de leurs functions des privileges et immunities diplomatiques." The English text is given above.

[2] Minutes, p. 479.

of the judges, when they are taking part in official ceremonies or demonstrations in the country where the Court
sits, or in foreign lands, or in their own. Do they, by
reason of their prerogative, march with the diplomatic
corps? What is their place in the diplomatic corps? It is
a complicated question, but it will be settled in a manner
satisfactory to all concerned, either by uniform national
laws regulating the diplomatic ceremonies, or by an international convention, or perhaps by the Assembly of the
League of Nations.

133. Another right conferred on the judges by the
Statute is of an economic nature. By Article 32, they are
to receive an annual indemnity to be determined by the
Assembly of the League, on the proposal of the Council.
It is expressly stated that the indemnity of a judge must
not be decreased during his appointment,—no doubt as a
guarantee to enable him to give up his other means of support without inquietude, when he accepts office.

The President receives a special grant, to be fixed in
the same way, also not subject to change during his term.
Moreover, the Vice-President, judges and deputy judges
receive a grant for the actual performance of their duties,
to be fixed in the same way; and the necessary travelling
expenses of the judges and deputy judges are paid. The
last two grants are also made to a national judge, appointed
by a party to a litigation not represented in the Court.

As will have been noted, the remuneration of the judges
is in two forms, one a fixed salary paid for the year, and
the other an allowance proportionate to the time spent in
the actual performance of duty. The first is fixed; the
second depends on the amount of work done, and is payable
only to those that take part in it. This is an ingenious
arrangement, but in certain cases it leads, perhaps, to criticisms rather humiliating to a judge's dignity. It would
have been better to reverse the arrangement, by deciding
on a certain fixed maximum, with proportionate deductions
to be made in cases where a judge, for whatever reason,
is unable to sit through all or part of a session, not includ-

ing in the deductions the case of a possible challenge of a judge by one of the parties to a litigation.

As the first system has been adopted in the Statute, however, the question of salaries had to be submitted to the Assembly of the League, which entrusted the necessary detailed work of preparing the schedule to a committee of which M. Costa was chairman. The committee met twice, on December 15 and 16, 1920, and after discussing the question in detail, proposed an arrangement which was accepted without change by the Assembly two days later.

By this arrangement the President of the Court receives an annual salary of 15,000 Dutch florins,[1] and a special allowance of 45,000 florins, making a total of 60,000 Dutch florins. The Vice-President receives the same annual salary, and an allowance of 150 florins per day spent in the actual performance of his duty, not to exceed over 200 days a year, thus giving him as a maximum 45,000 florins. Each judge receives an annual salary of 15,000 florins, and a grant of 100 florins per day of actual work, which may not exceed 200 days a year, which gives a possible maximum of 35,000 florins. The deputy judges receive an allowance of 150 florins per day of actual work, not to amount to over 200 days a year, which gives a possibility of 30,000 florins. These grants and allowances are reckoned from the day the judge leaves his country to the day he returns to it, naturally within the limits of a normal trip. In addition to this, the Vice-President and the judges and deputy judges receive a subsistence allowance of 50 florins a day while their presence at The Hague is necessary.[2]

134. The last paragraph of Article 32 provides that the Assembly, on the proposal of the Council, shall lay down a special regulation fixing the conditions on which retiring pensions may be given to the personnel of the Permanent Court. The Advisory Committee of Jurists discussed this question in connection with more than one proposal, but came to no decision on it, leaving it to be settled

[1] About $6,000.
[2] Documents relative, etc., p. 269 et seq.

THE JUDGES 141

by a special provision.[1] The Fifth Assembly adopted a
resolution on September 30, 1924, which provided that the
judges were entitled to a pension on retiring from office,
unless they had been dismissed for reasons other than
health; and a judge who has served less than five years is
not entitled to a pension, except by special decision of the
Court, which grants him the minimum amount. A pension
does not become payable till the person entitled to it is 65
years old, but here again the Court may by special decision
authorize its payment to him.

The maximum retiring pension is 15,000 florins a year.
The pension is calculated on the following basis: for each
twelve months of service, a judge is entitled to a pension
equivalent to one-thirtieth of his salary for that period,
salary being held to include his fixed annual salary, plus
a duty allowance for a minimum of 180 days. The President's duty allowance is reckoned as 35,000 florins, for this
purpose.

These retirement pensions correspond to the usual
administrative practice; they also help to make it possible
to find capable persons who are willing to change the course
of their lives for nine years if they are not to be entirely
helpless at the end of this relatively short term.

135. Another right which the judges possess—this a
right of an entirely different nature—is that accorded to
them by Article 57 of the Statute, which provides that if
the judgment does not represent, in whole or in part, the
unanimous opinion of the judges, dissenting judges are
entitled to deliver a separate opinion.

This decision was reached only after serious difficulties
and much controversy. The precedents of the Hague Peace
Conferences inevitably were invoked, and had some influence with the Committee. The arbitral convention of 1899
says, in Article 52, that the members who are in a minority
"may record their dissent when signing." In 1907, however, this phrase was suppressed in the revised convention,
which merely says, in Article 78, that "the tribunal reaches

[1] Minutes, p. 563.

its decisions in private and the proceedings remain secret,"
and that "all questions are decided by a majority of the
members of the tribunal;" the same provision was made in
the draft for the proposed Court of Arbitral Justice.

In commenting then [1] on this decision, the writer of this
book maintained that his individual experience, based on
extensive practice in judicial matters, justified him in saying
that the power and the prestige of Courts are not weakened
or diminished by the fact that one or more dissenting
judges state that they dissent and give the reasons why.
In international affairs, the custom of having the majority
and minority votes in arbitral decisions equally well known,
far from diminishing the authority of arbitration or the
obligatory force of the awards, has helped to protect
national *amour propre* from injury and has encouraged
compliance with the awards.

Moreover, as the writer then added, an eminent man
who accepts the honorable task of sitting on an arbitral
tribunal finds himself in a very disagreeable situation in
case an award is given with which he does not agree
if he has no right to protect his vote and make his own
opinion known. He must either break the seal of secrecy
imposed on the deliberations, thus failing in his duty, or
else he must pass as being opposed to vital rights, perhaps,
because his vote is fused into the fictitious unanimity of
a decision made by a mere majority. With the opposite
system, no one is made responsible for the opinions of
others; in international as in national affairs, no one ought
to stifle his individual conscience with the anonymous decision of an undetermined group. There can be no true
justice unless each judge feels and asserts his individual
responsibility.

The action of the Committee of Jurists was apparently
influenced by the fact that the question came up before
them from a different angle, with reference to the national
judges that the parties to a litigation may name to sit
in a case if there is not already a judge of their nationality
on the Court. M. de Lapradelle was afraid that a national

[1] de Bustamante—La 2a Conferencia de la Paz. Tome i, p. 205-6.

judge would always record his disapproval of a sentence unfavorable to his country. The Committee, perhaps as a compromise, allowed a judge to record his dissent, but without giving his reasons for it, or his reservations. This provision was made in Article 56 of the Committee's draft.[1]

Fortunately, by the time the question came up before the Council of the League, a committee appointed by the government of Sweden had already pointed out the advantages of allowing dissenting judges to state the reasons for their dissent.[2] The eminent M. Bourgeois, in his report adopted by the Council, pointed out that if the judges were permitted to state their opinions, together with their reasons, the play of the different judicial lines of thought would appear clearly; he therefore proposed that this be expressly authorized in the Statute. The Council agreed with this opinion, and this Article was changed to its present liberal and wise form.

Then it had to run the gauntlet again in the subcommittee to which the Assembly referred the draft for detailed study. M. Loder opposed the Council's provision, on the ground that it expressed ideas foreign to continental procedure and involving danger to the authority of the Court; MM. Ricci-Busatti and Fromageot supported him with more or less conviction. On the other side, M. Fernandes, the illustrious Brazilian, rejoiced at the Council's action, for which he had fought in vain in the Committee of Jurists; M. Politis also defended it, and Sir Cecil Hurst, speaking for England, gave very strong reasons in support of it. After this debate the Council's version was adopted by the subcommittee, and was accepted without comment by the Committee, and, still without any discussion, was finally adopted in the Assembly. This is a very fortunate result.

The Court has already had occasion to make use of this right. Its practice, in both judgments and advisory opinions, seems to be that judges who do not agree with the decision may so state, if they desire, giving their rea-

[1] Minutes, p. 531, 591, 741 et seq.
[2] Documents relative, etc., pp. 37, 44, 50, 136, 138, 213.

sons, and also that a judge who does agree with any particular arguments or statements made in it and who wishes
to present new or different reasons not accepted by the
majority, may do so.

136. It can hardly be said that the judges have the right
—at least not in the same sense as the rights that have
already been discussed—of asking a witness questions after
the President has done so, which Article 51 of the Rules
expressly authorizes them to do. The duties laid upon the
judges by the provisions of the Statute, and those that
devolve upon them by virtue of the charge confided to
them, are discussed below.

137. The first of their obligations—not explicitly stated
in any legal rule, but a natural consequence of their having
accepted the function of judge—is to be present at the sessions. When a judge has reasons that justify his absence,
he naturally notifies the Court through the President as
speedily as possible, so that a deputy judge may be called
to take his place.

Immediate notice must also be given to the President
of a more or less prolonged absence during a session that
has already begun, although in this case it would not be
necessary to call a deputy judge unless he was needed to
make up a quorum.

This obligation necessarily includes the duty to be
present until the session is ended and until the matters
requiring the attention of the judges are completed, unless
there are adequate reasons for absence or unless permission has been obtained from the Court. These are simply
matters of common sense which national legislatures regulate by law, but which this international legislation does
not cover, probably because there could be no doubt about
them.

138. On the other hand, Article 16 of the Statute
expressly provides that the ordinary members of the Court

—*i.e.,* the judges, not including the deputy judges—may not exercise any political or administrative function; it adds that any doubt on this point is settled by the decision of the Court. The particular points involved in this matter of incompatible functions were debated a long time by the Committee of Jurists and by the Assembly subcommittee, and yet it can hardly be said that what the drafters of the Statute meant is altogether clear.

While M. Ricci-Busatti pretended, greatly to the surprise of M. Descamps, that this matter should be left to the internal legislation of the different nations, several others of the jurists cited possible cases that might arise, some of which indicated that the double function should be prohibited, and some that it should be allowed. Lord Phillimore, for example, thinking of his own country, stated that in his opinion it was rather an advantage for an international judge to be at the same time on the bench in his own country, and suggested that as English judges were often members of the House of Lords, and as judges were in a similar position in other countries, it would be desirable not to consider membership in such a legislative body as a political function. He thought, however, that cabinet members ought not to serve as judges. M. de Lapradelle did not believe that jurisconsults attached to Foreign Offices could serve as judges (*i.e.,* while so attached). M. Altamira submitted a clear and comprehensive general provision to the effect that any one holding an executive position should be excluded.[1] M. Loder, for his part, saw no inconvenience in allowing a judge of the Court to exercise judicial duties at home, and M. Adatci thought that educational duties at home should also be allowable. Finally the following provision, prepared by Mr. Root and Lord Phillimore, was adopted by the Committee: "The exercise of any function which belongs to the political direction, national or international, of states by the members of the Court, during their terms of office, is declared incompatible with their judicial duties." Later, on Mr. Hagerup's mo-

[1] *I.e.,* that no one could continue to hold such a position while acting as judge.—Tr. note.

tion, the following phrase was added: "Any doubt upon this point is settled by the decision of the Court." Still later, M. Altimira said that he was afraid that if the import of this Article were not explained in the Committee's report, it would seem as though only national judges were eligible to be international judges, to which the President answered that it would be explained in the report that its object was only to exclude members of governments and persons holding positions of a political nature.

The report, prepared by M. de Lapradelle, contains this statement: "A great judge or a great professor, in whom the nations have sufficient confidence to call him to the Court, must be allowed to continue in his present functions —the judge to administer justice in his country, and the professor to give his lectures: no incompatibility exists in their cases. Similarly an eminent member of Parliament may retain his legislative function. On the other hand, a member of a government, a minister or under-secretary of state, a diplomatic representative, a director of a ministry or one of his subordinates, or the legal adviser to a foreign office, though they would be eligible for appointment as arbitrators to the Court of 1899, are certainly not eligible for appointment as judges upon our Court." The same incompatibility existed, he said, between the judicial function and active participation in the political control of a country or international political duties such as representing a nation in the Council or Assembly of the League, or as being the League's Secretary General; but it did not apply to membership in an international tribunal, especially in the Court of Arbitration of The Hague.[1]

When the draft plan reached the Council, one of the nations that studied it most carefully—Italy—proposed that this Article be clarified by stating expressly that parliamentary functions were not considered incompatible with service as judge, the English version of the text of the draft being: "any function which belongs to the political direction." The Swedish and Norwegian committees proposed another wording, simpler and more general, but with

[1] Minutes, pp. 191, 192, 193, 463, 494, 573, 646, 714, 715, 717.

much wider scope: "The functions of a judge are incompatible with any other public function. In doubtful cases the Court shall decide." The Council, however, did not amend this Article and sent it on to the Assembly just as it had come from the Committee of Jurists.

In the Assembly subcommittee the question was debated exhaustively, and the same arguments and instances were produced, finally taking shape in an amendment drafted by M. Fromageot, which was adopted by a vote of 8 to 2. It read as follows: "The exercise of any political or administrative function is incompatible with the duties of members of the Court." Afterward in the full committee, the Panama delegate, M. Arias, pointed out that this wording would apply to deputy judges too, and would make it impossible to find persons willing to serve; the point was considered to be well taken, and the provision was made applicable only to the ordinary (*i.e.,* the regular) judges. The Assembly gave its final approval to this wording, as it appears in the first sentence of this Number, 138.[1]

The Court has had to consider, more or less explicitly, several instances under this Article. At the very beginning it admitted as judges a Spanish Senator and a member of the British House of Lords. It also made no objection to service by a judge as a member of a conciliation commission appointed under an international treaty, or as an arbitrator appointed in the same way. And no doubt arose as to whether it was possible for other judges to continue to perform their duties, at least while the Court was not in session, as professors in official national universities or other educational institutions, or in the Academy of International Law at The Hague. When two functions are obviously compatible, they can easily be reconciled.

139. Article 17 contains two other prohibitions, which are so necessary and so justifiable that they need only be stated without comment: "No member of the Court can act as agent, counsel or advocate in any case of an international nature. This provision only applies to

[1] Documents relative, etc., pp. 28, 33, 101, 123, 125, 191, 208.

the deputy judges as regards cases in which they are called upon to exercise their functions on the Court. No member may participate in the decision of any case in which he has previously taken an active part, as agent, counsel or advocate for one of the contesting parties, or as a member of a national or international Court, or of a commission of enquiry, or in any other capacity. Any doubt on this point is settled by the decision of the Court."

140. Among the duties of the judges of the Permanent Court must be included that of preparing the reports entrusted to them and their opinions, together with the reasons for them, in every case submitted to them for judgment or opinion. They must also participate in the voting for a decision, and are not entitled to abstain from voting, although there is no specific provision to this effect. Such a privilege, however, is inconceivable in the administration of justice; if it were granted to one or more, all the others could avail themselves of it, and cases would not be decided. National laws often provide that a judge shall incur a penalty for refusing to vote on the ground that there is no law covering the case, or that the law is insufficient or not clear. The same rule should apply in international relations, particularly as this Court ought to be and can be a source of law.

141. Although the Statute and the Rules do not say so, all the judges are expected to reside during the sessions at The Hague, where the Court has its seat. Article 12 of the Rules, applicable only to the President, requires him to reside continuously within a radius of ten kilometres (about six miles) from the Peace Palace; and his main annual vacation may not exceed three months.

142. The Statute and the Rules do not expressly prohibit the judges from receiving honors or decorations from national governments during their term. A prohibition of this kind was made in several earlier drafts for a Court.

It was sensible to omit this provision; no judge possessing
the qualifications for being chosen would be capable of allowing his vote or his opinion to be influenced by the hope
of obtaining attentions flattering to his personal vanity,
or by gratitude for having received them; but it is just
as well that the credit and prestige of the Court should
not suffer from any suspicion that such a possibility were
conceivable.

143. There is a third class of judges which has not been
mentioned yet, and which should be described in this chapter. Article 31 of the Statute provides that if there is
upon the bench a judge of the nationality of one of the
parties to a case, but none of the other, the other party
may select from among the deputy judges a judge of its
nationality, if there be one, or, if there should not be one,
then preferably from among the persons who were nominated as candidates for election as judges. If there is no
judge of the nationality of either party on the bench, each
of the parties may choose a judge by the method just
stated. If there are several parties in the same interest,
they are, for this purpose, reckoned as one party only. Any
doubt on this point is settled by the Court.

These national judges represent a point of contact between the Permanent Court and the system of arbitration;
it is not an entirely plausible arrangement. They must
possess the same general qualifications as the other judges,
have the same obligations, and are subject to the same
prohibition as to incompatibility of functions and as to the
duty not to sit in cases with which they have previously
been connected.

144. There is one thing more to be said: when a member of the Court is dismissed during his term because, in
the unanimous opinion of the other judges, he has ceased
to possess the necessary qualifications for being elected, as
explained above, the registrar of the Court notifies the
Secretary General of the League, and the post becomes

vacant upon this notification. It seems necessary and logical that the same notice should be sent when a judge has ceased to perform his duties for any other reason, as, for example, if he resigns or dies.

CHAPTER IX

THE ORGANIZATION AND OPERATION OF THE COURT

145. The possible field of action of the Permanent Court is sufficiently restricted by Article 14 of the Covenant of the League, containing the provision for establishing it, which says that the Court "shall be competent to hear and determine any dispute of an international character which the parties thereto refer to it." This raised the question whether it was a judicial power for the world that was to be established, or whether it was arbitration that was to have henceforth a fixed institution, which would facilitate its use in any given dispute.

Certainly the Treaty of Versailles, in which the Covenant is incorporated, opened up the way for the first possibility, by establishing the compulsory jurisdiction of the Court for a considerable number of cases, as will appear in detail a little farther on in the book; but some doubt, nevertheless, remained, and the Advisory Committee of Jurists tried to settle this doubt by emphasizing the judicial character of the Court in the Statute it drafted for the new institution. This showed, as certainly more than one member of the Committee felt, the necessity of making the distinction clear between arbitration and the judicial power; there were long discussions on the nature and the results of this distinction. M. Ricci-Busatti twice maintained that there was no difference between them, and that progress had merely been made in the arbitral jurisdiction; but others thought that the work they had undertaken made it necessary to maintain the distinction.

M. Bourgeois, opening the work of the Committee in a very significant speech, indicated at once the nature of the future Permanent Court: "It is not to be a Court of Arbitration," he said, "but a Court of Justice." According to him, there is an essential difference between an arbitral award and the decision of a judge, as great as that between equity and justice.

It will be helpful, in trying to reach a final opinion on this point, to refer to the forms in which these two institutions appear in the domestic life of a nation. Each has its judicial power, with a detailed organization, open to all. A person claiming a right before this power obliges the other party either to appear to defend himself, or else to suffer judgment by default. In either case the judge or the Court, already in existence, working under rules of jurisdiction and of competence—two different things [1]— which precede and supersede the will of each party, decides in accordance with the laws in force or the applicable common law, and gives a legal solution to every question. Although sovereignty resides in the people and although all the public powers emanate from the people in democratic lands, the judicial power is not the concrete and special creation of all the parties to the suits; it exists before them and above them, and it operates from above as an authority and a force in relation to every question. The same thing is true as to the law that applies; it may correspond and usually does correspond to the national will, which creates the legislative power, and which is reflected in the legal usage; but it operates toward individual interests as a superior force, to which their disputes are submitted.

In the sphere of arbitration, which domestic legislation also admits for particular questions, with certain exceptions based on public policy, the parties choose and designate the judge or the court that they desire; and they may entrust to it the task of judging in accordance with the general law, or in accordance with special rules chosen by them, or simply in accordance with equity. It is fair to say that in arbitration everything is voluntary, personal, and private.

Is the situation the same in international relations? As there is no super-state, there cannot yet be a stable and

[1] See page 179. Tr. note.

fixed judicial power, set in operation by the will of the majority, and not by the consent of those interested. These interested nations, either for one specific case, or for a certain kind of questions, or for all questions not of a political nature that may arise between two or more of them, agree to submit their disputes or litigations to justice. In other words, the judicial power of the world, compared to that of each nation, has hitherto been determined by national law, and is, both in its origin and development, arbitral in its nature.

No doubt the existence of a common Court, created and maintained by all, and accepted as compulsory by all or by a large number of them as to certain problems, represents a considerable advance. It may be called the necessary link between arbitration and justice; seen from one side, it resembles arbitration, whence it comes; seen from the other side, it resembles justice, toward which it is going.[1]

And since this Court, as will be shown later on, decides *ex aequo et bono* when the parties agree to ask that it should, the analogy and the connection between the two institutions is very clear and evident. They do not seem incompatible on this account, however; and Article 1 of the Statute could say, without difficulty or violence, that a Permanent Court of International Justice was established, independent of the Court of Arbitration organized by the Conventions of The Hague of 1899 and 1907, and of special tribunals of arbitration, to which the states are always free to submit their disputes for settlement. This wording was kept by the Council and the Assembly, although one American nation, the Argentine Republic, proposed that the Arbitral Court already existing at The Hague should be totally suppressed. What is said here in Article 1 is not inconsistent with an intention to emphasize the clearly judicial character of the new institution.

The report of the Committee of Jurists, prepared by M. de Lapradelle, points out that in the Court of Arbi-

[1] See B. C. J. Loder, Le différence entre l'arbitrage internationale et la justice internationale. La Haye, 1923.

tration it is the parties who choose their judges, after the dispute has arisen, whereas in the case of the Permanent Court of International Justice the contesting parties no longer have that choice; "in the Court of Arbitration there is no permanent tie between the sitting judges, and consequently no *esprit de corps* and no progressive continuity in jurisprudence; the Permanent Court of International Justice, on the other hand, being composed of judges permanently associated with each other in the same work, and, except in rare cases, retaining their seats from one case to another, can develop a continuous tradition and assure the harmonious and logical development of international law. It is to be feared that the judges of the Court of Arbitration, being inclined to regard the case from a political standpoint, may not give sufficient weight to the rules of law. In the Permanent Court of International Justice law necessarily becomes more authoritative and also, possibly, more severe."

The Committee's draft of Article 1 contained the phrase, "to which parties shall have direct access," referring, of course, to the Court; in the Assembly the British representatives expressed the unwarranted fear that this phrase implied compulsory jurisdiction. This assumption was unjustified, but as this phrase might, strictly speaking, be considered unnecessary and as it did not add anything to the force or scope of the Article, it was dropped in the final revision.

146. One point that had to be settled was the residence and seat of the Permanent Court. A series of previous plans, official and otherwise, had chosen The Hague, especially after the attention centered on it in the two Peace Conferences of 1899 and 1907. The fact that Holland had remained neutral during the 1914-1918 war gave it a certain atmosphere of tranquillity that a judicial institution needs; moreover, the League of Nations had established itself in Switzerland, a permanently neutralized state, and it was obvious that the international political organization of the world and its international judicial organization should not be in the same place. It was for these reasons, no doubt, and for others, that the so-called Root-Phillimore plan, which was made the basis of the Committee's deliberations, provided in Article 24 that the Court should have its seat at The Hague.

Lord Phillimore, however, made the ingenious suggestion during the discussions that the choice of The Hague was perhaps only accidental and temporary; "who knows," he said, "but that one day it might be transferred, for instance, to South America." In a later session, on June 25, 1920, the Committee, after discussing the question, decided upon The Hague, for various reasons not completely set forth in the report. This is the provision that now appears in the Statute, in Article 22.

On July 12 a discussion took place that was very interesting and very much in point, on the question whether it should be possible for the Court to transfer its seat in any given case, with or without the consent of the parties, and by its own decision or by the decision of the League of Nations. Most of the members of the Committee were opposed to any such provision; some members, curiously enough, were afraid that it would tend to make the Court like an arbitral tribunal. The possibility that the Netherlands might be involved in a war apparently never occurred to anyone; the result of that situation would be that the Court would have to suspend its work indefinitely, or else carry it on during the roar of the cannon, without the presence of its members belonging to one or another of the belligerent states, and with the neutrals unable to bring suit against the enemies of Holland. The mere suggestion of this situation—and there are others quite as possible—is enough to show that if it had been brought to the attention of the Committee of Jurists, or of the Council or the Assembly, their common sense would have made them add the phrases necessary for qualifying this dangerous and prejudicial provision that makes the Court's seat so rigidly fixed.

Moreover, if America entrusts its cases to the Court, the Court may need the American atmosphere and may

need to be near the place where the parties are, in order
that its decisions may be entirely just. This will be referred
to later on.

147. Article 3 of the Statute provides that the Court
shall consist of fifteen members, eleven judges and four
deputy judges. This number may be increased hereafter
by the Assembly, upon the proposal of the Council, to a
total of fifteen judges and six deputy judges.

The question of the actual number of judges has, within
certain limits, very little importance. It is a curious fact,
however, that in the plans submitted to the Committee of
Jurists the number of regular judges ranged between seven
and twenty-one, and of deputy judges between five and
fifteen—not including the Italian plan, which proposed one
judge from each nation. The really serious difficulty, in
connection with a body relatively small in comparison to
the number of states accepting it, was whether the body
was to be large or small. M. Loder, on the one hand,
maintained that the number should be very much limited,
not only because it would be difficult to find a large number
of persons sufficiently qualified and at the same time willing
to accept the duties of judges, but also because a small
body would work together better than a large tribunal,
and its members would have a greater sense of responsibility. Others pointed out that with a sufficiently large
number of judges, each great power would have a place,
and the small powers would have the majority, and that
the different legal systems and different forms of civilization could then be represented. The Committee finally
agreed on eleven regular judges and four deputy judges,
as provided in the Article quoted above, without prejudice
to a minimum quorum of nine.

It was Mr. Root's idea to make the number elastic, by
providing that the present number may be increased within
set limits. He pointed out that half of the population of
Europe and the United States of America was outside
the League at that time and suggested that successive increases in the number of judges, in proportion as other

nations entered the League, would respond to the demands of its natural develópment.   Lord Phillimore supported this suggestion, and it was adopted in the final report of the Committee, submitted to the Council with the draft-scheme.

Without denying that the provision made by the Committee of Jurists has its advantages, and that it may have been opportune and necessary for political reasons, the writer of this book believes that a large Court works badly and slowly.   It becomes a sort of assembly instead of a court, and sometimes hands down lectures instead of decisions, which does not serve the supreme interests of justice.   This does not mean that the writer of this book is opposed, for the future, to the Italian proposition of one judge from each nation; the writer has upheld this plan in another book, in which it was proposed that the judges in this large body were not to sit as one Court, but were to be divided into a series of smaller chambers which, by rotation or by lot, were to take cognizance of litigations between nations.   There are a great many problems that would have to be solved under such a plan; life tenure for the judges would have to be a corollary of it.   At the present time, with not much work to be done, and with the world still divided by recent military and political events, perhaps no better arrangement could have been devised.

There is one point not covered in this article; it provides how the number of judges may be increased, up to a maximum limit, but it does not provide how it may be reduced in order to bring it down again to the minimum that is set.   If it is necessary to increase the number because other nations come under its jurisdiction, it would seem natural that it should be decreased if the same nations, or others, withdraw.   This hypothesis does not seem to have occurred to any one; probably it could be adjusted by a decision of the Council and Assembly.

M. de Lapradelle brought up before the Committee of Jurists a proposal that had been in a number of earlier plans.   In the session of June 24, 1920, he said, in effect, that in order to have all the great centers of civilization represented, it should be stipulated that the Court should contain so many Asiatic judges, so many American judges, and so many European judges. M. Descamps, the President, observed that this plan involved grave difficulties, and the subject was dropped. It came up again in the Assembly, however, and again without success; the Colombian delegation proposed that the Court should have fifteen judges and six deputy judges, of whom eight judges and three deputy judges were to be European in nationality, five judges and two deputy judges American in nationality, and two judges and one deputy judge Asiatic or African. The learned representative of Cuba, M. Aguero, proposed that the last group should be either Asiatic, African or Oceanic.[1]

The general election of the judges, as has already been seen, gave judges to all parts of the world, without any statutory provision, merely by the free and independent action of the electoral body.

148. Lord Phillimore insisted that the Court must always meet in plenary session, and that only thus would it deserve its name. Baron Descamps, President of the Committee, took the opposite view, advocating a division of the Court into chambers.[2] The first opinion won; Article 25 of the Statute provides that the full Court shall sit except when it is expressly provided otherwise. If eleven judges cannot be present, the number is to be made up by calling on deputy judges to sit. Article 4 of the Rules adds that in cases in which one or more of the parties is entitled to choose a judge *ad hoc* of its nationality, the full Court may sit with a number of judges exceeding eleven. This is what happened in the Wimbledon case and the Palestine mandate case, when the addition of a German judge in one case and of a Greek judge in the other brought the number of judges up to twelve. These provisions do not

[1] Minutes, pp. 54, 56, 169, 173, 185-6, 200, 441-2, 613, 711. Documents relative, etc., pp. 82 and 246.
[2] Minutes, pp. 169, 171, 175, 517.

apply to the special chambers nor to the chamber for summary procedure, mentioned at the end of this chapter.

149. The minimum number that may sit is not eleven, however, but nine, according to the last paragraph of Article 25 of the Statute; national judges may not be counted in the quorum, as the preceding paragraph refers only to judges and deputy judges. When eleven judges cannot be present, the number is made up by calling on deputy judges to sit, in the order laid down in a list prepared by the Court, with regard first to priority of election and secondly to age, beginning with the oldest. Articles 25 and 15 of the Statute and 2 and 3 of the Rules contain these provisions.

This last Article, going into details, directs that the deputy judges be called in their order on the list, *i.e.*, each of them is to be summoned in rotation till all the names are exhausted. If a deputy judge is so far away from the seat of the Court that, in the President's opinion, the summons would not reach him in sufficient time, the next on the list is to be summoned, and the one thus passed over is to be called, if possible, the next time that the presence of a deputy judge is required. If a deputy judge is summoned to sit in a particular case as a national judge, under the terms of Article 31 of the Statute, the summons is not considered as meaning that his name is to be passed over the next time it is reached on the deputy judge list.

While the Rules were being prepared, a discussion arose in the Court as to what was meant by priority of election; M. Negulesco submitted an argument, referring to the day and the hour of election by the Council and the Assembly, proposing that all the judges chosen at any one annual session should be considered as being elected on the same date.[1]

150. This question is settled in Article 2 of the Rules in the manner suggested above, and with reference to both judges and deputy judges. It provides that judges and

[1] Acts and Documents, etc., No. 2, p. 588.

deputy judges elected at an earlier session of the Assembly and Council of the League shall take precedence respectively over judges and deputy judges elected at a subsequent session, and that the judges and the deputy judges elected during the same session shall take precedence according to age, the judges taking precedence over deputy judges, and the national judges following in order of age.

The Vice-President sits on the right of the President and the other judges sit alternately right and left of the President, in the order given above.

Certain technical assessors may also form part of the Court; they sit, following the judges, in certain cases relating to labor and transit and communications. Their functions are explained later in the statement on the special chambers authorized and organized by the Statute.

151. The preceding rules apply to both public and private sessions. Article 31 of the Rules provides that the Court shall sit in private to deliberate upon the decision of any case or on the reply to any question submitted to it for an advisory opinion. During these deliberations only the judges, the technical assessors and the registrar may be present, unless some other person is admitted by virtue of a special decision taken by the Court, on account of exceptional circumstances; for example, an interpreter may be needed, on account of the normal and constant use of two languages in the same case.

152. Every member of the Court, including the national judges, must make what Article 20 of the Statute calls a solemn declaration, in open court; Article 5 of the Rules prescribes the following form:

> "I solemnly declare that I will exercise all my powers and duties as a judge honorably and faithfully, impartially and conscientiously."

At the public inaugural sitting held after a new election of the whole Court, the required declaration is made first

by the President, then by the Vice-President, and then by
the remaining judges in the order specified above.

153. In accordance with Article 21 of the Statute and
Articles 9, 10, 11 and 13 of the Rules, the Court elects its
President and Vice-President for three years; they may be
reëlected. The election takes place at the end of the
ordinary session preceding their term of office. After a
general election of the entire Court, the election of the
President and Vice-President takes place at the beginning
of the session following the election; in this case the President and the Vice-President take up their duties on the day
of their election, and remain in office until the end of the
second year after the year in which they were elected. In
the interval, before the election of these officers, the judge
entitled to precedence—*i.e.,* the oldest ordinary judge—per-
forms the duties of the President; he also acts in this capacity in case both of these officials are unable to be present,
or in case both appointments are vacant at the same time.

If either the President or Vice-President ceases to belong
to the Court before his normal term has expired, an election
is held to appoint a substitute for the unexpired part of the
term. The Vice-President takes the place of the President
only when the latter is unable to be present or during his
vacation, or, in case the office of President becomes vacant,
until the appointment of the new President. If necessary,
an extraordinary session of the Court may be called for
electing a new President.

The elections are by secret ballot and an absolute majority is required.

154. The Court appoints its registrar, in accordance
with Article 21 of the Statute. One of the drafts proposed
for the Court's organization provided that the Secretary-
General of the Permanent Court of Arbitration should
be the registrar of the new Court; the Statute makes no
such provision, however, limiting itself to the declaration
that the duties of these two offices are not to be deemed
incompatible. This last provision has had no practical

result so far, as the new Court organized its registry entirely independently of the Court of Arbitration.

Under Articles 17 to 26 of the Rules, the Court elects the registrar by a simple majority vote, by secret ballot, from among candidates proposed by the members. This term of office is seven years, beginning on January 1st of the year after the election; he may be reëlected. The reason why his term does not coincide with that of the judges is, no doubt, because the continuity of the traditions and practice of the Court is maintained through the registry as a channel. On the other hand, however, the registrar, with whom a contract is made, may not have confidence in a new Court, under the orders of which he might have to serve for a considerable time. If the registrar ceases to hold his office during his term, an election is held to appoint his successor; as the Rules make no provision on this point, his successor would presumably be elected for a full term.

Before taking up his duties, the registrar makes the following declaration at a meeting of the full Court:

"I solemnly declare that I will perform the duties conferred upon me as registrar of the Permanent Court of International Justice in all loyalty, discretion and good conscience."

The registrar must reside within a radius of ten kilometers from the Palace of Peace at The Hague, and his main annual vacation may not exceed two months.

The registrar is the channel for all communications the Court receives or sends; he is responsible for the archives, the accounts and all administrative work; he has custody of the seals and stamps of the Court, is responsible for drawing up the minutes of meetings and must be present in person, at all meetings of the full Court, and must either be present or else be represented by a representative approved by the President, at all sittings of the various chambers.

He also acts under special rules formulated by the Court, into the details of which it is not necessary to enter here. The regulations for the staff of the registry also do not need comment.

155. To conclude this statement of the organization of the Court: the first thing that should be said about its working is that it is to hold a session every year, which is to begin on June 15th, unless a different provision is made in its Rules. This date was not chosen arbitrarily; it is meant to commemorate the opening of the Second Hague Conference, on June 15, 1907, in the Salle des Chevaliers in the royal palace of Holland; no tribute could be more just than this, for at that Conference almost all the nations, for the first time officially, discussed the possibility of establishing a Permanent Court of International Justice and the basis on which it should be organized.

Moreover, the Assembly of the League of Nations meets at Geneva every September; as it may ask the Court for advisory opinions, the Court's answer would be ready if the Court met in June. With the diversity of climates and the particular situation of the Netherlands, June seemed to be the most suitable time for judges to come together from very different parts of the globe.

Without any apparent need, the Rules make one less sensible provision, that in the year following the election of the whole Court the annual session shall begin on January 15th. If June 15th or January 15th is a holiday in the place where the Court sits, the session begins on the following working day.

The President also has power, under the Statute, to summon an extraordinary session of the Court whenever it is necessary; this power has already been used rather frequently, but there are plenty of reasons why it should not become a constant practice. The President understands the circumstances.

156. The idea of creating special chambers to take cognizance of particular matters did not come from the Committee of Jurists. The Committee discussed on several occasions the question whether a chamber should be established for litigations in which private citizens, as well as states, might intervene; but this hypothesis was very quickly ruled out of the jurisdiction of the Court.[1]   The Council, too, in examining the Statute, made no change on this point; but the situation was very different in the Assembly.

M. Albert Thomas, the indefatigable director of the International Labor Office, submitted a report calling attention to the fact that Articles 415 to 418 of the Treaty of Versailles gave the Permanent Court of International Justice jurisdiction over a great many questions relating to labor, and that Article 418 entrusts to the Court the interpretation of the entire Part XIII, containing the labor provisions, as well as of all the conventions the contracting powers might subsequently make under the provisions of Part XIII.   He maintained that this made it advisable to set up a chamber, or special section, composed not only of judges of recognized competence in international law, but also of other judges of competence in labor legislation and social questions, and "known for their impartiality with regard to different economic contingencies."   Those judges were to be elected by the General Labor Conference and by the Administrative Council of the International Labor Bureau.   The chamber was also to have the assistance of experts particularly versed in the industrial matters involved.[2]

The British delegates, insisting that their proposal gave them priority, submitted three new articles.   One created a labor chamber, with five judges and four technical assessors, to deal with disputes arising under Part XIII of the Treaty of Versailles and the corresponding parts of the other peace treaties.   The second set up a chamber of three judges and two technical assessors for disputes relating to transit and communications, including those arising under Part XII of the Treaty of Versailles and the corresponding sections of the other peace treaties.   The third article authorized these special chambers to sit elsewhere than at The Hague, with the consent of the parties.

[1] Minutes, pp. 210-215.
[2] Documents relative, etc., pp. 74 et seq.

In the Assembly subcommittee M. Fromageot, the French delegate, stated that his government shared the views of M. Thomas that provision should be made for the representation of employers and workmen on the Court when labor cases were heard; the British representatives then expounded their views, which were discussed for some time. It was then agreed to draft three articles along these lines; these three are those that appear in the present Statute, except for certain changes made by the committee and approved by the Assembly (explained a little further on).

The first of these articles (now Article 26) provides that labor cases, particularly cases referred to in Part XIII of the Treaty of Versailles and in the corresponding portions of the other peace treaties, shall be heard and determined by the Court under the following conditions: The Court is to appoint every three years a special chamber of five judges selected, so far as possible, with due regard to the provisions of Article 9 (which prescribes that judges of the Court should each possess the qualifications required, and that the whole body should also represent the main forms of civilization and the principal legal systems of the world). Two other judges are to be selected, to replace a judge who finds it impossible to sit. This chamber is to sit only on the express demand of the parties; in the absence of such a demand the case is heard by the full Court. In either procedure, four technical assessors are to sit in the case, with no right to vote, chosen with a view to ensuring a just representation of the competing interests. If there is a national of one and only one of the parties among the judges that are sitting, the President is to invite one of the other judges to yield his place to a national judge chosen by the other party, as in other kinds of litigations. These technical assessors are to be chosen for each particular case, in accordance with rules of procedure under Article 30, from a list of persons, two nominated by each member of the League, and an equal number by the governing body of the Labor Office; half of those named by the governing body are to be representatives of the workers, and the other half representatives of the employers, taken from the list referred to in Article 412 of the Treaty of Versailles.

For litigated questions relating to transit and communications, especially those referred to in Part XII of the Treaty of Versailles and the corresponding parts of the other peace treaties, the special chamber is composed of five judges, with the same qualifications as in the labor chamber, and two deputy judges to replace any judge who finds it impossible to sit. It also has four technical assessors chosen from a list composed of two persons nominated by each member of the League.

These two chambers may sit elsewhere than at The Hague, with the consent of the parties; Sir Cecil Hurst said there were "reasons of convenience" for this provision; this is evident enough, but this same reasoning is quite as applicable to the full Court as to these particular sections.

A new paragraph was added to Article 26 in the Committee, proposed by Sir Cecil Hurst and M. Costa, giving the International Labor Office the right to furnish to the Court all relevant information in labor cases, and entitling the director of the office to receive copies of all written proceedings.

The Assembly made another change in Article 27, suggested by M. Loudon, providing that the technical assessors in transit and communication cases were to sit only when the parties desire it or when the Court so decides.[1]

The Rules complete and expand these provisions in Articles 14, 15 and 16. According to them, the judges of the special chambers are to be appointed at a meeting of the full Court by an absolute majority of votes, with regard to any preference expressed by the judges, so far as Article 9 of the Statute permits (as to representatives of the different legal systems and forms of civilization). This election is held at the end of the ordinary session of the Court, and the

---

[1] Documents relative, etc., pp. 70, 71, 74-76, 105, 106, 129, 148-150, 153-4, 209, 223, 227, and 254.

term of those designated begins on January 1st of the next year; but after a new election of the whole Court these chambers are elected at the beginning of the following session, and the term begins on the date of election. The Court also appoints the Presidents of these chambers, in full Court, but the President of the Court presides *ex-officio* in any special chamber of which he may be a member, as does the Vice-President, unless he and the President are both members of the same special chamber. Not more than five members may sit in these chambers, and deputy judges may not be summoned to complete them unless enough judges are not available.

Articles 7 and 8 of the Rules require the President of the Court to take steps to obtain all information that might be helpful to the Court in selecting the technical assessors, consulting the governing body of the International Labor Office when the labor chamber is concerned. The assessors are elected by an absolute majority of votes, either by the Court or by the special chamber dealing with the case in question. At the first sitting of the Court at which they are present, assessors are required to make a solemn declaration equivalent to that made by the judges, given above.

In the first three years of the Court's existence, neither of these two special chambers has ever been called on to meet, though they were appointed at the first session of the Court. This does not seem to indicate that the persons who insisted they were necessary had the gift of prophecy; but of course it is not possible yet to prove absolutely that they were wrong. The future will show whether or not their creation was a success.

157. There is one other special chamber, the chamber of summary procedure, proposed by the Committee of Jurists and approved by the Assembly; it comes from the reforms in the procedure in arbitral decisions introduced at the Second Hague Conference of 1907. It is composed of three judges, under Article 29 of the Statute, and is formed annually by the Court, toward the end of the regular session. The Rules apply the same provisions as to the designation of these judges and the election of the President, etc., as for the two other special chambers.

It also acts only at the request of the parties, in case it seems more swift and economical to them. This explains why it has already been called into service.

158. The votes in the full Court and in the special chambers require a simple majority, not an absolute majority. In case of a tie, the presiding officer—the President or his deputy—has the casting vote, according to Article 55 of the Statute.

To keep the material in order and to establish what cases shall come up at each session, a calendar or order of the day is prepared by the registrar, under the responsibility of the President, according to Article 28 of the Rules. It must include, for each session, all the questions submitted to the Court for an advisory opinion, and all cases in regard to which the written proceedings are concluded, in the order in which the documents submitting each question or case have been received by the registrar. If a question is submitted to the Court during a session, or if the written proceedings in regard to any case are concluded, the Court decides whether it shall be added to the calendar for that session.

The registrar keeps a separate roll showing the cases to be dealt with by the respective special chambers, made up, of course, of extracts from the complete roll. He also keeps a separate list of cases for revision.

159. These provisions do not suggest how the question is to be determined of whether the Court has or has not a legal personality, nor by what rules its action toward any given state, including the Netherlands, is to be regulated, in any relations outside of its judicial functions. This is an important question; some day or other it will be raised. It will be solved by a convention between the nations that have accepted the Statute.

CHAPTER X

THE FINANCIAL SITUATION OF THE COURT.

160. The actual financial status of the Court is much more important than it may seem at first thought, although the Advisory Committee of Jurists and the writers of several of the proposed drafts paid little attention to it.[1] The drafts submitted to the Advisory Committee either made the Court's expenses payable by the League of Nations, as in the Netherlands plan, or divided the expenses equally among the nations in the Court, as in the Danish, Norwegian and Swedish plans. The subject was not even mentioned in the drafts sent in by Switzerland, Italy, Germany, Austria, the Interparliamentary Union and the Union Internationale Juridique.

The maintenance of the Court, with which this chapter deals, must not be confused with the costs of each party to a case; these costs are discussed later in the chapter on the Court's Rules and procedure (see page 230). The statement in the Root-Phillimore draft, which was used as the basis of the Advisory Committee's discussions, to the effect that the expenses of the Court shall be borne by the League of Nations, refers only to the maintenance of the Court.

The scheme of dividing the expenses equally among the nations was speedily abandoned. Its supporters based it on the principle of the legal equality of nations; but this is just as fallacious as to say that in a democracy a rich man and a poor man should pay the same annual taxes because they are equal before the law. Every international organization in the world that is supported by the nations that belong to it receives contributions from them, not in

[1] See Morellet, J., L'Organisation de la Cour Permanente de Justice Internationale. Paris, 1921.

equal amounts but according to a sliding scale based either on their economic importance or on the material benefits they obviously derive from it.

It was for this reason, perhaps, and perhaps also because a well-known arrangement already in operation somewhere is more likely to be adopted than some new plan, that the Advisory Committee adopted the Root-Phillimore plan, applying to the Court's expenses the same principle used for apportioning the expenses of the League of Nations, *i.e.*, on the basis not of equal, but of proportionate, contributions from its members. In order to leave a margin for possible changes, a phrase was added to Article 33 of the Statute so that the whole sentence is as follows:

> "The expenses of the Court shall be borne by the League of Nations, in such a manner as shall be decided by the Assembly upon the proposal of the Council."[1]

161. Although the League of Nations regards the Permanent Court of International Justice as an autonomous institution, like the International Labor Office, and has so stated in several official documents, it incorporates the entire cost of the maintenance of the Court in its general budget, and pays this cost out of its general receipts.

The Covenant of the League, in the last paragraph of Article 6 of the Treaty of Versailles, provided that the expenses of the Secretariat should be voted by all the members in accordance with the apportionment of expenses in the International Bureau of the Universal Postal Union. It was plain at once that this arrangement might be inequitable and might have inconvenient results. The Second Assembly adopted the following amendment, subject to ratification by the majority of the members of the Assembly and by all the nations represented in the Council:

> "The expenses of the League shall be borne by the members of the League in the proportion decided by the Assembly."

[1] Documents relative, etc., pp. 96, 326, 495, 578.

By September, 1923, twenty-seven nations, including all the members of the Council, had ratified this amendment, and it accordingly has been in effect since then. In 1923 the Assembly, acting under the authority of this amendment, drew up the following schedule of contributions for 1924, keeping the Postal Union principle of allotting to each country a definite, but variable, number of units.

1 unit:	Albania, Austria, Costa Rica, Guatemala, Honduras, Liberia, Luxemberg, Nicaragua, Panama, Paraguay, Salvador.
2 units:	Abyssinia and Haiti.
3 "	Esthonia and Latvia.
4 "	Hungary and Lithuania.
5 "	Bolivia and Venezuela.
6 "	Persia.
7 "	Bulgaria, Colombia and Uruguay.
9 "	Cuba.
10 "	Finland, Greece, Ireland, New Zealand, Peru, Portugal and Siam.
11 "	Norway.
12 "	Denmark.
15 "	Belgium, Chile, South Africa and Switzerland.
18 "	Sweden.
20 "	The Netherlands.
25 "	Poland.
26 "	Australia and the Kingdom of the Serbs, Croats and Slovenes.
31 "	Rumania.
35 "	Argentine, Brazil, Canada and Czecho-Slovakia.
40 "	Spain.
61 "	Italy and Japan.
65 "	China and India.
78 "	France.
88 "	Great Britain.

Subsequently the Reparations Commission reduced

Hungary's quota to three units, that of Greece and Portugal to nine and Rumania's to twenty-nine.

This, then, is the proportion in which the states mentioned above contribute to the maintenance of the Permanent Court of International Justice.[1]

162. Two anomalous situations arise from this arrangement. One is that since a nation may be a member of the League without joining the Court or being bound by it, these nations that neither approve of it nor want it nevertheless are obliged to help to maintain it. They are forced to contribute to its financial support, although they make no use of it.

The second case concerns nations not members of the League that nevertheless are obliged, under international treaties, to accept its jurisdiction in certain situations, or that have the right to have recourse to it under certain conditions. Germany is put in this position by the Treaty of Versailles and Turkey by the Lausanne Treaty. These nations may make use of the Court without being under the slightest statutory obligation to pay any part of its expenses. This situation has already arisen twice with reference to Germany, once in the Wimbledon case in 1923, and again in 1925 in the case, still pending, of its complaint against Poland in connection with the expropriation of certain holdings in Poland. Both Germany and Turkey have also been concerned in advisory opinions given by the Court, although in these instances it was the Council, and not either nation, that made the request to the Court.

In certain other cases provided for in the Council's resolution of May 17, 1922, which will be discussed in the following chapter, the Court is to state, at a given point in the proceedings, the contribution each shall pay to the cost of those proceedings, in accordance with the last paragraph of Article 35 of the Statute.

---

[1] In September, 1925, a new scale of units was adopted by the Assembly for the apportionment of the expenses of the League in 1926, 1927 and 1928.—*Tr. Note.*

163. Just after the Court was established, and while it was still completing its organization, the Secretariat of the League took direct charge of its financial administration. Very soon, however—on February 21, 1922—the President and the Secretary of the Court took over the accounts and the administration of the funds, although the final approval of the annual budget and of the accounts of each period still remains with a Supervisory Commission of the League. The Court now receives directly from the League the proportionate amount for its work from each nation's contribution to the League, except for deductions to offset advances it may have obtained for the payment of current bills, under Article 26 of the rules for the financial administration of the League.

164. The proposals in the budget must be approved by the Court, but a practical difficulty arises from the fact that the Financial Commission of the League, which prepares the budgets, meets after the regular annual session of the Court, which begins on June 15th; consequently the instructions for the Secretariat provide that the President of the Court may accept provisionally a tentative budget prepared by the Secretariat, without prejudice to the right to amend it later reserved by the Court and admitted by the League in Articles 14 and 19 of its financial regulations.

In accordance with a resolution adopted by the Fourth Assembly, the budgets of these autonomous organizations must follow the form used by the Secretariat for the general budget of the League, so far as is possible with due regard to the varying needs of each organization. They must be formulated in certain terms and according to precise regulations stated in the resolution; and they are subject to the final approval of the Assembly, which meets annually at Geneva in September. The Assembly also approves the accounts.

165. Until now the regular charges and services covered by the Court's budget for the calendar year are as follows: annual salaries, including those of the judges, the registry and the employees; traveling expenses; a contribution to the Carnegie Foundation for the use of part of the Palace of Peace; and administration expenses.

The budget approved by the League for the year 1922, the first year of its existence, was 900,000 Dutch florins, 822,616.32 of which were used. The League Commission's estimate for 1923 was 987,895.95 florins, which was reduced by the Assembly to 935,625.70; 745,990.54 florins were used. The amount approved by the League for 1924 was 1,920,108 gold francs, equivalent to 938,139.83 florins; the amount expended was only 590,327.30 florins, as the number and length of the sessions was less than had been expected. The estimated budget for 1925 is 921,196.76 florins.

166. Reading these provisions, one is instantly struck by the insecurity and the precarious financial situation of this new institution, circumstances which may have great importance in its future. Two radically different institutions are financially joined—the League of Nations, essentially a diplomatic and political organ, in spite of its varied functions in other fields, and the Permanent Court of International Justice, essentially a judicial organ. Any tempest that beats down on the League will inevitably react on the Court. Suppose another general war were to break out in Europe, lasting for several years, and ending with a new peace treaty, which, by the familiar hazard of conflict, might not be influenced by the same considerations that ruled the Paris Peace Conference: all the tremendous progress implied in world-wide justice might vanish, carried down by the destruction of another institution, more easy to overwhelm, but perhaps not less lamentable.

This financial partnership has already begun to do harm in other connections. A certain powerful nation, staying outside the League of Nations because of its traditional policy of keeping aloof from the domestic affairs of Europe, would have to overcome great obstacles in order to join the Court; this causes continual discord in its Congress and in its elections. Another important nation, this one in Latin

America, legally a member of the League though having actually withdrawn from its deliberations, has not been meeting its social obligations, thus not only diminishing the resources of the League of Nations, with the actions of which she does not agree, but also reducing the income of the Permanent Court, of which she has no cause to complain. Other countries find it difficult to make their payments, on account of their precarious financial situation, and in some countries the legislators or governments are more or less lax in meeting this international obligation; these conditions inevitably affect the Court, but will not, it is to be hoped, hamper its course.

167. To look at the situation from another point of view, even assuming that none of these other inconveniences was present: as long as the Court's existence is dependent on assessments payable by over forty nations, some poor and others rich, some stable and others insecure, some proud of their foreign credit and others callous to the results of their slowness or failure to pay, the Court will be in a situation annoying to its prestige and its future. As the writer has already said in discussing one of these questions before the Academy of International Law at the Hague,[1] we can easily imagine how much influence one national legislator might have, and how he might feel when he compared the sums which his country would have to pay in several years toward maintaining a Court his country has never yet used, with the sums needed for domestic services that are not provided for. When we realize this, and further realize that the need of meeting the assessment for maintenance might keep nations with limited resources out of the Court, the possibility of international complications arising from this source is obvious.

It may be true that other bureaus and institutions have lived and may still function under this arrangement, carrying on various administrative services for the common weal, obeying instinctively or as a matter of habit this same rule; but the Permanent Court, which ought really

[1] See page 51.

to be considered extra-national or super-national, rather than inter-national, needs a different outlook and a different budget or financial basis.

168. The remedy for this situation lies in the endowment of the Court. The present economic conditions in the world, still violently disturbed by the last war, make it impossible for the member nations to provide the amount of capital required for such endowment all at once, or even to guarantee a loan of the necessary amount. When the Court owns its own funds, has its own private fortune, so to speak, administered either by the Court or by an international board of trustees, it will have infinitely more authority and its future will be much more secure. With the income from its own capital covering all its expenses, it could dispense justice to all the world,—justice, which, according to the phrase used in the constitutions of certain American republics, ought to be free to all who need it.

In the present state of civilization, there should be nothing amazing in the idea that an international institution should have its own resources. Even now the League of Nations and one of its autonomous organizations, the International Labor Organization, are preparing to own their own palaces, built on land belonging to them alone, which was either given to them or else bought with the joint funds of the nations which provided the necessary capital. This first step suggests others, and shows how the work may be carried on. Obtaining capital in order to have one's own building and not pay rent is precisely like getting capital together in order to use the income for any other purposes.

169. How can this be done? Many methods will suggest themselves; a few are mentioned briefly here. For example, a certain percentage of the necessary funds might be included in the annual budget of the Court, as the amount of the capital to be provided in that year; in this way the different states that support the Court could supply the necessary amount, in installments that need never be burdensome. It would take some years to obtain it; but very speedily, as the sum capitalized increased, the percentage would increase in proportion to the amount of its revenues which the Court allotted to its regular expenses, or else the quota of the different states would be lowered until it disappeared entirely.

Or by a similar method of building up the necessary capital slowly, the Court might transfer to this account its unexpected balances from year to year, and the contributions to the costs made by non-member states appearing before it.

Another method, suggested above, and practically equivalent to these others, may not be practicable now, but it will become so when a general improvement takes place in national finances. This consists of making a public loan, which should be large enough to give to the Court, at one stroke, the income it requires for its present needs and for those likely to arise in the near future. The nations that are making annual contributions now to the maintenance of the Court would undertake to pay the interest and also a sufficient yearly amount for the amortization of the loan; the annual amount required to meet these two charges would not be much greater than the amount they pay now for its maintenance alone, and in a relatively short time they would have met the entire obligation.

The very great increase in private fortunes in certain countries since 1900 suggests the possibility that large personal gifts may be made, which would help to solve this problem. One American philanthropist alone built the palace at Cartago for the Central American Court of Justice, and gave a large sum toward the construction of the Palace of Peace at The Hague, where the Permanent Court of Arbitration and the Permanent Court of International Justice both have their seats. Others will no doubt emulate or imitate him. It would be hard to find a better way of using the surplus of a great personal fortune than in supporting this lofty and noble conception of justice.

Such a foundation would be the complement and the most important consequence of the legal personality of the

Court, to which a brief allusion was made at the end of the last chapter. This is a subject that must be considered. The aim here has been merely to raise the question, in the confidence that through the experience and knowledge of others the correct solution can eventually be reached.

The progress of the world depends on justice between nations, and justice between nations cannot be had without firm foundations and without sufficient guarantees that it can resist and can endure. The more stable the institution can be made which, under the shelter of law, makes it possible for two peoples to avoid the necessity of settling a dispute by force of arms, the nearer will be the day when force will be defeated and justice will take its place. A single step toward this goal is a victory.

Earlier in this chapter it was pointed out that the subject of this chapter is of vital importance, although most of the plans for the Court and the writers and publicists who advocated and defended them either did not realize its importance, or else considered that the essential thing was to establish the Court first. This, luckily, has been done.

CHAPTER XI

THE JURISDICTION OF THE COURT[1]

170. In order to know what cases and questions the Permanent Court of International Justice may take cognizance of, it is necessary to consider first what may be called its two-fold jurisdiction, *ratione personae et ratione materiae, i.e.,* its jurisdiction over persons and its jurisdiction over the subject matter, and to examine the various contentions that have been made on this subject by writers, associations, conferences and congresses, officially or individually. It will then be easy to see what may and may not be expected from the Court as now organized.

171. As to its jurisdiction over persons: it will be convenient to consider in ten groups certain individuals, private legal persons, and international associations which, though official, are not states or nations, grouping and subdividing them on the basis of the differences resulting from the existence of the League of Nations and from their membership or non-membership in it.

172. Some writers have maintained that disputes involving individuals and private legal persons[2] could be submitted to an international court, whether all the parties were of the same nationality or not, provided the dispute arose out of the application,—extra-territorial or internal —of international principles, or, to put it more clearly, if it arose out of the application of those rules of private

---

[1] The title of this chapter in the original Spanish text and in the French translation is The Competence and Jurisdiction of the Court. The distinction between these two terms as they are used in the civil law may be illustrated as follows: a criminal court has jurisdiction over criminal offenses, but is competent to try only those criminal offenses that are committed in the Court's district. In the official English text of the Statute, however, the one word *jurisdiction* is used for both the word *juridiction* and *compétence* in the official French text.—*Tr. note.*

[2] Such as corporations.—*Tr. note.*

international law which would be in point in the compulsory arbitrations contemplated in the draft convention of the Second Hague Conference.

So far as individuals are concerned, and keeping in mind that it is jurisdiction over persons that is now being discussed, the writer does not believe that this hypothesis is justified. Private international law is applicable, within the legislative competence of nations, only in reference to legal relations that are subject to the domestic legislation of more than one nation. Consequently, while public international law affects the direct relations of international legal persons in their external life, taken as a whole, and considered, as units, as subjects of law, private international law, on the contrary, affects only one of the aspects of national activity, *i.e.,* its legislative function, in both the enactment and the application of the law governing the case. Only the state—not in its external function as a member of the international community, but in its internal function, exercising one of its social duties—only the State itself can decide whether it is competent to regulate by its statutes certain legal relations in which private persons, whether individuals or associations, are concerned.[1]

Whether a dispute is of an international character does not depend on whether a nation is acting directly in the normal exercise of its external functions, but rather on whether its laws do or do not permit the laws of another nation to apply to private legal relations within its territory. From this point of view, the law now under consideration is both private and international, and so far as the individuals or private legal persons are concerned, the question is not distinguishable from the question of applying or interpreting any other legal rule. As in other cases,

[1] In other words, public international law deals only with the relations of nations, as such, to each other; private international law, so called, relates only to the legal situation of private individuals who are brought, by the circumstances of their lives, under the workings of the domestic laws of two different nations, as, for example, in the question of succession or of inheritance by a widow, when the property is located in two countries, and when the parties to the marriage were of different nationalities, and when their marital status was differently regulated by the laws of the two nations.—*Tr. note.*

a suit does not usually arise between an individual and a nation, but between two individuals or private legal persons, who may avail themselves of the usual domestic courts, with the same official national sanctions as for the decision in any other kind of case. And in order that citizens and aliens may sue each other, an international court is not necessary now, and never has been.

It may also be pointed out that a jurisdiction of this character would naturally be expected to apply the international rules and principles of law recognized by all or by certain of the nations, whereas, as a matter of fact, although there are several different national systems or conceptions of private international law, there is no universal or general private law. And for the application of these national systems, there already are the national courts.

When the rules of private international law have been drawn up in an international convention, or when nations have agreed on a code of private international law, then, and not until then, will it be possible to argue the scope of this convention or code before an ordinary court, independent of disputes or suits that may arise between private citizens in each country over the domestic or internal application of the same rules. If it were made possible to take cases of this kind before a super-national Court, it would make it a court of appeal from the national courts, in derogation of their sovereignty. These considerations, to which another may be added—the right of action of one nation against another before the Permanent Court for a denial of justice to its citizens or subjects on matters of private international law—explain the observations made on this subject in the Advisory Committee of Jurists [1] and in a recent important book on international justice. [2] As a matter of positive law, and in accordance with the thesis developed above, the Statute of the Court does not contain any provision authorizing private citizens to bring such matters before it. On the contrary, it does contain a general rule excluding them, which will be discussed later on.

---

[1] Minutes, pp. 210-215.
[2] Politis, N.—La justice internationale, p. 250. Paris, 1924.

173. The second group consists of complaints brought by private citizens or by private legal persons against their own nation, involving the interpretation or application of international principles of a contractual, unilateral, or customary nature. One instance of this sort of jurisdiction was contained in the treaty which established the Central American Court of Justice for ten years, and it has already been pointed out in this book that this form of jurisdiction may have been one of the causes of the regrettable ending of this Court.

As a matter of principle, the disputes between a state and its citizens or subjects are not and cannot be of an international character. They are problems that relate to the nation's sovereignty within its borders, and they should be solved by the exercise of that sovereignty; this fact is not altered or modified by the international character of the applicable principle. Except in very special and transient cases, it would constitute an irritating act of intervention, which a third state would be performing if it had a voice or a vote in the litigation, and the situation would not be appreciably changed by the fact that it would be under an extra-national jurisdiction. They are questions between the sovereign power and the subject or the citizen, the adjustment of which, in substance and form alike, lies within the competence of the sovereign state in which they arose.

It must not be forgotten, however, that the Treaty of Berlin of June 13, 1878, made a timid step in this direction, and that the treaties made after the end of the World War inaugurated and developed, this time openly and with careful regulations, a system of protection for racial, religious and linguistic minorities, with lofty and generous provisions. The victorious powers, however, eluding the various attempts, specific and disguised, to undermine the principle of sovereignty, did not make themselves responsible for the administration of this intervention, but put it under the authority of the League of Nations, as an impersonal agency, which, from the point of view of political ambitions, will make its action seem gentler.

In addition to this,—and this is a new and important admission of the exclusive nature of sovereignty between the state and the citizen—neither these minorities, nor groups of them, nor any individual members of them are given authority either to bring a complaint to set the machinery of the League in motion, or to bring the case before the Permanent Court of International Justice; the complaint may be brought only by another state specified in the particular treaty the protection of which is invoked.

This will be illustrated later in the analysis of the cases submitted to the compulsory jurisdiction of the Court. It is sufficient to say here, by way of summary, that the Permanent Court will not take jurisdiction in any case brought by private citizens or private legal persons against the nation to which they belong for the application of international principles. Like the first group, this second group is also excluded from the Court's jurisdiction over persons.

174. The Central American Court of Justice was made competent, by Article 2 of the Treaty of Washington that created it, to hear and determine questions which individuals of one of the contracting nations might raise against any of the other nations, because of the violation of treaties and in other cases of an international character, whether their own government supported their own claim or not, but provided they had exhausted the remedies afforded by the laws of that country for such a violation or claimed that justice had been denied them.

This group of cases is like the preceding group, in that they are between private citizens and governments, but different in that the private citizen here is an alien, not a national. In the Central American system, it was also essential for the alien to show that the remedies of the local laws had been exhausted or that justice had been denied.

Any admission that the Court was competent in such cases would involve two things that are not in accordance with current doctrines and teachings of international law. First of all, it implies the admission that private citizens possess an international personality of their own in the public affairs of nations. The true and just standard, however, is that the international legal community consists only of public persons that possess an external treaty-making sovereign power and maintain diplomatic relations, and that the nation acts and appears for the private persons that compose it. Only in one exceptional case—the International Labor Office—has a voice and a vote in international affairs been given to any one who does not represent, directly and completely, an international legal person; and this case affects not individuals, but economic groups of employers and employees. International law requires that only the state to which the aliens belong may appear in their interest as against the other state.

The second principle that would be violated if alien individuals were allowed to appear against a nation is that of the legal equality of citizens and aliens, obtained only with great difficulty in modern laws. Now that the alien is not to be judged by special domestic courts, because he has won the right to appear, to accuse and to defend himself before the same courts as the citizen, it would be impossible to make a special provision allowing aliens to carry before special courts, nothing less than supra-national in character, the same disputes that a native born citizen may only take to the ordinary domestic courts. The principle of civil equality is broken as much by the privilege to one as by the exclusion of the other. Luckily the Permanent Court of International Justice does not possess this dangerous and unjust jurisdiction.

175. It has been proposed that criminal liability for certain specified offenses should be adjudicated under an extra-national jurisdiction. The first step toward establishing such jurisdiction as a matter of positive law was taken in the Treaty of Versailles of June 28, 1919. In Article 227 the Allied and Associated Powers publicly arraigned William II of Hohenzollern, formerly the German Emperor, for a supreme offense against international morality and the sanctity of treaties. A special tribunal was to be constituted to try the accused, thereby assuring him the guarantees essential to the right of defense. It was to be composed of five judges, one appointed by each of the following powers: the United States of America, Great Britain, France, Italy and Japan.

In its decision the tribunal was to be guided by the highest motives of international policy, with a view to indicating the solemn obligations of international undertakings and the validity of international morality. It was to be the tribunal's duty to fix the punishment it considered should be imposed. The Allied and Associated Powers were to address a request to the government of the Netherlands for the surrender to them of the former Emperor in order that he might be put on trial.

In Article 228 the German government recognized the right of the Allied and Associated Powers to bring before military tribunals persons accused of having committed acts in violation of the laws and customs of war. Such persons, if found guilty, were to be sentenced to punishments laid down by law. This was to apply notwithstanding any proceedings or prosecution before a tribunal in Germany or in the territory of her allies. The German government was to hand over to the Allied and Associated Powers, or to whatever one of them should so request, all persons accused of having committed acts in violation of the laws and customs of war, who were specified either by name or by the rank, office or employment they had held under the German authorities.

Article 229 established the jurisdiction, providing that persons guilty of criminal acts against the nationals of one of the Allied and Associated Powers were to be brought before the military tribunals of that Power, and that those guilty of criminal acts against the nationals of more than one of these powers were to be brought before military tribunals composed of members of the military tribunals of the powers concerned. In every case, the accused was to be entitled to name his own counsel.

In the last Article, 230, the German government undertook to furnish all documents and information of every kind, the production of which might be considered necessary to ensure the full knowledge of the incriminating acts, the discovery of offenders, and the just appreciation of responsibility.

Two American nations at least, one a great power and one not at all great, went on record officially in the Paris Peace Conference against this doctrine, which involves defining an act as a crime *a posteriori* (after it has been done), and courts set up by the victors *ex professo* (for this particular purpose) after the acts had been committed, with an arbitrary and unfamiliar procedure for the trial of the cases, and with penalties not stipulated in advance but set by the judge—in short, a procedure that is not at all in conformity with the fundamental principles of criminal jurisdiction in the modern civilized world, nor with the constitutional guarantees of private citizens as against the judicial power in democratic countries.

These provisions of the Treaty of Versailles had no practical result, because the Netherlands refused to return the former German Emperor, who had taken refuge on her soil, and because it was finally agreed that one of Germany's own courts should try some of the other accused persons, under guarantees set by the victorious powers.

176. Nevertheless these provisions, though unsuccessful, served as the germ of penal justice in international affairs. They came to light again before the Advisory Committee of Jurists; Baron Descamps took the initiative, presenting on June 21, 1920 a proposal for the organization of international justice, Article 4 of which reads as follows:

"The High Court of International Justice shall be competent to hear and determine cases which shall be submitted to it by the Assembly of the League of Nations or by the Council of the League, and which concern international public order, for instance: crimes against the universal Law of Nations." [1]

In the very interesting session of July 13, he developed this proposition as follows:

[1] Minutes, p. 142.

"Article 1. A High Court of International Justice is hereby established.

"Article 2. This Court shall be composed of one member for each state chosen by the group of delegates of each state upon the Court of Arbitration.

"Article 3. The High Court of International Justice shall be competent to try crimes against international public order and the universal law of nations, referred to it by a public full meeting of the Assembly of the League of Nations, or by the Council of the said League.

"Article 4. The Court shall have power to define the character of the offense, to fix the penalty, and to decide the means by which the terms of the sentence are to be enforced. The Court shall lay down the procedure to be used in this case in its internal regulations." [1]

MM. Loder, Hagerup and Ricci-Busatti were strongly opposed to this proposal, and other members of the Committee also expressed certain general ideas which it may be worth while to summarize here. Mr. Root, for example, pointed out that unless there is a penal law to be broken, there can be no penalty for breaches of it; and he then called attention to the distinction between the acts of individuals or officials whose government accepts responsibility for their acts, and those which it disapproves or disowns, citing as an example of the latter class of cases persons engaged in the slave trade, who are deprived of the protection of their government, *i.e.,* are outlawed. For such outlawed criminals, he suggested a special classification, to be followed by the creation of a special tribunal to try these crimes, which would be set in operation by a special request from governments themselves. The jurisdiction of this tribunal could be extended gradually.

M. de Lapradelle added another example under this classification, *i.e.,* pirates. He observed that it was one of the duties of the League of Nations to see that inter-

[1] Minutes, p. 521.

national justice was done, and suggested that the new Permanent Court should have jurisdiction over such cases; they would occur only rarely, and would not impose a heavy burden on the Court. The Court could also establish a uniform jurisprudence on the subject.

Lord Phillimore also gave a general outline of this doctrine. He asserted that three groups of cases must be differentiated. The first group consisted of acts committed in time of peace, for which a competent national jurisdiction always exists; for these, therefore, an international court would be not only useless, but a hindrance. The second group consisted of acts of war; he was not opposed to an international jurisdiction for them, because an applicable law was in existence,—the regulations respecting the laws and customs of war on land, adopted in 1907. As to the third group, consisting of the crime of having made war, he hesitated to entrust jurisdiction over this offense to a tribunal like the one proposed, with no recognized procedure, no definite laws, and composed of forty or fifty persons, with more or less political tendencies.

As the result of this debate, the Committee of Jurists, in one of its final recommendations (*voeux*), recognized the great importance of Baron Descamps' proposal and recommended it to the consideration of the Council and Assembly of the League of Nations.[1]

177. The Council adopted a report on these recommendations prepared by M. Caclamanos, representative of Greece. It proposed that certain international law associations should study two preliminary questions,—whether a high court of justice should be established for the purposes and with the jurisdiction suggested in Baron Descamp's proposal, and, if so, whether this criminal jurisdiction should be given to the Permanent Court or whether there should be a separate Court. The answers of these associations to these two questions were to be submitted by the Council to the governments of the States that were members of the League of Nations.[2]

[1] Minutes, pp. 142, 498-516, 748.
[2] Documents relative, etc., p. 53.

The Third Committee of the Assembly, to which this question was referred, was of the opinion that there was no international criminal law recognized by all the states, but that, if it were possible to refer certain offenses to any international jurisdiction, the most practical arrangement would be to organize a special chamber of the Permanent Court for that purpose. It therefore proposed that the Assembly take no action. M. Lafontaine, who prepared the Committee's report, explained this opinion before the full Assembly on November 18, 1920, adding that the proposal was useless and that consideration of the qquestion would be premature. No one opposed these views, and the recommendation of the Committee of Jurists was adopted without debate and almost without a vote.[1]

178. At the meeting of the International Law Association at Buenos Aires in August, 1922, a very interesting communication from Lord Phillimore was read, containing a detailed explanation of the reasons that influenced the Committee of Jurists in favor of an international court for criminal offenses of the three classes to which reference has already been made. A profound study of this question was summed up in another paper read at this session, prepared by the English professor, Sir Hugh H. L. Bellot; its main ideas are summarized below. These two papers indicate the theoretical and practical interest in the subject.

After stating the facts on which his views were based, including various precedents of the North American Civil War and the Boer War, as well as the work of the Paris Conference and the consequences of the peace of Versailles, M. Bellot proposed that a tribunal be established composed of fifteen judges and ten deputy judges, who must have been members for fifteen years of their highest national criminal courts, to be chosen by a procedure analogous to that used in the present Permanent Court, and for the same term of nine years. It would have jurisdiction in peace over all punishable offenses which a state could not punish and in which it asked the Court to intervene; during war,

[1] Documents relative, etc., p. 52.

and at the end of a war, it would have jurisdiction over all offenses submitted to it both by the nations and by individuals, the latter requiring the approval of the proper department of their respective governments.

For the law it was to apply, it was to take the formula used in the preamble to the Hague Convention: "The principles of international law, as they result from the usages established between civilized nations, from the laws of humanity, and the requirements of the public conscience." The theory that obedience to superior orders was to absolve the offender was entirely suppressed. The Court was to establish its own rules.

The discussion turned particularly on this last point, of the excuse of superior orders, reference being made to the 1922 Washington convention on the use of submarines.[1] Professor Bellot withdrew that part of his report, after which the Association, by a vote of 31 to 22, declared it to be urgent and essential to the interests of justice that an international court for criminal offenses be established.[2]

179. The movement in favor of penal justice over criminal offenses in international relations has not died down; it appears in new forms every day. In 1923 M. Quintiliano Saldaña, the noted Spanish criminologist, asserted that the Permanent Court of International Justice might take cognizance of penal offenses by an individual delinquent, at the request of a nation. He mentions, first of all, cases where jurisdiction might be doubtful, not with reference to the competence of the Court, but as to whether it could take cognizance of the causes of the criminal affair. It should also have jurisdiction over international criminal cases, by which the author means such acts as piracy on the high seas and boarding another airship in the free zones of the air; and it should also sit in questions of national protection of delinquents, native born or naturalized, and of the application of international penal privileges, such as pardon,

---

[1] By which the orders of a governmental superior did not constitute an excuse.—*Tr. note.*

[2] Report of the 31st Conference of the International Law Association, at Buenos Aires. Vol. I, pp. 49-86. London, 1923.

limitations, and double jeopardy *(non bis in idem)*. It should also take cognizance of international offenses where the social defence fails because the extradition of accomplices or receivers is refused, and also over alien delinquents who have taken flight and are found in a third country, not their own nor the one in which the offense was committed.

M. Saldaña divides international criminology into extra-national crimes, international crimes, and typical criminal forms of international participation. He includes, from the political point of view, violations any constituent part of which takes place outside of the geographical limits of any state, or that are planned, carried on and finally completed on the territories of different states. Among extra-national crimes he mentions fraudulent boarding, on air or sea, between ships of different nationalities, and damages caused by an airship outside of the national air zone or in free space. Among the crimes properly termed international, he mentions anarchistic attempts and the white slave traffic. By international participation he means acting as accomplice or as receiver, with reference to the present difficulties of extradition. All this seems to him to correspond to the natural action of international courts.[1]

180. M. Politis also speaks of international jurisdiction in penal affairs, in his recent interesting book to which reference has already been made. He reminds his readers that such jurisdiction presupposes that the states recognize the power of a joint organ, to act in the general collective interests for the sake of justice. He asserts that the Assembly of the League thought that this reform would be premature, and that there is no international penal code whatever, and not even a convention on the general subject of these crimes.[2]

181. If international crimes are taken to mean acts or intentional omissions in violation of the law of nations

[1] Saldaña, Quintiliano.—La justicia penal internacional, pp. 31-44. Madrid, 1923.
[2] Politis, N.—La justice internationale, pp. 251-2. Paris, 1924.

punishable by an international law, which the separate states do not want to prevent or cannot prevent, a distinction would still have to be made between those which individual citizens commit, and which do not imply any responsibility on the part of the state unless it stands back of the criminal, directly or indirectly, and those acts which are done by employees, public officials or diplomatic representatives in the exercise of their respective charges, which imply national responsibility unless the state expressly repudiates them or claims that the acts are outside of the official powers and functions of the persons committing them.

In every case in which a state is faced with a delinquent and prosecutes and judges him, international jurisdiction is superfluous, because the national jurisdiction is adequate. When there is doubt about the good faith or the authority of a state, the resulting international problem is of a different character, of a preliminary or interlocutory nature, and its solution concerns, not the individuals, but the states as sovereign organisms. If it be assumed that the state wishes to punish the delinquent and is not able to do so, because it has no applicable extradition treaties or agreements, whether by reason of the nationality of the accused, the nature of the punishable act, or the degree of complicity in it, the remedy is to change by international agreement the rules and practices that favor impunity; changing the judge is not the remedy. The first remedy, of stopping up the loopholes, is simpler than the second; and it is, moreover, in conformity with the procedural rules of justice, because it gives the accused a guarantee of defense and gives the judges a guarantee of success and approval, at the place where the offense was committed or in its immediate neighborhood, and not at the more or less distant point where the international court would sit. Moreover, it is not easy to see why a state would refuse to surrender accomplices to their natural judges and would agree to surrender them to this special tribunal. If the League of Nations has the moral or material influence needed to overcome a state's resistance, it could put it to better use by inducing the nations to assist each other properly in the repression and punishment of ordinary crimes.

When a nation, in war or peace, makes common cause with a delinquent, and even applauds or rewards him, the individual problem is absorbed in one of a different nature, the practical solution of which has depended hitherto on international complications, in time of peace, and on the hazard of victory, in time of war. In all cases, however, it comes around again to a problem between two nations, which can be solved by forcing one of them to proceed in justice. International jurisdiction is not indispensable in this situation either.

The difficulty of establishing international jurisdiction in criminal affairs is aggravated by the fact that it is not enough to set up preliminary definitions of international crimes, because it is essential to fix in advance the penalty of each one. Penalties are very difficult to determine in an international code; if they are to consist of imprisonment, international prisons become necessary, and the Court has no prisons at its disposal; if they are to be pecuniary, carrying a right of attachment against property, it would be necessary to have recourse to coercive measures in the place where the property is situated; and if they are to consist of the total or partial loss of civil or political rights, here again the assistance of the nation to which the guilty person belongs is essential. And even supposing that the international court or the institutions of which it would be a part had sufficient power at its disposal, as opposed to a powerful conquerer, to enforce this national coöperation, —much more real progress would have been made, and by a simpler and juster method, if what had been done had been to obtain that international criminals would not go unpunished in any part of the world, but would be punished under the appropriate national jurisdiction.

182. The statute attacks this problem at its root, by expressly providing that only nations or members of the League of Nations may appear before the Court. Its competence, therefore, does not extend to private persons under any circumstances, whether they are natural persons or legal persons, except when the representation of their interests is in the hands of one nation which as their representative pleads against another nation. The Committee of Jurists discussed this question and solved it in this way, with more common sense than was displayed in the Washington convention establishing the Central American Court of Justice.

A different proposal made by the International Labor Office was rejected; in fact, it may have had some influence in the production of this Article (34) in its present form, which was made a little more definite and exclusive by the Assembly, though its meaning remained the same as in the Committee's draft.

183. This wording of Article 34 is also an obstacle to a fifth group of possible parties before a Permanent Court of International Justice—*i.e.,* international unions and bureaus, and the League of Nations itself; differences of a legal nature may arise between any one of them and a state, with reference to the interpretation or application of international conventions or to the execution of their respective obligations; delicate questions come up between two of these unions or bureaus as to their respective competence and powers, like those that arose around the International Labor Organization and the Institute of Agriculture at Rome; there may be similar difficulties between the League of Nations and any one of these unions and bureaus, aside from those arising under Article 24 of the Treaty of Versailles, which, subject to the consent of the parties, puts such associations under the direction of the League; or between the Assembly and the Council of the League some irreducible opposition may arise: from the legal or judicial point of view, they are all without a common superior today.

If the unity or centralization of international administrative life provided for in Article 24 of the Treaty of Versailles becomes a matter of fact, the possible problems suggested in the preceding paragraph may come before the

Permanent Court, as others have, under the guise of advisory opinions, if not of litigations; and if unhappily any conflict should arise between two organisms of the League having the same powers over divers matters, it is possible, or probable, that the same advisory function would be used to settle it. The entire procedure, in this case, in view of execution, encounters at present the difficulty that the Statute limits the competence of the Court to states and to members of the League of Nations, terms that are not synonymous.

Article 14 of the Treaty of Versailles of June 28, 1919, which is the legal genesis of this new institution, says only that the Court shall be competent to hear and determine any dispute of an international character which the parties thereto submit to it. Although the word parties—always with a capital P in the different texts of the Treaty—is used in the other articles and in the preamble as synonymous with states and with autonomous public international persons that took part in the convention, it seems at least possible that the contracting parties could decide to submit to the Court suits between unions and bureaus organized and maintained by all or by a part of them, or between themselves and the unions or bureaus. This would open the door, in a possible amendment of the Statute, for the revision of Article 34 in a new form which would permit it. Perhaps it has not been done because no one has thought of it at a suitable moment. The change would be not only plausible, but suitable in every sense. The Court and the cause of justice would benefit by it.

184. An incidental reference was made in the preceding number to the sixth group of possible parties who do not yet come within the complete international category of states properly so-called. These are the new international legal persons, outlined or suggested years ago, which began to grow during the World War and appeared, completely developed, by the time it ended, during the negotiations at Paris. Without possessing complete political independence, and while still an integral part of another nation, they nevertheless have obtained sovereign diplomatic representation in foreign affairs, thus constituting a new form of contemporary public law. The Dominions and autonomous colonies of Great Britain had direct representation in the peace negotiations and have mounted higher since then; they have kept their international personality and their separate representation in the Assembly of the League of Nations.

The Dominion of Canada, Australia, the Union of South Africa, the Dominion of New Zealand, and India all took part in the negotiation of the Treaty of Versailles, with special plenipotentiary delegates. They are not mentioned in the preamble, which names only Great Britain, and they do not appear in the place where they belong alphabetically. In the list of representatives of the High Contracting Parties, the delegates of England are given, without reference to the part of the Empire from which they come; and immediately after come the five regions mentioned above, by groups corresponding to their locality. From the first Article of the Treaty on, however, this new international orientation is plainly marked; the second paragraph says that any fully self-governing state, dominion or colony not named in the Annex may become a member of the League if its admission is agreed to by two-thirds of the members of the Assembly, provided it shall give effective guarantees of its sincere intention to observe its international obligations and shall accept such regulations as may be prescribed by the League in regard to its military, naval and air forces and armaments. And the Annex, which honors the principle of the legal equality of states, by listing all the powers, great and small, in alphabetical order (in French) puts Canada, Australia, South Africa, New Zealand and India under the British Empire, although slightly indenting their names, as if to indicate that they are a part of it as a political unit.

Does this mean that a definite change is being brought about in external public law, from the influence of a transformation in the constitutional organization of the British

Empire, the results of which cannot yet be foreseen clearly? Does this amount to the first step toward the independence of these colonies or dominions? Is international law, as some recent writers have been bold enough to suggest, giving them at their conception the rights that they ought not to acquire till their birth, according to the old Roman formula? This is not the place to discuss that. Article 14 of the Treaty of Versailles requires that the plan for the Permanent Court of International Justice be submitted by the Council to all the members of the League of Nations. The statute is merely complying with this provision when it declares, in Article 34, that states or members of the League may appear before it.

If some convention or national law were passed tomorrow that extended the Court's jurisdiction to that extent, the colonies and dominions in the League of Nations might plead before the Court against the mother country, or vice versa. Perhaps that would be possible even now, under certain stipulations of the Treaty of Versailles and subsequent conventions closely connected with the Treaty.

It should be noted that a new member, the Free State of Ireland, not in existence in this form when the Treaty of Versailles was signed, is now a member of the League of Nations and is consequently included in Article 34 of the Statute. The five others mentioned above signed and ratified the Versailles Treaty separately from Great Britain.

185. Article 35, developing the provision in Article 34, says that the Court shall be open to members of the League and also to the states mentioned in the Annex to the Covenant.

The list of the first group, members of the League, is essentially subject to change, but for the moment it constitutes the nucleus of the Court's jurisdiction over persons *(ratione personae)*. No difficulty arises here except a very slight one: it would seem only natural that the nations in this situation would accept and ratify the Statute, since they must do so to benefit by it. The great majority of them have done so, and the others will certainly do so, thus removing this question.

186. The Annex to the Covenant, referred to above, divides the nations into two groups. The first group consists of the original members of the League of Nations, signatories to the Treaty of Peace; it includes the United States of America, Belgium, Bolivia, Brazil, the British Empire,—with Canada, Australia, South Africa, New Zealand and India,—China, Cuba, Ecuador, France, Greece, Guatemala, Haiti, Hedjaz, Honduras, Italy, Japan, Liberia, Nicaragua, Panama, Peru, Poland, Portugal, Rumania, the Serb-Croat-Slovene State, Siam, Czechoslovakia and Uruguay.

Although some of these nations, like the United States and Ecuador, have not ratified the treaty and do not belong to the League of Nations, the fact that they are mentioned in the Annex gives them full right of access to the Court, if they desire it.

The second group of states consists of those "invited to accede to the Covenant," according to the phrase that precedes their names; these are the Argentine Republic, Chile, Colombia, Denmark, the Netherlands, Norway, Paraguay, Persia, Salvador, Spain, Sweden, Switzerland and Venezuela. As is easily seen, not all of the nations then existing are included in these two groups. There is a third group, mentioned below.

187. What was to be the situation with reference to the Permanent Court of this last group of states, excluded from the Annex to the Covenant by special political conditions existing at the time when the Coverant was signed, or because they were not on cordial terms then with certain of the contracting powers? Among these states Russia may be mentioned, in Europe, and in America, Mexico, the Dominican Republic and Costa Rica. And the new nations set up after the Treaty of Versailles are in a similar situation. From the ruins of the Russian Empire alone several new states have arisen, which may or may not enter the League of Nations; the same thing is true of those states that will arise in the future.

The Statute makes a provision for this situation in the second paragraph of Article 35; it states that the conditions under which the Court may be open to these other states, subject to special provisions in treaties in force, shall be laid down by the Council, but that in no case shall these provisions place the parties in a position of inequality before the Court.

This provision was carried out on May 17, 1922, by the adoption of the following resolution by the Council.

"The Council of the League of Nations,

"In virtue of the powers conferred upon it by Article 35, paragraph 2, of the Statute of the Permanent Court of International Justice, and subject to the provisions of that Article,

"Resolves:

"1. The Permanent Court of International Justice shall be open to a State which is not a Member of the League of Nations or mentioned in the Annex to the Covenant of the League, upon the following condition, namely: that such State shall previously have deposited with the Registrar of the Court a declaration by which it accepts the jurisdiction of the Court, in accordance with the Covenant of the League of Nations and with the terms and subject to the conditions of the Statute and Rules of Procedure of the Court, and undertakes to carry out in full good faith the decision or decisions of the Court and not to resort to war against a State complying therewith.

"2. Such declaration may be either particular or general.

"A particular declaration is one accepting the jurisdiction of the Court in respect only of a particular dispute or disputes which have already arisen.

"A general declaration is one accepting the jurisdiction generally in respect of all disputes, or of a

particular class or classes of disputes which have already arisen or which may arise in the future.

"A State in making such a general declaration may
accept the jurisdiction of the Court as compulsory,
ipso facto, and without special convention, in conformity with Article 36 of the Statute of the Court, but
such acceptance may not, without special convention,
be relied upon *vis-a-vis* Members of the League of
Nations or States mentioned in the Annex to the
Covenant which have signed or may hereafter sign the
'optional clause' provided for by the additonal protocol of December 16, 1920.

"3. The original declarations made under the
terms of this Resolution shall be kept in the custody
of the Registrar of the Court. Certified true copies
thereof shall be transmitted, in accordance with the
practice of the Court, to all Members of the League
of Nations and States mentioned in the Annex to the
Covenant, and to such other States as the Court may
determine, and the Secretary-General of the League
of Nations.

"4. The Council of the League of Nations reserves the right to rescind or amend this Resolution
by a Resolution which shall be communicated to the
Court; and on the receipt of such communication by
the Registrar of the Court, and to the extent determined by the new Resolution, existing declarations
shall cease to be effective except in regard to disputes
which are already before the Court.

"5. All questions as to the validity or the effect
of a declaration made under the terms of this Resolution shall be decided by the Court."

188. The mere reading of the text of this resolution,
given here in complete form because of its importance,
suggests several doubts and comments. The first is that
it follows the defective wording of Article 35 of the
Statute, and does not mention anything except states,
which would exclude any self-governing dominion or colony

that had not previously become a member of the League of Nations. For example, taking this resolution literally, Ireland would not have been able to adhere to the Court before entering the Assembly at Geneva. It is not easy to see any motive of a legal nature for this arrangement, even considering any political reasons according to which the League of Nations might wish to have a sort of visa for the international personality of the nations in this situation. It is more easily understood if regarded as a mere inadvertence; if the case arose, it probably would not cause any difficulty.

As to the conditions laid down, they seem very natural and logical, except that it is not quite clear why some of them should apply to the states in this third group. For instance, the agreement to accept the Rules of the Court, which the members of the League are not required to accept expressly. And as to the undertaking to carry out in full good faith the decision of the Court and not to resort to war against a state complying with it,—this applies to permanent justice the provisions made with reference to arbitration in Article 13 of the Covenant (in its original form, when still not modified by the compulsory provision).

The provisions in the paragraph numbered 4 in this resolution, however, are very significant. Taking the text as a whole, the Court is faced with the question of the recognition of new states that arise, or pretend to arise, in international life. Recognition is often a political question. The Permanent Court ought to admit their declaration, or to refuse it if need be, and thus pass, at least provisionally, on the question of the legal status of such nations. It would seem that in such a situation the Court ought to act according to the facts, in conformity with its own impression of the reality of the situation, and taking no account, in this connection, of the attitude of the nation to which the new nation formerly belonged, nor of the attitude other nations may take.

The same difficulty may arise in relation to *de facto* governments, not recognized by most of the nations, who are confronted with nations that have been recognized and admitted as such for a long time. The Court ought not to be the judge of their legitimacy, even incidentally or indirectly; and it ought not to be placed between the public power and a part of its nationals, in order to turn the scale. The Court ought to consider nothing but the facts, and ought to regard as the representative of any nation whatever government exercises its material power.

No inconveniences whatever, as against the other nations in the international community, could arise from this attitude, as it would be based on the obvious material facts and would expressly reserve questions of law for formal adjustment at the proper time. Such admission to the Permanent Court of a state or government existing *de facto* but not completely *de jure* would not serve in any case to allow it to cite before the Court any nation that had not recognized it, or to intervene in any litigation already pending for or against a nation that has not recognized it; the final paragraph of the provision numbered 2 of the resolution safeguards this situation. The Court cannot be used as an indirect method of forcing recognition, which, as a general rule, is political and completely free and voluntary.

This provision No. 4 of the Council resolution does not deserve favorable criticism. A body exercising a political function reserves to itself the right to close the access to the Court, and to put out of Court countries that have made the required declaration and that the Court has already admitted. This provision really annuls all the rest of the resolution; in fact, it cancels paragraph 2 of Article 35 of the Statute. No nation will come to discuss its problems before the Permanent Court if it comes within this group and if the Council of the League of Nations has the right to block its path and deny it justice. The declaration required from a nation ought not to be subject to revocation at the will of a third party, and access to the Court ought not to depend for any nation on what may suit the interests or the convenience, in any given political situation, of the reduced nucleus of the nations that forms the Council of the League.

189. The last group to be mentioned consists of those nations that do not belong to the League, are not mentioned in the Covenant, and have not adhered to the Court since it was established, but who are nevertheless obliged to submit a certain category of differences to it, as plaintiffs or defendants, under the provisions of treaties in force. This is the situation of Germany, under the Treaty of Versailles of June 28, 1919, and that of Turkey under the Treaty of Lausanne of July 24, 1923.

190. To summarize what has been said as to the jurisdiction of the Permanent Court of International Justice over persons *(ratione personae)*: the Court is not qualified to take cognizance of any dispute which individuals or private legal persons might like to submit to it, nor litigations in which permanent international unions or bureaus, or the Assembly or the Council of the League of Nations might wish to appear as parties.

On the other hand, its competence has been recognized for the suits of members of the League of Nations that are not nations, but only parts of nations; for the suits of nations mentioned in both the first and the second group of nations in the Annex, although they have not entered the Court; and for the suits of the remaining nations of the world, under the conditions of the Council resolution of May 17, 1922, if they expressly declare that they accept its jurisdiction; and the suits of nations obliged under general international treaties to allow their disputes to be settled in this way,—although there is no precedent for any of these situations.

191. The jurisdiction over the subject matter *(ratione materiae)* of the Permanent Court was defined in a rather general manner at the outset by Article 14 of the Covenant. It says that the Court "shall be competent to hear and determine any dispute of an international character which the parties thereto submit to it." Article 36 of the Statute, still more general, speaks of "all cases which the parties refer to it," without any qualification as to their nature, adding, to lay any doubts, "all matters specially provided for in treaties and conventions in force." But the same Article, in the following paragraph, the "optional clause" referring to compulsory jurisdiction, is careful to limit it to "all or any of the classes of legal disputes concerning" the interpretation of a treaty, any question of international law, the existence of a fact which, if established, would constitute a breach of an international obligation, or the nature and extent of the reparation to be made for such a violation.

The difference in wording can easily be justified. If two countries agree to submit a particular dispute to the Permanent Court, they know the situation in detail and accept the possibility of a decision on legal principles, or, if they so decide, on equitable grounds (*ex aequo et bono*). On the other hand, when they make a general agreement, for questions yet to arise and as yet unknown, it is necessary that the character of these questions shall justify and permit a strictly legal settlement. Hence the adjective "legal" (*juridique*) employed in the provision on obligatory jurisdiction in the last part of Article 36 of the Statute.

Another question arises: just what is a legal dispute? On what basis can a dispute be called legal? It does not explain the situation to recall that the international existence of a nation develops along three lines, political, legal, and economic, because the first and the third are not incompatible with the second; their form, their foundation, and their defense is almost always legal. It is almost impossible to draw complete boundaries for it, in spite of the fact that there is a radical difference between these three aspects of existence when each is considered within its own domain.

Consequently the general jurisdiction of the Permanent Court is not limited to legal questions, using the word in its restrictive sense. And moreover, between nations, just as between individuals, the judicial power governs litigations in which it is not the actual law that is being debated, since all the parties accept it, but the exactitude of the facts that would make the application of the law necessary or possible. The intention in using this phrase was to refer to judicial or justiciable questions rather than to juridical problems; the framers of the Statute characterized these legal questions by the fact that it would be possible to arrive at a solution for them by applying principles of law.

Even within this limited sphere, in the field of arbitral jurisdiction, the nations have usually excluded anything that might affect the vital interests, the honor, the independence, or the constitution of the state: witness the Second Hague Conference. It is *de rigueur* to take shelter behind the excuse of necessity for not applying the law in a normal manner, and this excuse of necessity implies that there is a simple legal principle at the bottom of the dispute. Every state arrogates unto itself the right to decide alone whether or not one of these elements is present, and, for the same reason, to decide whether it is possible to exclude from arbitration every dispute in which it is afraid of justice. One forward step was taken when the decision whether one of these elements was present was left to the Court itself, even though an affirmative decision would take the case out of the Court's hands.

The report prepared by M. de Lapradelle that was sent with the draft statute by the Advisory Committee of Jurists to the Council suggests that the legal character of disputes is defined by the enumeration in Article 36 of the Statute, and that this list is taken from the statement in Article 13 of the Covenant of cases suitable for arbitration.

Nevertheless, it is clear that a list of possible cases suitable for arbitration may or rather must be different from an enumeration of the questions submitted to the judicial power.

It was only logical that the Institute of International Law, the learned organization whose mission it is to express the legal conscience of the civilized word, should attack this most delicate of questions. At its 1922 meeting at Grenoble, after a detailed and conscientious report by MM. Brown and Politis, it took the following action:

"The Institute of International Law, while expressing the hope that all the powers that have not yet
adhered to the optional clause of Article 36 of the
Statute of the Permanent Court of International Justice, will adhere to it, recommends to the states the
adoption of the following resolutions:

"Article 1. All disputes of whatever origin or
character are, as a general rule, and with the reservations stated below, susceptible of a judicial decision
or an arbitral solution.

"Article 2. In every case in which a state cited
to appear before the Court claims that the dispute
is not susceptible of judicial settlement, the preliminary question of determining whether it is justiciable shall be submitted for examination by the
Permanent Court of International Justice, which
shall decide it in accordance with its ordinary procedure.

"If, by a three-fourths majority the Court declares
this claim to be without foundation, it shall retain
the affair for judgment on its merits.

"In the contrary case, the affair is sent back to
the parties, who shall be free, in default of amicable
adjustment by diplomatic means, to bring it ultimately
before the Court, after an agreement has been reached
upon the powers to be given to the Court in order
that it may act usefully."

The position taken by the Institute, on the matter of
compulsory jurisdiction, coincides with that part of Article
36 of the Statute of the Court that refers to optional
jurisdiction. Its jurisdiction is to comprise all cases the
parties refer to it and all matters specially provided for
in treaties and conventions in force. Moreover, when
one of these treaties or conventions provides for the reference of a matter to a tribunal to be instituted by the
League of Nations, the Permanent Court is to be that
tribunal, by Article 37. And as a question as to whether
the Court has jurisdiction is to be settled in accordance

with the last paragraph of Article 36 (*i.e.*, by the Court), the resemblance is all the more striking. It is only for the obligatory jurisdiction set up by the treaty itself and by the additional protocol that the phrase "legal disputes" is applied or developed, with reference to certain hypotheses under this rule.

It should be remembered, however, that in the majority of cases, the compulsory jurisdiction, happily and wisely left flexible, arises out of treaties and conventions which are almost imperceptibly becoming more numerous and more inclusive, taking in even the powers the most opposed to this jurisdiction. It is an example of social and legal penetration; the invariable law of progress will triumph here in the end.

Actually, then, so far as its jurisdiction over the subject matter (*ratione materiae*) goes, the Court has two missions, equal in development but different in origin. It is at the disposition of nations that agree to submit any kind of a dispute to it. It is the judicial power of the nations that have covenanted to accept it, temporarily or permanently, with or without reciprocity, for all kinds of legal questions or for only certain kinds, and which therefore have submitted to its compulsory and obligatory jurisdiction.

Article 36 of the Statute, to which reference has frequently been made, declares, in effect, that for legal disputes—analyzed above—the members of the League of Nations and the states mentioned in the Annex to the Covenant, when signing or ratifying the Protocol or at a later time, may declare that they recognize the jurisdiction of the Court as compulsory *ipso facto* and without special agreement, in relation to any other member or state accepting the same obligation. This declaration may be made unconditionally or on condition of reciprocity on the part of several or certain members or states, or for a given time.

192. The Court's jurisdiction is obligatory today in the following cases in accordance with the Statute and its protocol and subsequent conventions, treaties and mandates:

I. Between the states, enumerated below, that have accepted the additional protocol (the optional clause), as to legal disputes concerning the interpretation of a treaty, any question of international law, the existence of any fact which, if established, would constitute a breach of an international obligation, or the nature and extent of the reparation to be made for the breach of an international obligation:

(a) Esthonia, Haiti and the Dominican Republic have accepted this clause permanently, without reciprocity;

(b) The following nations have accepted it permanently, but on condition of reciprocity, and one of them has not yet ratified it: Bulgaria, Costa Rica, Liberia, Panama, Portugal, Salvador and Uruguay;

(c) The following nations have accepted it for five years, on condition of reciprocity, and with two ratifications pending: Austria, China, Denmark, Finland, Latvia, Lithuania, Luxembourg, the Netherlands, Norway, Sweden and Switzerland;

(d) Brazil accepted it for five years, on condition of reciprocity, and on condition of acceptance by two of the powers permanently represented on the Council of the League;

(e) France accepted it for fifteen years, on condition of reciprocity, subject to ratification, and reserving the right of denunciation should the Geneva Protocol lapse.

To sum up, without including the last two nations: the additional protocol has received the approval of twenty nations.

II. Between the states that have signed and ratified the Treaty of Versailles of June 28, 1919, which was signed by twenty-seven powers and ratified by all but three, viz.: the United States of America, Ecuador and the Hedjaz:

(a) As to the necessary measures to remove any obstacle or danger to navigation, and to ensure the maintenance of good conditions of navigation, on the internationalized part of the Elbe from its confluence with the Moldau and the Moldau from Prague, the Oder from its confluence with the Oppa, the Niemen from Grodno, and the Danube from Ulm, as to the riparian states and the states represented on the international commissions: under Article 336, of the Treaty of Versailles.

(b) As to the same states, in any question of new works of a nature to impede navigation in the international sections of the rivers, or, under certain conditions, of relative rights in connection with irrigation, water power, fisheries and other national interests; under Article 337 of the same treaty.

(c) As to the states in the same situation in the matter of the construction of a deep draught Rhine-Danube navigable waterway; Article 353.

(d) As to all the interested powers, in disputes that may arise in connection with the interpretation and application of Sections I, II and III of Part XII of the Treaty of Versailles, referring to ports, waterways and railways: Article 376.

(e) As to the same states, in the clauses relating to the Kiel Canal, which is to be maintained free and open to the vessels of commerce and of war of all nations at peace with Germany on terms of entire equality: Articles 380 to 386.

(f) As to the same states, over any question or dispute relating to the interpretation of Part XIII of the Treaty of Versailles, Articles 387 to 427, or of any subsequent convention concluded by the members of the International Labor Organization in pursuance of these provisions of the Treaty: Article 423.

III. Between the British Empire, France, Italy, Japan and Poland, which signed and ratified the special Treaty of Versailles of June 28, 1919:

(a) As to the stipulations for the protection of racial, religious and linguistic minorities: Article 12.

(b) As to the river régime of the *Vistula,* including the Bug and the Narew: Article 18.

IV. Between the states that signed and ratified the

Treaty of Saint-Germain-en-Laye of September 10, 1919, signed by nineteen powers and ratified by all except three, *viz.*: the United States of America, Panama and Poland:

(a) As to Austria and the nations that are members of the Council of the League, as to the conventions for the protection of racial, religious and linguistic minorities: Article 12.

(b) As to the matters mentioned in II (a), (b) and (c) above: Articles 297, 298 and 308.

(c) As to Austria and Czechoslovakia, as to the right given to Czechoslovakia to run trains over certain parts of Austrian territory: Article 324.

(d) As to the same states, as to questions relating to the use and servitudes of telegraph and telephone lines: Article 327.

(e) As to all the interested powers, in disputes that may arise in connection with the interpretation and application of Sections I, II and III of Part XII of this treaty, referring to ports, waterways and railways: Article 328.

(f) As to the same states, over any question or dispute relating to the interpretation of Part XIII of this treaty, Articles 332 to 367, or of any subsequent conventions concluded by the members of the International Labor Organization in pursuance of these provisions of the treaty: Article 368.

V. Between the British Empire, France, Italy, Japan and the Kingdom of the Serbs, Croats and Slovenes, which signed and ratified the special Treaty of Saint-Germain-en-Laye of September 10, 1919:

(a) As to the stipulations for the protection of racial, religious and linguistic minorities: Article II.

VI. Between the four powers first mentioned in V and Czechoslovakia, which signed and ratified the other special Treaty of Saint-Germain-en-Laye:

(a) As to the same stipulations about minorities: Article 14.

VII. Between the nations parties to the convention regulating aerial navigation signed at Paris on October 13,

1919, by twenty-one powers, eleven of which have ratified it, to which Bulgaria and Persia subsequently adhered:

(a) As to any dispute that may arise between two or more nations as to its interpretation: Article 37.

VIII. Between the states that signed and ratified the Treaty of Neuilly-sur-Seine of November 27, 1919, which was signed by sixteen powers, twelve of which have ratified it, and to which Rumania subsequently adhered:

(a) As to Bulgaria and the nations in the Council of the League, as to the convention for the protection of racial, religious and linguistic minorities: Article 57.

(b) As to all the nations interested in the international régime of navigable waters, in all cases similar to those indicated above under the Treaties of Versailles and Saint-Germain: Article 225 and 226.

(c) As to the stipulations relating to ports, waterways and railways: Article 245.

(d) As to the regulation of labor: Article 285.

IX. Between the nations that signed and ratified the Treaty of Trianon of June 4, 1920, signed by eighteen powers and ratified by thirteen:

(a) As to the protection of minorities: Article 60.

(b) As to the international waterways: Article 224.

(c) As to the right to run trains across Hungarian territory: Article 307.

(d) As to telegraph and telephone communication with Czechoslovakia: Article 310.

(e) As to the régime of ports, waterways and railways: Article 311.

(f) As to the regulation of labor: Article 451.

X. Between the British Empire, France, Italy, Japan and Greece, under the Treaty of Sèvres of August 10, 1920:

(a) As to questions relating to the protection of racial, linguistic and religious minorities: Article 16.

XI. Between the first four powers mentioned in X and Armenia, under the same treaty:

(a) As to the same protection of minorities: Article 8.

XII. Between Poland and the Free City of Dantzig, under the Treaty of Paris of November 9, 1920:

(a) As to the same protection of minorities: Article 33.

XIII. Between the British Empire and all other members of the League of Nations, under the mandate of December 17, 1920, for Nauru:

(a) As to any dispute relating to the interpretation or application of the provisions of the mandate which cannot be settled by negotiation: Article 7.

XIV. Between the same nations, under the mandate of December 17, 1920, for German Samoa, which is to be exercised by the Government of the Dominion of New Zealand:

(a) As above: Article 7.

XV. Between the same nations, under the mandate of December 17, 1920, for the German possessions in the Pacific Ocean south of the Equator, of the same date, which is to be exercised by the Government of the Commonwealth of Australia:

(a) As above: Article 7.

XVI. Between the same nations, under the mandate of the same date for German South West Africa, to be exercised by the Government of the Union of South Africa:

(a) As above: Article 7.

XVII. Between the same nations, under the mandate of July 20, 1922, for the Cameroons:

(a) As above: Article 12.

XVIII. Between the same nations, under the mandate of July 20, 1922, for Togoland:

(a) As above: Article 12.

XIX. Between the same nations, under the mandate of July 24, 1922, for Palestine:

(a) As above: Article 13.

XX. Between the same states, under the mandate of July 20, 1922, for East Africa:

(a) As above: Article 13.

The states that are members of the League of Nations may likewise bring any claims on behalf of their nationals for infractions of their rights under this mandate before the said Court for decision: Article 13.

XXI. Between Japan and all other members of the League of Nations, under the mandate of December 17, 1920 for former German colonies in the Pacific Ocean north of the Equator:

(a) As to any dispute relating to the interpretation or application of the provisions of the mandate which cannot be settled by negotiation: Article 7.

XXII. Between Belgium and all other members of the League of Nations under the mandate of the same date for East Africa:

(a) As above: Article 17.

XXIII. Between France and all other members of the League of Nations, under the mandate of the same date for the Cameroons:

(a) As above: Article 12.

XXIV. Between the same nations, under the mandate of the same date for Togoland:

(a) As above: Article 12.

XXV. Between the same nations, under the mandate of July 24, 1922, for Syria and Lebanon:

(a) As above: Article 20.

XXVI. Between the nations that have signed and ratified the Barcelona convention and statute of April 20, 1921, on freedom of transit, signed by forty powers, ratified to date by twelve, and subsequently adhered to by two other nations:

(a) As to any dispute that may arise as to the application or interpretation of the statute, unless, under a special agreement or a general arbitrative provision, no other action can be taken: Article 13.

XXVII. Between the nations that signed and ratified the convention and statute of the same date and place on the régime of navigable waterways of international concern; signed by forty nations, ratified to date by nine, subsequently adhered to by four, two reserving ratification:

(a) As above: Article 12.

XXVIII. Between the twelve nations that signed and ratified the convention relating to the statute of the Danube, signed at Paris on June 23, 1921, now ratified by all the signatory nations:

(a) On appeal from a decision of the International Commission on the ground that it is *ultra vires* or violates the convention: Article 38. The convention does not say who is to be regarded as the defendant.

(b) When a nation neglects to carry out a decision taken by the International Commission by virtue of the powers it holds under the convention: the same Article 38.

XXIX. Between Denmark and Norway, under the convention of Copenhagen of July 27, 1921, on air navigation:

(a) As to any disputes between the contracting states affecting the application or interpretation of this convention or its annexes, which cannot be settled by direct negotiations: Article 40.

XXX. Between Albania and every member of the Council of the League, in accordance with the declaration of Albania at Geneva on October 2, 1921:

(a) As to any dispute over questions of fact or of law relating to the articles concerning racial, religious and linguistic minorities: Article 7.

XXXI. Between the states that have ratified the agreement of Porto-Rosa of November 23, 1921, on international railway traffic:

(a) As to any dispute relating to its interpretation or application: Article 13.

XXXII. Between Austria and Czechoslovakia, under the political agreement signed at Prague on December 16, 1921:

(a) As to any disputes that may arise in the future between them, which may also be submitted to an arbitrator or arbitrators chosen *ad hoc*: Article 7.

XXXIII. Between Lithuania and the nations in the Council of the League, under the declaration made by Lithuania at Geneva on May 12, 1922:

(a) As to any dispute over questions of fact or of law relating to the Articles concerning racial, religious or linguistic minorities: Article 9.

XXXIV. Between Poland and Germany, under the accord signed at Geneva on May 15, 1922:

(a) When, in discussing whether new provisions for the division of land and for labor legislation may be substituted for those already in force, a mixed commission decides that the case is suitable for submission to the Court: Article 2.

(b) As to differences of opinion respecting the construction and application of Articles 6 to 22: Article 23.

XXXV. Between Germany and any member of the Council of the League, under the same convention:

(a) As to questions of fact or of law relating to racial, religious or linguistic minorities: Article 72.

XXXVI. Between Switzerland and Poland, under the commercial convention signed at Warsaw on June 26, 1922:

(a) As to disputes relating to the interpretation or executions of the convention that cannot be settled by diplomatic means nor by a conciliation commission: Paragraph 2 of the final protocol.

XXXVII. Between the British Empire and Mesopotamia, according to the treaty signed at Bagdad on October 10, 1922:

(a) As to any dispute that may arise between the contracting parties as to the interpretation of its provisions: Article 17.

XXXVIII. Between Austria and Hungary, under the arbitration treaty of April 10, 1923:

(a) For reasons of expediency, the two governments may submit disputes to the Permanent Court of International Justice: Paragraph 3 of Article 1.

XXXIX. Between Norway and Sweden, under the convention on air navigation signed at Stockholm May 26, 1923:

(a) As to any dispute affecting the interpretation or application of the convention and its annexes which cannot be settled by direct negotiations: Article 40.

XL. Between the British Empire, France, Italy, Japan, Greece, Rumania and Turkey, under the Peace Treaty of Lausanne signed on July 24, 1923, which extends the same rights to all members of the Council of the League:

(a) As to the provisions relating to Turkish nationals that are not Musulmans.

XLI. Between the forty nations and British colonies and dominions that have accepted the Geneva convention of September 12, 1923, for the suppression of the circulation of and traffic in obscene publications:

(a) As to all disputes that may arise on the subject of the interpretation and application of the convention which cannot be settled by direct negotiation. In case either or both of the parties to the dispute should not be parties to the protocol of the Permanent Court, the dispute shall be referred, at the choice of the parties, either to the Permanent Court or to arbitration: Article 25.

XLII. Between Germany, Belgium, the British Empire and France, in accordance with the London Protocol of August 15, 1924, on the economic evacuation of the Ruhr:

(a) As to any disputes that may arise between the allied governments or one of them, on the one side, and Germany on the other side with regard to the agreement, that cannot be settled by direct negotiation: Article 10.

XLIII. Between the thirty-one states that signed the convention for the simplification of customs formalities of November 3, 1923, at Geneva:

(a) As to disputes concerning the interpretation or application of its provisions that are not settled directly by the Council, which are to be referred to the Permanent Court on the request of either party: Article 22.

XLIV. Between the twenty-two states that signed the Geneva convention and statute of December 9, 1923, on the international régime of railways:

(a) As to disputes concerning the interpretation or application of its provisions not settled otherwise: to be submitted to arbitration unless the parties decide to bring it before the Permanent Court: Article 35.

(b) As to the same disputes: any questions of international law or the legal meaning of the convention that arise in the course of arbitration to be submitted to the Permanent Court at the request of either party: Article 36.

XLV. Between the fourteen states that signed the Geneva Statute and Convention of the same date for the international régime of maritime ports:

(a) As to disputes arising in case one of the contracting powers suspends the equality of treatment provided in the convention, in which case either state has the right to apply to the Permanent Court: Article 8.

(b) As to disputes arising as to the interpretation or application of the statute, not settled after submission for an advisory opinion to the advisory and technical organization of the League for matters of communication and transit, to be referred to arbitration, and any legal question of international law to be referred to the Permanent Court as in XLIV (b) above: Article 22.

XLVI. Between France and Czechoslovakia, under the treaty of alliance and friendship of Paris of January 25, 1924:

(a) As to any disputes arising in the future not settled by friendly agreement or through diplomatic channels,

which are to be submitted either to the Permanent Court
or to one or more arbitrators chosen by the Court:
Article 6.

XLVII. Between the British Empire, France, Italy,
Japan and Lithuania, under the convention concerning the
transfer of the Memel territory signed at Paris, May
8, 1924:

(a) Any difference of opinion in regard to questions of
law or of fact concerning the provisions of the convention
is to be regarded as of an international character and
shall, on request, be referred to the Permanent Court:
Article 17.

193. It is really surprising that within three years after
this Court was organized and set in motion, forty-seven
treaties and international agreements can be listed (even
if the unratified Treaty of Sèvres were not counted in, or
any other of doubtful interpretation) in which the jurisdiction of the Court is accepted as compulsory in matters
of the most different kinds, ranging from those that arise
out of the Treaty of Versailles to simple commercial agreements.[1] And it seems all the more wonderful when one
considers the list of the fifty-one nations that have signed
one or more of these conventions and that have turned,
without reservation or distrust, to the judicial power of
the Court, in matters of every kind or in more or less
general classes of disputes. These fifty-one nations are
as follows: Albania, Armenia, Austria, Belgium, Bolivia,
Brazil, the British Empire, Bulgaria, Chile, China, Colombia, Costa Rica, Cuba, Czechoslovakia, Dantzig, Denmark, Ecuador, Esthonia, Finland, France, Germany,
Greece, Guatemala, Haiti, Hedjaz, Honduras, Hungary,
Italy, Japan, Latvia, Liberia, Lithuania, Luxembourg,
Mesopotamia, the Netherlands, Nicaragua, Norway,
Panama, Paraguay, Peru, Poland, Portugal, Rumania, Sal-
vador, the Serb-Croat-Slovene State, Siam, Sweden,
Switzerland, Turkey, Uruguay and Venezuela.

---

[1] Publications of the Permanent Court of International Justice. Series D,
No. 3. International Agreements Affecting the Jurisdiction of the Court.

All the races, all the continents, all the forms of civilization are before the Court. Swiftly, and finally, the conception and practice of law and justice in international relations has conquered the world.

CHAPTER XII

PROCEDURE AND JUDGMENT

194. The provisions about procedure in the draft plans submitted to the Advisory Committee of Jurists were very defective; usually they consisted only of references to previous arbitration treaties. The reason for this omission probably was that the able and distinguished men who drafted them, while having a broad grasp of public affairs and international matters and a theoretical knowledge of law, did not realize the practical importance of the procedure, as a practicing lawyer or a judge learns to do from long experience.

This was—and is—an obvious mistake, for a court of justice, which may have a long calendar at times, cannot allow suits to be delayed or retarded; its success and the tranquillity of its suitors depends on its applying a uniform system, never varying as does the procedure in arbitration. In arbitration proceedings the parties who have set up the proceedings indicate the rules and regulations they wish to have followed, and as there is only the one case before each group of arbitrators, there may be postponements of every nature, without much prejudice to either contestant.

The Advisory Committee of Jurists, like the makers of the proposals, did not make any vigorous attempt to establish the procedure; it adopted a few general rules (discussed below) and then got rid of the problem by handing it over to some one else—to the Court; Article 30 of the Statute provides that "the Court shall frame rules for regulating its procedure. In particular, it shall lay down rules for summary procedure." The composition and the real purpose of the Council and of the Assembly naturally made them unsuitable bodies for drawing up Rules of Court.

195. As the quotation above indicates, there were to be two forms of procedure in cases before the Court, the usual procedure before the full Court, and a shortened or summary procedure—the latter a suggestion from the draft plan approved at the Second Hague Conference. As a number of the Rules apply to both forms of procedure, on matters both of detail and of the essence, these rules of universal application are discussed first, and then the Rules applicable only to one or the other form.

196. A fixed quorum is set for every case. For the full sessions—and all sessions are of the full Court unless the Statute expressly provides otherwise—eleven judges must be summoned, that being the number of the full Court; if all the eleven cannot be present, enough deputy judges are called to make up the number. Article 25 of the Statute, containing these provisions, overlooks the fact that the Assembly may increase the number of judges to fifteen, in which case the deputy judges would not be called until after all the fifteen judges had been summoned. If there are not eleven available, of the judges and deputy judges together, a quorum of nine is sufficient to constitute the Court.

The persons who drafted the Statute and those who drew up the Rules both forgot completely to make any provision for a quorum in case the Assembly does increase the number of judges to eleven; Article 4 of the Rules even says that in the case where one or more of the parties has the right to designate national judges, the full Court may sit with more than eleven judges. It would seem that the specification of this one exception to the usual number—contrary to the usual rule of statutory construction—should not be held to exclude other instances, and that where the Rules set the number at eleven, that being the present number of judges, it could be taken to mean twelve, thirteen, fourteen or fifteen, according to the actual number of judges at the time.

One point, which may become important, has not been covered: whether national judges may be counted in to make up the quorum of nine. There are reasons for and against including them; the principal reason for counting them is that it is important that the Court should be able to function, and that justice should be done.

197. The special chambers for labor cases and for transit and communication cases consist of five judges, never more nor less, according to Articles 26 and 27 of the Statute and Article 15 of the Rules. If there is a national of one and only one of the parties among these five, the President of the Court invites one of the other four to retire so that a national judge of the other party may be' designated.

The chamber of summary procedure sits with three members, never more nor less. This number is set in Article 29 of the Statute, and although Article 21, making the general provision about national judges, does not expressly state that they are not to sit in cases before this chamber, Article 15 of the Rules was drafted on the basis that the number was set at three, and was not to be modified.

There has been no occasion yet for the Court to make a ruling on these doubtful points and on those mentioned in No. 196.

198. Some of the possible cases where the number of available judges is reduced or where there is no quorum may result, of course, from natural causes, such as death, illness, inability to be present, or leave of absence. They may also, however, result from the provision for the withdrawal or disqualification of a judge in Article 24 of the Statute. The proposal that it should be possible for a litigant to challenge one of the judges was the subject of considerable discussion; it was not adopted, and the provision for national judges is in a way a substitute for it. Nevertheless the Statute provides, in Article 24, that if one of the judges considers that for some special reason he should not take part in the decision of a particular case, he is to inform the President of that fact; or if the President considers that for some special reason a judge should not sit, he is to give him notice accordingly. If the President and the judge do not agree, the question is to be settled by the Court.

199. The parties, *i.e.*, the states or members of the League of Nations, that are parties to a case, are represented in the proceedings by what are termed agents; they may also employ counsel. As there is no international bar, to which counsel may be admitted as to the bar of their own country, a person duly admitted in his own country may appear before the Permanent Court. There is no rule covering their credentials, nor any procedure for determining, if doubt should arise, whether counsel is duly qualified. This point will be regulated as soon as the number of cases before the Court makes it necessary. Here, as in the national courts, it is a great privilege and honor to defend a cause or a principle; a professional duty of so lofty a nature should be entrusted only to lawyers of high personal qualities who have thoroughly prepared themselves for it.

Nations will inevitably try to choose counsel of the first rank as their representatives; this will make it easier to obtain agreement on suitable qualifications for appearing before the High Court of International Justice.

Article 25 of the Rules makes the logical provision that service of papers upon the official representatives or agents of the parties is to be considered as service upon the parties themselves.

200. The President fixes the dates and hours of the sessions, by Article 29 of the Rules. The hearings are under the control of the President, or, if he is absent, of the Vice-President; if he too is absent, the senior judge presides (Article 45 of the Statute). Article 45 adds that the hearings shall be public, unless the Court shall decide otherwise, or unless the parties demand that the public be excluded. This last provision, which allows the parties, not the Court, to decide this point, is another survival from the arbitral procedure.

201. The official languages of the Court, as has already been said elsewhere in this book, are French and English. Article 39 of the Statute, which makes this express provision, adds that the use of the one or the other depends on the agreement of the parties, in default of which each uses the one he prefers, and the decision is given in both languages, the Court determining which text is to be considered authoritative. The same rules apply to all documents submitted. The registrar arranges for the translation from French to English or from English into French of all statements, questions and answers, if the Court so directs. On account of the composition of the Court, this direction is almost always given.

At the request of the parties, the Court may, according to the last paragraph of Article 39 of the Statute, authorize a language other than French or English to be used. This case has already arisen; German was allowed in an oral report, although the question was raised whether it was enough that one party alone asked for it, or whether it was necessary for all the parties to agree; the text uses the plural. In such a case as this, Article 44 of the Rules puts the burden of the necessary translations of its documents, proofs and reports on the party concerned.

202. Minutes are made at each hearing; they must be signed by the President and the registrar. These minutes are the only authentic record, according to Article 47 of the Statute. Article 55 of the Rules provides that they must include the names of the judges and of the agents, advocates and counsel; the names, Christian names, description and residence of witnesses heard; a specification of their evidence produced; any declarations made by the parties; and all decisions taken by the Court during the hearing. These minutes are made in both French and English, on account of the use of the two languages; so far both have always been used.

203. The Rules, following the Statute, and so still perpetuating the mistake of asssimilating this Court of Justice to an arbitration proceeding, provides, in Article 32, where the provisions for contentious procedure begin, that the rules contained under this heading shall in *no way preclude the adoption by the Court of such other rules as may be jointly proposed by the parties concerned, due regard being paid to the particular circumstances of each case.

In judicial life, it is allowable for the parties to dispense with the prescribed formalities, in order to expedite the work of the Court; but it is not permissible that the procedure shall be regulated according to their choice.

204. If the parties do not reach any such agreement, cases are brought before the Court, either by the notification of the special agreement *(compromis)*, or by a written application; both are sent to the registrar. The subject of the dispute and the contesting parties must be indicated. The registrar forthwith communicates the application to all concerned; he also notifies the members of the League through the Secretary-General. This last formality is not necessary, except in certain hypotheses, such as disputes over the application of a treaty or a general convention. In these cases, too, the notice should be sent directly to the nations concerned.

205. The Court has the power to indicate—presumably at the request of the parties or *ex officio,* although Article 41 of the Statute, covering this point, does not expressly say so—any provisional measures that ought to be taken, if it considers that circumstances so require. Pending the final decision, notice of the measures suggested must be given at once to the parties and to the Council. This makes it seem as if the Statute made the Council the Court's executive organ.

Article 57 of the Rules does not so interpret this provision, however; for after having given to the President the power to indicate such protective measures when the Court is not sitting, it merely adds that the refusal by the parties to conform to these suggestions is to be placed on record.

206. Article 43 of the Statute says that the procedure shall consist of two parts, written and oral. The first, which will be described first here, consists of the communication to the judges and to the parties of cases, counter cases and finally the reply and the rejoinder, as well as all papers and supporting documents. These communications are made by the registrar, in the order and within the time set by the Court. A certified copy of every document produced by one party must be communicated to the other party.

207. If the proceedings have been instituted by a special agreement, and provided no agreement to the contrary has been made by the parties, the following documents are presented in the order given, under Article 39 of the Rules: (a) a case, (b) a counter case, and (c) a reply. The rule adds that each must be submitted by each party within the same limit of time. It is strange, and, considering our clear and logical Latin procedure, it is really incomprehensible that a legal debate should consist of each side handing in each paper or complying with each formality at the same time as his adversary, so that neither one knows what the other claims or is going to claim. If they did it twice consecutively, one would understand that the second set were to answer the opposed arguments in the first set, but why three times?

If the proceedings are instituted by an application,— again provided the parties have made no agreement to the contrary—the documents are presented in the following order, which is a much more practical arrangement than in the other case: a case by the applicant, a counter case by the respondent, a reply by the first, and a rejoinder by the second.

208. The case must contain: (a) a statement of the facts on which the claim is based; (b) a statement of law;

(c) a statement of conclusions; and (d) a list of the supporting documents.

The counter case must contain: (a) the affirmation or contestation of the facts stated in the case; (b) a statement of additional facts, if there are any; (c) a statement of law; (d) the conclusions based on the facts stated, including counterclaims if they come within the jurisdiction of the Court; and (e) a list of the supporting documents.

These details are found in Article 40 of the Rules, which make no reference to the contents of the reply and rejoinder. Article 35 adds that the original application must indicate, in addition to the subject of the dispute, the names of the parties concerned, a succinct statement of the facts, an indication of the claim, and the address at the seat of the Court to which subsequent notices and communications about the case are to be sent. This article contains a similar provision as to an address for the special agreement or for the communication by which notice of it is given to the Court.

One thing attracts attention immediately: a perfectly useless difference between the rules for the first demand and for the case. Everything that belongs in the second could and ought to be in the first, as is done in the domestic procedure of any well organized country, in order to gain time and avoid cost and mere formalities.

All documents of the written proceedings presented to the Court must be accompanied by not less than thirty printed copies certified as correct. The President may order that additional copies be supplied.

209. For every case, the Court fixes the time limits, by setting a definite date for the completion of the various acts of procedure, having regard, as far as possible, to the desire of the parties. The Court may extend these time limits, and may decide that some act or proceeding done after the time limit is valid. If the Court is not sitting these powers are to be exercised by the President, subject to any subsequent decision of the Court (Article 33 of the Rules).

This system does not seem altogether satisfactory. It would be better to have the time limits set in the code of procedure; they would thus be known in advance to the parties; this arrangement could not cause any difficulty, because the time would begin to run from the notification, and because, as a general thing, the time limits could be extended for a fixed portion of the regular period. This would make the case move more swiftly, which would be to the advantage of all; a judgment is always a little unjust if it is retarded.

210. For the service of all notices on any person except the agents, counsel, or advocates, the Court applies directly to the government of the state upon whose territory the notice is to be served. Article 44 of the Statute makes this provision; it applies also whenever steps are to be taken to procure evidence on the spot. This provision is likely to result in many practical difficulties.

211. The Court takes all the necessary measures in connection with the production of evidence; these measures are not defined in either the Statute or the Rules. Article 45 of the Rules says that in every case the Court is to decide whether the production of the evidence is to come before or after the representatives of the parties address the Court; it would seem a little strange if they addressed the Court afterward.

The Court may, nevertheless, as indicated in Article 49 of the Statute, call on the agents of the parties, even before the hearing begins, for any documents or explanations, if it sees fit. Formal note is taken of any refusal to comply with such a demand. Under Articles 50 and 51, the Court may also, at any time, entrust the task of making any inquiry or giving an expert opinion to any individual, body, bureau, commission or other organization it may select; and the person or organization so chosen may ask any relevant questions of the parties or the witnesses during the hearing.

After the Court has received the proof and evidence

within the time set, it may refuse to accept any further oral or written evidence that one of the parties wishes to submit unless the other side consents. Article 52 of the Statute makes this provision.

212. Articles 47 to 54 of the Rules contain various provisions about the production of evidence. At a sufficient time before the oral pleadings begin, each party must inform the Court and the other party of the evidence it intends to produce and of the names, Christian names, description and residence of the witnesses whom it desires to have heard. A general indication of the point or points to which the evidence is to refer must also be given. Part of this information is to be given with the case, counter case, reply and rejoinder, and the rest shortly before the production of the evidence, after the written pleadings.

The Court may ask the parties to call witnesses or to procure additional evidence on points of fact on which the parties do not agree. The Court, or the President, if the Court is not sitting, takes any necessary steps for the examination of witnesses out of Court; it may do this at the request of one of the parties, or on its own initiative. There is no provision about the authority before whom such testimony is to be taken, nor about the form of the citation, nor about counter-interrogatories, nor about whether both parties must consent.

Before giving evidence each witness must make the following declaration: "I solemnly declare upon my honor and conscience that I will speak the truth, the whole truth, and nothing but the truth." The representatives of the parties examine the witnesses, under the control of the President; the President and the other judges may also ask the witnesses questions. The indemnities of witnesses called by the Court are paid out of the Court's funds.

Every report or record of an inquiry made at the request or order of the Court, and every report furnished by experts on order of the Court, must be sent at once to the parties. A record is made of the evidence taken; the portion containing the testimony of each witness is read to him, and must be approved by him. The Court decides whether a stenographic record is to be made for its use of all or of any part of the other oral proceedings.

213. The oral proceedings, which consist of the hearing by the Court of witnesses, experts, agents, counsellors and advocates, begins at a date fixed by the President after the written proceedings are completed. The Court fixes the order in which the advocates, counsel or agents shall be called on to speak, unless the parties have made an agreement on that point, as they may do under Article 46 of the Rules. Before the oral proceedings are concluded, each party may present his bill of costs. This provision contained in Article 56 of the Rules, is hardly plausible, aside from the influence it may have on the decision as to the costs, because the Court considers that failure to present the bill of costs is a renunciation of them. It is illogical to call for the bill of costs except at the necessary and useful moment; the fitting time, established in every code of procedure or practical system, is after the decision; and then only the party in whose favor a judgment carrying costs has been given should be called on to state his costs.

214. Article 54 of the Statute says that when the agents, advocates and counsel have completed the presentation of their case, subject to the control of the Court, the President shall declare the hearing closed and the Court shall withdraw to consider its judgment. Article 31 of the Rules provides that during these deliberations only the judges and the registrar may be present, except under a special decision of the Court caused by exceptional circumstances.

Among these possible cases is that of an interpreter, under the bi-lingual system provided in the Statute.

Each member of the Court expresses his opinion, stating the grounds on which it is based; the conclusion adopted by the majority, after the final discussion, determines the result. Before voting on any question, any judge may demand that it be formulated in concrete terms, in writing, and distributed to the Court in both official languages.

This system, in which no one is an arbitrer, has the advantage that every judge must study every case, so that no one can rest on the labor and pains of one or more of the others; but it has the disadvantage of retarding the decisions and of provoking long and often useless discussions.

All decisions are made by the majority of judges present. In case of a tie, the President, or his deputy, may cast the deciding vote. These rules, in Article 45 of the Statute, raise a question that apparently was never decided or brought up. When there is on the bench a judge of the nationality of one of the parties, the adversary has the right to name a national judge *ad hoc;* this was done, no doubt, to balance opinions and votes; but it hardly raises the dignity or the feeling of justice or independence of the judges in this situation. When this occurs, however, it raises the normal number of judges to twelve, and consequently a tie vote is possible. If the President is of the nationality of one of the parties, his casting vote would have the same weight as two votes, and the desired balance would vanish. The question could be solved by providing that a judge of the same nationality as one of the parties could not preside during the trial. This suggestion is not offered as an ideal arrangement, for the actual system of *ad hoc* judges, a remnant from arbitration, does not seem to the writer the most suitable arrangement, but it is indicated here as a possible improvement in harmony with the present regulations.

215. There is one case, very logical and simple, in which the Court does not come to a decision. If the parties conclude an agreement on the settlement of the dispute, and send a written notice of agreement to the Court before the end of the proceedings, the Court merely records this fact. The same action is taken if the parties notify the Court, by mutual agreement, that they intend to break off proceedings. Two points on which there may be a difference of opinion ought to be mentioned in connection with Article 61 of the Rules, containing these provisions about the settlement out of Court. The first is, that it is not clear why the parties cannot arrive at a solution themselves *after* the end of the proceedings; even after the judgment, they could do so if they liked, whether the Court was willing or not.   There is no reason why they should be deprived of this power after the discussions are closed, because to say that they may not do so would be equivalent to maintaining the impossible and attaining the unrealizable.

It is also odd that the consent of both parties is required to end the case.   This may be admissible in certain conditions of arbitration, or in a procedure based on a *compromis,* but in the ordinary legal action there is no reason why the plaintiff should not have power to stop, at his own risk, of course.   Domestic legal systems allow it, and it is the only good one in practice.

216. The Statute has provided for the possibility that a defendant may not appear, or that one of the parties may not defend his case after having appeared; Article 53 provides that in such a case the other party has the right to ask the Court to decide in its favor.   The Court may do so, after being satisfied itself that it has jurisdiction and that the claim is well founded in fact and in law.

217. Another possibility has been foreseen and regulated in both the Statute and the Rules,—that a third nation, not cited, might want to intervene in a case.   This may occur in two situations covered in Articles 62 and 63 of the Statute; a nation may consider—and certainly a member of the League of Nations that is not a nation may take the same action, in spite of the wording—that it has an interest of a legal nature in the case, and may ask the Court to be permitted to intervene as a party.   The Court decides this request.   It may also be possible that a case involves the construction of a treaty binding on states not connected with the case; in such case the registrar notifies these other nations of the litigation when it begins, and they have the right to intervene; if a state does intervene, the interpretation of the treaty in the decision is binding upon it.

The Rules give three Articles, 58 to 60, to this subject.

The first two refer to intervention on account of an interest of a legal nature; here the application for permission to intervene must be sent to the registrar before the oral proceedings begin; but under exceptional circumstances the Court may consider an application made at a later stage. This provision gives rise to complaints and to involuntary acts of injustice, and it would have been better not to allow later applications; this provision makes it necessary to go back in the proceedings, perhaps to change all the evidence, and causes confusion and disorder that do not help in doing justice. If a third party learns too late that it has legal interests in a pending case,—aside from the fact that its officials must be at fault, because the Court proceedings are all public,—it does not lose anything, because, in international as in national justice, a sentence has no binding force except over the parties between which it was given.

This application for permission to intervene must contain (a) the specification of the case in question; (b) a statement of law and of fact justifying the intervention; and (c) a list of supporting documents. The application is communicated at once to the parties, so that they may answer within the time set by the Court, or by the President of the Court, if not sitting.

If, however, a state—or a member of the League of Nations—desires to exercise its right of intervention in a litigation over the interpretation of an international treaty to which it is one of the contracting parties, all that it has to do is to inform the registrar in writing before the oral proceedings begin. The Court, or the President if the Court is not sitting, takes the necessary measures to enable the intervening state to see the documents in the case (called, in Spanish, *autos*), so far as they relate to the interpretation of the convention in question, and to submit its observations to the Court. There are no further provisions as to formalities, time limits, or proofs for the third nation. These omissions will be filled in practice.

218. Chapter II of Section C of Rules is taken up with rules for summary procedure. They are contained in three

Articles, 67 to 69 (so far as procedure before judgment is concerned). They were made rather hastily. They begin with a general provision making the rules for procedure in the full Court, ordinary or general, applicable to these proceedings also, except when these special rules provide otherwise.

Then it says that after the registrar receives the document beginning the proceedings in a case which, by agreement of the parties, is to be dealt with by summary procedure, the President is to convene this special chamber as soon as possible. This rule calls forth two observations. For one thing, it requires the preliminary agreement of the parties, and thus unnecessarily excludes the hypothesis that the plaintiff, giving his consent in advance, might leave it to the defendant to consent that the question be judged in this manner. In the second place, it makes the equally unnecessary provision, contrary to all ordinary procedure, that the chamber must be convened before the commencement of the written proceedings, which could and should be dealt with entirely by the President, with the help of the registrar.

Each party presents a case—whether at the same time or one after the other, the Rules do not say—and the registrar sends them to the judges of this chamber and to the opposite party. These cases must refer to all the evidence the parties desire to produce. Thus there is no debate or argument, which would seem essential in every instance. And it has never been expressly decided that notice of the demand must be given to other states that have signed or adhered to the convention the construction or application of which is under consideration. Nevertheless Article 63 of the Statute, which prevails over the Rules, leaves no doubt of the necessity for such notice, and provides for no exceptions.

Only when the Court considers that the cases do not furnish adequate information may oral proceedings be instituted, "in the absence of an agreement between the parties," Article 69 of the Rules says; this situation is really very curious. What would the Court decide if the parties decided not to have oral proceedings when the Court wanted to institute them because it had not obtained sufficient light on the situation from the written proceedings?

If a hearing is held, the Court may call on the parties for oral explanations It may also sanction the production of any evidence mentioned in the cases, and the witnesses and the parties must be available for appearance before the chamber when required.

219. The silence of these Rules of procedure on several very important matters that may arise at any time is notable. It has been mentioned before that the Court decides on its own competence, if any one has doubts about it. In other words, any one of the defendants or a third party intervening may dispute its competence, either by raising a preliminary question—which is called a dilatory motion in national legislation—or incidentally in relation to those who have intervened. How are these proceedings regulated? Absolute silence in the Statute and the Rules. One case that has already come up, in which incompetence was raised as a preliminary question, caused differences of opinion; there was a case, a counter case, and oral proceedings.

And there is no regulation of the proceedings or examination of other possible situations, such as attacks on witnesses, counter-interrogatories, intervention of all the parties in case evidence is taken out of Court, the competent authorities for taking such evidence, taxing of costs, and other questions of procedure. As has been said elsewhere, these Rules do not possess the precision and the foresight of Latin laws of procedure, inherited from the legal genius of Rome, and fortified by the experience of centuries; but it may be better to have vague and intermittent rules for a new institution, until its practice, in operation, permits less elasticity in written Rules and less arbitrariness in the powers of the Court and the President. It is fortunate that this does not depend on a treaty or an international statute, requiring discussion and the agreement of most of the nations for any change, large or small, but on a set of Rules which the Court itself makes and which can be modified at the pleasure of the judges. Although there naturally is a certain resistance to changes or additions that may seem premature, nevertheless the constituent power is in hand and almost always at work; therefore one may hope that it will not be long until the international procedure of the Permanent Court reaches the height demanded by the nature and the elevation of its mission.

220. As to the judgment, when the moment comes to render it, the Statute and the Rules contain provisions for its form and its substance. Article 62 of the Rules provides that it must contain (a) the date on which it is pronounced; (b) the names of the judges participating; (c) the names and style of the parties; (d) the names of the agents of the parties; (e) the conclusions of the parties; (f) the matters of fact; (g) the reasons in point of law; (h) the operative provisions *(dispositif)* of the judgment; (i) the decision on the costs, *i.e.,* under Article 64 of the Statute, which provides that if there is no special decision of the Court or of a chamber as to costs, each party is to pay its own. The opinions of dissenting judges are attached to the opinion if the judges desire it, whether they refer to the operative provisions or to the reasons on which they are based. This last point is based on a precedent; Article 56 of the Statute, which contains very few provisions, undoubtedly refers to the points mentioned above as (f) and (g); recognizing that justice must not only command but also convince, it requires that the reasons for the judgment be set forth. Finally, as to the details of its form, Article 58 of the Statute requires the President and the registrar to sign the judgment.

There are two methods of preparing judgments in the judicial practice of the world. One consists of writing them out in a sort of narrative form, like a brochure or a magazine article. In the other, they are arranged in a clear, precise outline; they are divided up into one series of paragraphs containing what the civil law calls "resultandos," and another series of concrete, compact paragraphs, technically called "considerandos," containing the legal principles. The Court had to choose between these two systems, as there is no rule on this point in the provisions under which the Court is governed. The majority voted for the narrative form, thinking, perhaps, that in this form the judgments would be more comprehensible for the general public, and in a sense less technical. This choice was probably influenced by the present practice in the countries from which the judges come, and perhaps also by the precedents of arbitral procedure, which reflected the same impulses.

221. As soon as the judgment is signed, it is read in open public session, due notice being given to the agents of the parties. This provision, found in Article 58 of the Statute, is completed by Article 63 of the Rules, which requires the registrar to communicate it forthwith to all parties concerned and to the Secretary-General of the League of Nations. The judgment is final and without appeal, except by the procedure for revision described below.

In the event of any dispute as to the meaning or scope of the judgment, Article 60 of the Statute authorizes the Court to construe it, on the request of either party; but errors due to a slip or an accidental omission may be corrected by the Court, or by the President if the Court is not sitting. The final Article of the Rules, Article 75, makes this provision.

222. The two legal documents, the Statute and the Rules, authorize an application for revision of a judgment, and regulate the procedure for it. Article 61 of the Statute provides that the application may be made only when it is based on the discovery of some fact of such a nature as to be a decisive factor, which, when the judgment was given, was not known to the Court nor to the party claiming revision,—always provided, however, that its ignorance was not due to negligence.

The proceedings for revision begin by a judgment of the Court expressly recording the existence of the new fact, recognizing that its character is such as to open the case for revision, and declaring the application admissible. The Court may require compliance with the terms of the judgment before admitting the application for revision.

The application for revision must be made not later than six months after the discovery of the new fact. No application may be made after ten years from the date of the judgment.

According to Article 66 of the Rules, the application, made in the same form as the application opening a case, must refer to the judgment impeached and the fact on which the application is based, and must contain a list of the supporting documents. The registrar gives immediate notice of the application to the interested parties, who may submit their observations within a time set by the Court, or by the President if the Court is not sitting.

The application for revision must be dealt with by the same chamber as gave the judgment, even though the terms of some of the judges that gave it have expired. The Rules do not say what is to be done if a quorum cannot be obtained because some of them are dead or cannot be present; but common sense, and the necessity to get the work done would force the Court to substitute others.

If the Court makes the admission of the application depend on previous compliance with the judgment that is attacked, the registrar must make this condition known at once to the applicant; the proceedings are stayed until proof of compliance has been received by the registrar and approved by the Court.

These provisions represent an advance over the precedents established by the Hague Peace Conference and over the proposals examined by the Committee of Jurists; this is commendable, from the point of view of the authority of the judicial power in international relations, and because of the need for assuring prompt and final justice.

223. The binding force of the judgment begins on the day on which it is read in open Court, according to Article 64 of the Rules. It would seem natural that if the Court or a chamber adds interpretations or if errors are corrected, it would be the publication of the last form that would fix the beginning of its binding force, so far as the interpretation or correction is concerned.

In any case, as *res judicata (chose jugée)*, the judgments are not binding except between the parties and in respect to that particular case; this is expressly provided in Article 59 of the Statute; as this provision relates to an entirely different matter, it has no effect on its efficacy so far as international jurisprudence is concerned. For this reason, among others, an official collection of the judgments is printed and published, under the responsibility of the registrar (Article 65 of the Rules).

224. A little while ago a very important question connected with that of the judgments was passed over so that it could be given special study here. This is the question of the law that ought to be applied; it has been the subject of many discussions in conferences and in official and unofficial congresses.

In the proposals examined by the Committee of Jurists, agreements between the parties were suggested, the rules of the law of nations, and the general principles of justice and equity. Baron Descamps submitted a proposal out of which eventually came Article 31 of the Committee's draft; it was formulated in these terms:

"The following rules are to be applied by the judge in the solution of international disputes; they will be considered by him in the order given below:

1. Conventional international law, whether general or special, being rules expressly adopted by the states;

2. International custom, being a practice between nations accepted by them as law;

3. The rules of international law as recognized by the legal conscience of civilized nations;

4. International jurisprudence as a means for the application and development of law."

The first two rules did not create any serious difficulty; but the discussion of the others took a wide range, covering the most important aspects of the question. Some of the jurists thought they involved compulsory jurisdiction, and they recalled that the International Prize Court, proposed at the Second Hague Conference of 1907, had been rejected in Great Britain, because no agreement had been reached on the general law to be applied, in the absence of a convention and of universal customary rules. As long as every country, it was said, has its own public international law on certain questions, international or national, it would never consent to submit (and the Monroe Doctrine was mentioned here) to a judicial authority that had power to apply in certain circumstances international law as it was understood by some other nation.

Others discussed the possibility of converting the judges into legislators, and of having them, in their judgments, prepare codes for the whole world, which, in derogation of national sovereignty, would not have the sanction of the separate governments. Others, with a different point of view, asked whether the Court, in the absence of any treaty or custom, could refuse to decide a question, leaving the parties without a solution. After a series of amendments and proposals, the final draft of the Committee was worded as follows:

"The Court shall, within the limits of its jurisdiction as defined in Article 34, apply in the order following:

"1. International conventions, whether general or particular, establishing rules expressly recognized by the contesting states;

"2. International custom, as evidence of a general practice which is accepted as law;

"3. The general principles of law recognized by civilized nations;

"4. Judicial decisions and the teachings of the most highly qualified publicists and of the various nations, as subsidiary means for the determination of rules of law."[1]

225. The first change in this text was proposed in the Council. It consisted of adding at the beginning of No. 4 a phrase referring to Article 37a, by which the decisions would be binding only on the parties, or, in other terms, indicating in rather a confused manner the difference, not discussed by any one, between jurisprudence as a source of law and the effect of *res judicata*. No reform is ever too large or too small to propose.

In passing through the third stage of its evolution, in the subcommittee and committee of the Assembly, this Article, which is number 38 of the present Statute, underwent several interesting alterations. One of them cut out the opening phrase, reducing it to "The Court shall apply." The unnecessary reference to the Court's jurisdiction, already sufficiently distinct, was fortunately suppressed, as was the provision requiring the four sources of law to be applied in the order given. This last requirement might not always be possible; and it certainly was dangerous.

In addition to certain other changes in the wording of No. 3 and No. 4, special mention should be made of the addition of a new paragraph stipulating that these provisions about the law to be applied should not prejudice the power of the Court to decide a case *ex aequo et bono,* if the parties agree thereto. This provision makes the new institution both a judicial power and a court of arbitration.

226. The final revision of this Article slightly diminished, in No. 4, the obligatory force of international jurisprudence. Its creative legal power, in the absence of written or customary law, is limited to being an auxiliary method for determining its rules.

There is, however, no standard, outside of jurisprudence and the doctrines of its most highly qualified publicists, for

[1] Minutes, pp. 293-5, 306-322, 331-8, 344, 584, 620, 729-730.

determining what are the principles of law recognized by the civilized nations. This is the field for the intervention of national rules applicable to international life or of international rules, properly so called.

CHAPTER XIII

SANCTIONS

227. How, and by whom, are the decisions of the Permanent Court of International Justice enforced? This question is very much in the minds of persons concerned about the judicial power of the world; the accounts in earlier chapters of the evolution of this power and of the preparations for establishing it have indicated that this is a question that should be answered now.

As a matter of fact public opinion on the subject seems to be divided; one group believes that the Court should have power to enforce its decisions; the other group believes that force would be useless or even harmful. Wehberg[1] points out that in the 1911 Lake Mohonk Conference Foulke maintained that an effective sanction was desirable, while Tripp, at the 1907 Conference, had strenuously opposed the idea. This German writer, who is opposed to sanctions, lays great stress on the difference between enforcing judicial decisions in a nation with several million inhabitants, and enforcing them in an international society composed, at the time when he was writing, of less than fifty states. The moral influence of a decision does not operate in the same way in these two situations; moreover, since this form of human jurisdiction is purely voluntary, arising only when the parties will it, it is all the more necessary that the judgments should have binding force.

228. Wehberg is right, as a matter of principle; and the results of arbitration support his position. As a recent writer has said, the distinction must be kept clear between force, which is the physical instrument of authority, and

---

[1] Wehberg.—The Problem of an International Court of Justice, pp. 105-109. Oxford, 1918.

authority, which is the moral support of force. Authority
may maintain itself without any great amount of force,
as in the case of the priest, the father of a family, the
apostle preaching his doctrine, or the master in his school;
but without a certain degree of authority force immediately
becomes unendurable tyranny, leading to revolution or
reaction.[1] This Court should possess the maximum authority between the nations, and then it would need only a
minimum of force in order to obtain respect and obedience
for its decrees.

As the writer recently pointed out before the Academy
of International Law at The Hague,[2] experience shows that
the execution of judgments in suits between individuals depends in most cases on the nature of the individuals. Nations are litigants of the first rank; the implacable eye of
public opinion and of history is fixed upon them, now and
forever. For this reason law and justice often find that
it is public opinion, the most intangible and yet the most
powerful of human forces, that gives them their irresist-
ible authority.

The statistics of international arbitration prove this beyond a doubt. The celebrity of the Alabama case, which
had so much to do with the extensive use of this procedure
since then, was due largely to the fact that a very powerful
nation, defeated by the decision, yielded voluntary obedience to orders without sanctions, and carried them out as
it never would have done if any attempt had been made to
execute them by force. There have been, of course, arbitral decisions that were not obeyed, but the state refusing
to carry out the award has always maintained, in good
faith, that there was some element in the situation which
weakened the moral authority of the judges or of their
action. This is really one of the defects of arbitration, but
it does not often arise.

229. And even arbitral sentences are not without all
possible material sanctions. Even before the League of

[1] Ferrero, Guillermo.—Lectures to the Deaf. Paris, 1924, pp. 74-75.
[2] See page 51.

Nations was established, it was admitted that if the loser
in an arbitration refused to carry out the award, the successful party still had at its disposition all the measures
recognized by international law by which one nation may
obtain what is due to it from another, even including war.

For example, in the convention adopted at the Second
Hague Conference on the limitation of the employment of
force in the recovery of contract debts, the contracting
powers agreed not to have recourse to armed force for
the recovery of contract debts claimed from the government of one country by the government of another country
as being due to its nationals; but it was very carefully
stipulated that this agreement was not to apply if the
debtor state refused to submit to the award after it had
been given.

This is something; but it is not much. International law
cannot feel satisfied today in allowing one nation to make
war on another after a decision has been given, instead of
sustaining it once it has been given. On the other hand,
to charge one of the contestants with executing the award,
whether by hostile or pacific means, would not tend toward
international concord, and would afford but slight guarantee that only a scrupulous and equitable fulfillment of the
award would be exacted from the defeated nation.

230. The first thought that comes to one's mind is that
this function might be given to the Court itself; but the
Court would have to be provided with sufficient forces to
enable it to overcome those the defaulting nation might
employ. This would be very difficult; it might even turn
the Court into a belligerent. The very thought of the
actual organization of the world shows that this idea is
impracticable. None of the various proposals on this subject mentioned in this book, all more or less fantastic, has
been able to change this impression.

231. There is a third possibility; and the current is
turning in this direction. Since all or almost all the nations
and their colonies and self-governing dominions now form

one social organism for certain joint purposes, this organism, which must have force and authority, might well assume the duty of enforcing the judgments of the Permanent Court of International Justice, in case the defeated nation resists the decision.

The Covenant of the League of Nations provides this joint sanction for certain possible situations, including possible international arbitrations. The idea of the Permanent Court was not in the original draft of the Covenant; it was inserted later. The preamble of the Covenant speaks of the necessity for the maintenance of justice in the dealings of organized peoples with each other, in order to promote international coöperation and to achieve international peace and security. In Article 12 the members of the League agree that if there should arise between them any dispute likely to lead to a rupture, they will submit the matter either to arbitration or to enquiry by the Council. Article 13 adds that if the dispute is one which they recognize to be suitable for arbitration or judicial settlement, and which cannot be satisfactorily settled by diplomacy, they will submit the whole subject-matter to arbitration or judicial settlement; certain cases are listed as being among those which are generally suitable for submission to arbitration or judicial settlement.

The last paragraph of this Article, which is the most significant provision in connection with this subject, states first that the members of the League agree that they will carry out in full good faith any award or decision that may be rendered, and that they will not resort to war against a member of the League which complies therewith. And then come these words: "In the event of any failure to carry out such an award or decision, the Council shall propose what steps should be taken to give effect thereto."

According to Article 16, which deals expressly with sanctions, if a member of the League resorts to war in disregard of its covenants under Articles 12, 13, or 15, it shall *ipso facto* be deemed to have committed an act of war against all other members of the League, who undertake to subject it immediately to the severance of all trade or

financial relations, the prohibition of all intercourse between their nationals and the nationals of the covenant-
breaking state, and the prevention of all financial, commercial or personal intercourse between the nationals of the
covenant-breaking state and the nationals of any other
state, whether a member of the League or not.

In such a case it is the duty of the Council to recommend to the several governments what effective military,
naval or air forces the members of the League shall sev-
erally contribute to the armed forces to be used to protect
the covenants of the League.

The members of the League agree, further, that they
will mutually support one another in the financial and economic measures which are taken under this Article, in
order to minimize the loss and inconvenience resulting
from them. They agree to support each other mutually
in resisting any special measures aimed at one of their
number by the covenant-breaking state, and to take the
necessary steps to afford passage through their territory
to the forces of any of the members of the League which
are coöperating to protect the League's convenants.

Any member of the League which has violated any covenant of the League may be declared to be no longer a member, by a vote of the Council, concurred in by the representatives of all the other members of the League represented thereon.

232. In the second session of the Assembly, in 1922,
these articles, and others, were amended so as to add,
wherever arbitration was mentioned, the words, "or solution or judicial decision." Thus the result of this amendment would be to make all the League sanctions identical,
by making the sanctions now provided for arbitral decisions applicable to judicial decisions as well. This is the
logical arrangement; it would give to the Permanent Court
in the Covenant a definitive situation as to the sanc-
tioning power; undoubtedly this would have been
done at the Paris Conference when the final form of the
Covenant was drafted, if the Court had been from the

beginning one of the institutions the framers had in mind.

At the present time, however, these amendments have not gone into effect, because they have not yet been ratified by all the nations in the Council and by the majority of the nations represented in the Assembly (required under Article 26 of the Treaty of Versailles).

At the opening session of the Advisory Committee of Jurists, M. Léon Bourgeois, representing the Council of the League, was asked what effect a judicial decision could have if it did not possess, in a strong organization of international institutions, what might be called in technical terms an executory force for its decisions. M. Bourgeois was undoubtedly counting on the ratification of these amendments, when he answered without the least hesitation that the Covenant provided different forms of sanctions, judicial, diplomatic, economic, and, as a last resort, and within fixed limits, military sanctions as well.

In the present circumstances it is rather difficult to accept this statement, in spite of its indisputable authority.

It is very desirable that this situation should be cleared up, and that the execution of decisions by joint will and action should be assured. Both material and political difficulties are involved in the matter, but they ought to be overcome, as similar difficulties have been overcome in national or international affairs. Confidence in the good effect of these amendments is justified, in these surprising times when new and fertile ideas are swiftly winning approval.

233. In certain cases the benefits of Article 13 of the Covenant have already been made applicable to the Court's decisions, by special agreements. The text authorizes the Council of the League to recommend the economic, political and military measures, as Article 16 puts it, that are necessary to ensure compliance with an award or decision.

The treaty of peace with Austria, signed at Saint-Germain-en-Laye on September 10, 1919, contains certain stipulations for the protection of racial, religious or linguistic minorities, under the collective guarantee of the League

of Nations. The last paragraph of this section, which has
already been discussed in an earlier chapter, provides that
any questions of law or fact arising out of these articles
between the Austrian government and any one of the principal allied and associated powers or any other power that
is a member of the Council shall be held to be a dispute of
an international character under Article 14 of the Covenant, and shall be referred, if the demand is made, to the
Permanent Court of International Justice; and the last
sentence adds: "The decision of the Permanent Court shall
be final and shall have the same force and effect as an award
under Article 13 of the Covenant." This is the first example
of the application, foreseen and duly regulated, of effective
sanctions for the judgments of the Court,—arranged even
before the Court was created.

This provision naturally was reproduced in the subsequent peace treaties. The special treaty of June 28, 1919,
with Poland; the treaty of Neuilly-sur-Seine of November 27, 1919, with Bulgaria; the treaty of Trianon of June
4, 1920, with Hungary; and all the other agreements and
declarations for the régime and protection of minorities
cited in Chapter XI [1] contain the same provisions, providing in these cases an administrative force chosen beforehand and not otherwise connected with the case, to see that
the Court's decisions are obeyed.

234. The Treaty of Versailles of June 28, 1919, by
which peace was made with Germany, tried to provide a
sanction, outside of the Court itself, for one particular situation, created by the terms of the Treaty. By Article 405,
referring to the work of the International Labor Conference, each member agrees that within one year or, under
exceptional circumstances, within eighteen months from the
end of a session of the Conference, it will submit the
recommendations or draft conventions of the Conference
to the national authority or authorities within whose competence the matter lies, for the enactment of legislation or
other action. If complaint is made that a nation, after

[1] See pages 209-215.

ratifying a convention, has failed to secure its effective observance within its jurisdiction, the governing body of the Labor Organization may appoint a Commission of Enquiry for investigation and report.

In both of these situations, according to Articles 415, 416 and 423, the Permanent Court of International Justice may intervene at the request of either party; and Article 418 adds that the Permanent Court may affirm, vary or reverse any of the findings or recommendations of the Commission of Enquiry, if any have been made, "and shall in its decision indicate the measures, if any, of an economic character which it considers to be appropriate, and which other governments would be justified in adopting against a defaulting government." Any member, whether a party to the case or not, may adopt any of these economic measures against the defaulting state.

The difference between this situation and those mentioned under Number 233 are obvious. In the latter group it is the Council of the League that is to recommend the measures that are necessary to ensure compliance with the Court's decisions; and these may be political, economic, or military measures. In the labor cases it is the Court itself that indicates them; here, however, they may be only economic, and their execution is entrusted to any one of the states belonging to the International Labor Organization. Evidently the solution of this problem will have to be worked out as a matter of positive law, and in the end the arrangement that gives the most satisfactory results in actual practice will be adopted. Perhaps several different arrangements will be adopted, varying according to the nature of the case.

235. Actual practice suggests another method by which the Permanent Court of International Justice could intervene directly to determine the sanction, in a way that would exert a more or less stimulating effect on the good will of the loser.

In a recent litigation where damages payable immediately were claimed, the nation making the complaint asked the Court to oblige the defendant to pay moratory interest, by raising the rate of interest considerably if the award was not carried out within a certain time. This would automatically provide a penalty for the delinquent party. This suggestion implies the assumption that it would be impossible to enforce compliance with the judgment, which is not flattering to the authority of the Court nor to the credit or honor of the state to which the sanction would apply. It is always better to begin with the opposite assumption, which is the only desirable one and which conforms with established practice.

236. The Committee of Jurists made no actual attempt to solve these problems, fearing, perhaps, that any ruling on this subject might raise irreconcilable differences of opinion that might endanger the adoption of their draft. The question came up incidentally, however, in connection with other topics. Lord Phillimore, asserting that the Court must have behind it a material force to ensure the execution of its decisions, so that nations would not be able to evade complying with them, maintained that this was one reason why the great powers must all have jurists of their nationality on the bench. "The great powers," he said, "are the police of the world, and by obliging them to have a direct interest, they would be compelled to act when the situation demanded."

M. de Lapradelle wanted to know what would happen under this arrangement if the judges of the great powers happened to be a dissenting minority, not in agreement with the decision of the majority of the judges. He might well have raised another point: that the great powers do not always agree among themselves. MM. Hagerup and Rici-Busatti insisted that what the Court needed was great moral force.

Of the many drafts examined by the Committee of Jurists, only those of the five central powers, of Switzerland and of Austria dealt with this question. The first two of these, in somewhat different terms, contained a rather vague provision placing the decisions under the guarantee

of the League of Nations; the third required the members
of the League to coöperate in enforcing them.[1]

The subject was not taken up in either the Council or
the Assembly, and consequently the Statute contains no provision on this question of sanctions.   Unless or until the
provisions of the Covenant are amended, they are left to
whatever arrangements may be made in separate treaties.
The force of public opinion will tend to increase the number of these separate agreements and to prepare the way
for converting them into a universal international convention.

[1] Minutes, etc., pp. 94, 95, 105, 125-128.

CHAPTER XIV

THE ADVISORY FUNCTION OF THE COURT

237. The last sentence of Article 14 of the Treaty of Versailles says, as has already been pointed out, that the Permanent Court of International Justice *will give (donnera)* an advisory opinion on any dispute or question referred to it by the Council or by the Assembly. At least, this is what the French text says; the English text uses the words *may give,* which do not mean exactly the same thing. Both these texts are official, under the bi-lingual system adopted by the Paris Conference and confirmed in the final provisions of the Treaty.

A North American internationalist, John Bassett Moore, who has studied the subject carefully, thinks that the conflict between these two versions ought to be decided in favor of the second. He asserts that several persons who collaborated in the negotiation of this treaty state that the English text is the original and that the French text is a translation of it; he does not give the names of these witnesses. He therefore thinks that the English text is the controlling one, especially because, in his opinion, the question involves giving the Court a function "admittedly inconsistent with and potentially destructive of the judicial character with which the Court has undoubtedly been invested." [1] M. Altamira expressed the same opinion, in the discussion over the Court Rules, and proposed inserting a statement to the effect that the Court could refuse to give an advisory opinion. Lord Finlay objected, and M. Weiss observed that the provisions already in force implied that right. [2]

The writer is not convinced that these opinions on this

[1] Acts and documents, p. 384.
[2] *Ibid.,* p. 161.

question, however entitled to respect, are altogether exact.
On reading carefully the English version, it does not seem
to contradict the French text.   In the English text, after
having stated that the new institution is to render justice
by solving the disputes which are submitted to it, it is
added that the Court may also give an advisory opinion
to the Assembly or to the Council of the League of Nations.   The word *may* in the sense in which it is used here,
implies the grant of an additional function for the new
organism, but that does not mean that the exercise of this
function is in the discretion of the Court.   The idea is
not that the Court may refuse to give the advisory opinions
which are asked, but that the Council and the Assembly
may or may not ask for them.   These bodies are given
power to ask for the opinions, but the Permanent Court
has not the power to give them when it wishes to do so, as
an act of grace, or to refuse them for any reason whatever.

The Treaty of Versailles simply placed the Court, for
the creation of which Article 14 provides, at the disposition of the League as a consulting body.   It is useless to
argue whether this task is or is not compatible with the
judicial function, or to assert that it compromises the
Court's prestige and future; it is not a question of arguing
about Article 14, but of applying it; and these reasons are
not strong enough to modify it.

238.   The power to apply to the Permanent Court for
advisory opinions is limited to the Council and the Assembly of the League of Nations.   When the Statute was
before these two bodies for consideration, the International Labor Office made a vain attempt to have this privilege extended to it and to the Labor Conference, and Ar-
gentina also demanded, in vain, that it be extended to the
governments of all the nations in the League.[1]

Fortunately, these two proposals were rejected.   It is
a good thing that they were, not only because they would
have done much harm to the work of the Court, but also
because they would have made it possible to bring before

[1] Documents relative, etc., pp. 68 and 79.

the Court, under the guise of advisory opinions, disputes
which the other party did not want to submit to the Court
in the form of a litigation; it would have been a clever
way of finding out what the Court's decision would be in
a subsequent litigation, or of learning what would be the
best reasons for refusing to compromise or to arbitrate the
question.

239. What is the subject matter of the opinions? "Any
dispute or question referred to it by the Council or by the
Assembly," are the precise words of Article 14 of the
Covenant. M. de Lapradelle ingeniously maintained in
the Committee of Jurists that a "dispute" was an actual
case, whereas a "question" was theoretical; the Committee
made no objection to this distinction, except that Mr. Root
thought that the power to give an advisory opinion with
reference to an existing dispute was a violation of all juridical principles.

The report of the Committee to the League of Nations,
prepared by M. de Lapradelle, observes that the dispute
must be of an international character. This would apply
also to a question. This must have been generally understood, or else it would have been necessary to stipulate that
the Court could not give an opinion on matters of any
other kind. This point has no bearing on the question
whether it is obligatory on the Court to give the opinions,
and does not need to be discussed.[1]

240. M. de Lapradelle made a distinction between a
point of law and a dispute, which is very difficult to apply
in certain cases, not as a matter of scientific obligation or
of pure empiricism, but because a Court, differently constituted, has to concern itself with both of them. If the
advisory opinion does not relate to any actually existing
dispute, then, says his report, "as the question may subsequently be brought before the Court in its judicial capacity,
either on account of its character, or because the parties
make a special agreement to that effect, the Court must be

[1] Minutes, pp. 584-5, 701, 730-2.

so constituted that the opinion given in the abstract upon the theoretical question does not restrict the freedom of its decision, should the question come before it later in practice and no longer as a theoretical problem, as a concrete case and not merely in the abstract." The Court, in such cases, must therefore, he thought, "be differently constituted" and reduced to a smaller number.

In accordance with these views, the Committee of Jurists' draft made the following provision, in Article 36:

> "The Court shall give an advisory opinion upon any question or dispute of an international nature referred to it by the Council or Assembly.
>
> "When the Court shall give an opinion on a question of an international nature which does not refer to any dispute that may have arisen, it shall appoint a special commission of from three to five members.
>
> "When it shall give an opinion upon a question which forms the subject of an existing dispute, it shall do so under the same conditions as if the case had been actually submitted to it for decision." [1]

241. The first objection came from the Council for Diplomatic Litigation attached to the Italian Ministry of Foreign Affairs; the Italian government endorsed the objection. The Council was of the opinion that the last paragraph quoted above gave to the functions and opinions of the Court a character scarcely in conformity with Article 14 of the Covenant. If this provision referred to the power of the Council and the Assembly to send the parties *ex officio* before the Court, more exact and definite rules should be formulated. The second paragraph quoted above should be so modified as to limit this power. An amendment was proposed by Italy, in line with these criticisms, reading as follows:

> "When the Court shall give an opinion upon a question of international law, it shall appoint special

[1] Minutes, p. 732.

commissions to perform the duty of preparing the requested opinion." [1]

242. In the first discussion in the Assembly sub-committee—rather confused discussions, to judge from the printed minutes—the third paragraph of Article 36 quoted above was struck out, by a vote of six to three, and the Italian amendment was accepted in principle (*i.e.*, the wording was reserved).

Two days later, however, in the next meeting, M. Fromageot declared that it would be better to suppress the entire Article; according to Article 14 of the Covenant, the Court could not refuse to give advisory opinions, and it was not necessary to include a rule to the same effect in the Statute of the Court. He added, a moment later, that the question of the conditions under which the Court could give opinions was not included in that of the organization of the Court, which was the only question that could be studied at the moment. A vote was taken, and it was unanimously agreed to suppress the entire Article.

The report of the sub-committee, which was adopted by the committee and laid before the Assembly, sets forth other reasons. This report says, first of all, that these opinions should, in every case, be given with the same quorum of judges as that required for the decision of disputes, and that the distinction established in this respect by the draft scheme between cases referring to disputes that have actually arisen and theoretical cases was lacking in clearness and was likely to give rise to practical difficulties. It added that on this point the draft went into details which concerned rather the rules of procedure of the Court. For these reasons it proposed that the article be suppressed. This explanation, drafted by M. Hagerup, ought to be considered as the official statement on the subject, rather than the preceding statement of M. Fromageot, but both must have influenced the votes, especially the first statement in the subcommittee because it pre-

[1] Documents relative, etc., pp. 29 30.

ceded its vote, and the second in the Assembly, for which it was prepared.[1]

This account shows, first of all, that it was the desire of the Assembly, based on Article 14 of the Covenant, that the full Court, and not sections, commissions or chambers, should study and decide these questions. In the second place, the result is that, thanks to all these misunderstandings, the Statute of a Court charged with judging litigations and giving advisory opinions does not say a word about its latter function.

243. This omission had to be remedied, as far as possible, in the Rules, prepared by the judges who were present at a preliminary meeting; these judges agreed unanimously that advisory opinions should always be given by the full Court. They so provided, in the first paragraph of Article 71 of the Rules.

Since then two opposed opinions have been developed, based mainly on practical considerations. It is a tenable proposition that since there is a special chamber for summary procedure, sitting in urgent cases, which is able to meet quickly, this chamber might well give an advisory opinion when it is important to get the opinion quickly. It may also be maintained that since the power of asking for the advisory opinion belongs to the Council and the Assembly, there is no reason why they should be allowed to ask eleven judges for it, but not allowed to base their action on the judgment of the three or five in the chamber of summary procedure or in the special chambers for labor cases and transit and communications cases; and in the last group, it might even be an advantage. In every respect, *dura lex, sed lex.* For the present,—partly by the fault of the Assembly and of the Rules, but also partly due to the wording of Article 14 of the Covenant, which though sufficient, is doubtful, and still harder to alter,—all the advisory opinions must be given by the full Court.

244. In M. de Lapradelle's very remarkable report,

[1] Minutes, pp. 145, 146, 156, 211.

sent in with the draft-scheme of the Committee of Jurists, it is said, in the comment on Article 36, that when the opinion asked for refers to an existing dispute, the Court ought to allow the appointment of national judges *ad hoc*.[1] After Article 36 was suppressed, it can hardly be maintained that these observations are still in point; but the question is a practical one and may come up at any time. It is carefully studied in an important book on the Permanent Court of International Justice received while this chapter was being written.[2]

The author of this last book is inclined to answer the question, as to national judges in connection with these opinions, in the negative; and so far this seems to be the feeling of the Court, although no official request has yet been made in this connection, as the presence of the judges has never been required. In these advisory matters, there are no parties who plead and are bound by the judgment; there are only the nations and associations that have been invited to furnish information; and their presence is not indispensable or obligatory. Moreover, the Rules, in the section on the advisory procedure, do not say one word from which the necessity of admitting the national judges can be deduced.

245. The Rules on advisory matters are very simple, so far as procedure is concerned. Under Article 72, questions on which the advisory opinion of the Court is asked are laid before the Court by means of a written request, signed either by the President of the Assembly or by the President of the Council of the League of Nations, or by the Secretary-General of the League acting under instructions from the Assembly or the Council. This request contains an exact statement of the question upon which an opinion is required, and is accompanied by all the documents likely to throw light on the question. Under the

---

[1] Minutes, pp. 731-2.
[2] Salvioli, Gabriele.—La Corta permanente de Giustizia internazionale, pp. 154-156. Rome, 1924.

practice adopted by the Council, from which all the requests for opinions have come so far, the Secretary-General is expressly authorized to furnish all necessary assistance for the examination of the question and, if need
be, to take measures to be represented before the Court.
The Council also sees to it that interested nations or associations may be heard or may intervene.

In preparing Article 72 of the Rules, which was Article
76 in the draft under discussion, certain members of the
Court insisted that the Court ought to receive the entire
official report out of which the request arose;[1] frequently
the Court avails itself of its right to receive the documents
by demanding supplementary information, either by a
general agreement or at the request of several of the
judges.

246. After he has received the request for the advisory
opinion, the registrar, in accordance with Article 73 of the
Rules, gives notice of it forthwith to the members of the
Court, and to the members of the League of Nations
through the Secretary-General, and to the states mentioned in the Annex to the Covenant. Under the same
Rule, it is also sent to any international organizations that
are likely to be able to furnish information on the question.
The drafting of this Article caused much discussion
among the judges. M. Anzilotti wanted to expand its provisions, so that the notice would be sent to all the states
that could appear before the Court; but M. Beichmann
maintained that it ought not to be made known to any one
except the judges, adding one very good reason that has
since been repeated: that it is the person who consults,
not the person consulted, that ought to decide how much
publicity is given to the request. Lord Finlay showed that
the arrangement proposed in the draft would permit the
nations to furnish all useful information; and M. Beichmann's proposal was rejected by a majority vote. Later
M. Anzilotti proposed to strike out the reference to the

---

[1] Acts and Documents, etc., pp. 159, 160, 471-2.

states mentioned in the Annex to the Covenant, but the provision was retained, on a divided vote.

As a matter of fact, the consultations are denatured and in urgent cases the opinion is greatly delayed, by the sending out of these notices to the far corners of the horizon to get suggestions or information from any international legal person that desires to send them in. In private relations such a practice would be indelicate, and would constitute an obvious violation of professional duty. The consultant can be required to furnish all necessary evidence and information, and if it fails to do so and the Court thus remains in ignorance of something of real importance, it is the consultant, and not the Court, that is responsible. But after it was once decided to send out notices of the requests for opinions before the questions had been examined and answered, it was necessary to choose between two systems: of giving notice only to members of the League of Nations, as collectively represented, or of making it known to all the world. The Rule does neither; it orders that the notice be sent to the members of the League and to the states mentioned in the Annex to the Covenant, whether members of the League or not, which is explicable only on the ground of the search for information; but it suppresses the notice for other countries, although they may be obliged to appear before the Court in certain cases or may have adhered to the Court and expressly submitted to its jurisdiction. And then, after suppressing the notice to these countries, which may seem unnecessary on account of the completeness of its information, the Court notifies mere international associations that could never appear before it as parties to a litigation.

247. The procedure explained in the preceding number (246) has the advantage of absolutely preventing any secret consultations. In the League of Nations, and in the light of our present conceptions, the publication of the Court's acts and results is an obvious necessity. The Court cannot be a secret organ helping to uphold responsibilities and decisions under cover. This is not the same thing, however, as serving as a publicity agency, and the two things ought not to be confused.

In discussing its Rules, the Court went on record against secret consultations almost unanimously, by a vote of eleven to one, Lord Finlay and Mr. Moore rightly maintained that not only was every secret decision incompatible with the Statute, but also that a practice of giving opinions that would not be known and published would destroy the Permanent Court as a judiciary body.[1]

248. The Rules do not say a word about the procedure in advisory opinions. In practice, this omission has been made good by the establishment of a written procedure and oral pleadings, as in cases up for judgment. The interested nations that have answered the notice, and international associations in the same situation, present cases and counter cases and produce documents and replies to enquiries, in public, through their agents, counsellors or advocates. In other words, the procedure before the full Court is used as a model for these proceedings, which so far form much the largest part of the work of the Court. But as everything depends in each instance on the standards and the will of the Court, it has hitherto been easy for it to prevent the privileges it has granted from getting out of bounds and becoming an abuse or a political device for delaying urgent and necessary solutions.

249. These formalities over, the Court makes its decision, by a majority vote; and the opinions of dissenting judges may, at their request, be attached to the opinion of the Court; this is expressly stated in the second paragraph of Article 71 of the Rules. This provision caused the same discussion as in the case of the judgments; but an additional argument for publishing the dissenting opinions here was brought forward, the strength of which is undeniable; it is that any person that consults another is seeking for enlightment, and he does not lose anything

[1] Acts and Documents, p. 160.

by learning the reason for the opinions that are manifested; it helps him to form his own opinion. It is not necessary to repeat here, from the point of view of the Court and of the judges, what has already been said with reference to dissenting opinions in connection with the Court's judgments, nor to insist on other more or less important aspects of the question.

As to the form of the advisory opinion, the rules say nothing. In the first draft the word *motivé* (accompanied by the reasons on which it is based) appeared in one of the provisions about the opinions; but this word disappeared later on. But this does not indicate that the Court may limit its answer to a mere yes or no; an advisory opinion needs reasons and arguments just as much as a judgment does. Its value is in direct ratio to the reasoning it sets forth. This practice has been established; and hitherto, with more reason than in judgments, the narrative form has been used. Only the President and the registrar sign the advisory opinions; each judge or group of judges dissenting on the substance of the opinion or on certain of the reasons for it signs his own opinion; or if a dissenting judge merely declares his dissent, it is so stated at the end of the advisory opinion.

250. How and when should an advisory opinion be published or announced? The Rules do not cover this point; they only make a provision for printing them, which will be discussed later. When the Article containing this provision was being discussed, M. Huber proposed to add the following: "Provided, that the publication of each advisory opinion that has been completed will not take place until the end of the session in which the request for it was made." It was rejected by ten votes to two, after Lord Finlay had asserted that these opinions should be read in open session, and after the President, M. Loder, had maintained they ought to be sent first to the body that asked for them.

No vote was ever taken on this last suggestion; in practice, exactly the opposite of what the President rightly suggested is done. The advisory opinions are read in the solemn open session of the Court as soon as they have been formed, and the consultant learns the result from the daily papers, although the representatives of the interested nations or the consultants are given a copy of the opinion, if they are present.

All the advisory opinions and the requests in response to which they were given are printed in a special collection for which the registrar is made responsible, by Article 74 —the last of the Rules on this part of the Court procedure.

251. The Court's opinion in these cases has only moral value. A person who asks for advice in good faith either follows it or does not follow it, according to his own convictions. Nevertheless the authority of the Court is so great that the Assembly and the Council would not be in a very good position before the world, if they paid no attention to an advisory opinion after obtaining it.

It is evident, in this connection, that the parties may obligate themselves in advance to the Council or the Assembly to conform to the Court's opinion and to make it the basis of their subsequent negotiations. In 1922 two great powers, England and France, debated before the Council the question whether certain decrees promulgated in Morocco and Tunis were of a national or an international character. The Council decided to submit this question to the Permanent Court of International Justice, in the form of a request for an advisory opinion; the resolution making the request stated that the two governments had agreed to accept the Court's opinion as the rule for their future conduct. This agreement was carried out to the letter, which raised some doubt as to whether this was a true advisory opinion or a judicial decision.

It is by all means important not to forget, as M. Ricci-Busatti said in the Committee of Jurists,[1] that as a general thing it is not possible to assimilate an advisory opinion to a judgment, in origin, in method of examination, or in legal effect.

[1] Minutes, p. 226.

252. One of these legal effects relates to jurisprudence; it concerns international law and its development, as much as it concerns the Court itself. In the report of the Advisory Committee of Jurists, the statement is made that because the Court's opinion is given in the abstract, in a purely advisory capacity, it is necessary that, if the opinion came back to them again in a concrete form, the Court would not be bound by its preceding opinion. This fear seems rather exaggerated, both in the Committee's report and in other commentaries.

Suppose that two nations, interested in a general convention, came to a dispute over the interpretation of one article in it and decided to submit their difference to the Permanent Court. No other of the contracting nations intervenes, and the Court gives its advisory opinion, which has binding force only on the parties to the litigation. Months, or even years afterward, two other nations get into a dispute over the same question and submit it again to the Court, one of them basing its main argument on the earlier decision. Would any one contend that the Court should not take cognizance of the second case because it had decided the first? And if this situation can arise and does arise very often before the national courts, of two similar or identical actions, what real inconvenience could there be if a litigation arose on some matter after it had been the subject of the advisory opinion? The Courts always give their decision according to what is appealed to and is proved before them, and if information on matters of fact or conclusions of law are produced in the second case that were not known at the first case, the decisions might even be contradictory without any implication of scandal or of injustice.

253. If a person were giving a theoretical opinion as to whether it would be suitable to give to a Supreme Court of Justice advisory functions in connection with executive and political organisms, he would instinctively feel inclined to answer in the negative. Two powers so different as the executive and the judicial powers, the one that administers and the one that judges, ought not to be confused, because this confusion would be likely to denature them and to injure them both.

Suppose the consultative system has been accepted, and the question then, still purely theoretical, is whether it would be suitable for the body that is consulted to call the interested parties before it and to apply the same forms of procedure, written or oral, in the debates as in those for a judgment,—once more the professional conception of the consultation and of its usefulness leads one mechanically to answer in the negative, and to base the answer on very serious grounds.

Nevertheless there is one case in which the mixture of these two apparently irreconcilable functions has produced good results, and has even created a new form for the solution of international difficulties that is helpful toward harmony and pleasant relations between peoples. Perhaps this is partly due to the fact that the Assembly and the Council, in the actual international organization that has only just made its *début,* are not exclusively executive or administrative bodies, because they have semi-judicial functions that make it easy for a Court of Justice to give an impartial and disinterested opinion, technical competence not being essential. Perhaps, too, as in the case between England and France, the situation is influenced by the advantage of an arbitral solution without arbitration and a judgment without proceedings; this provides diplomacy with new formulas for its agreements, without delays, costs or solemnities, and sometimes without the constitutional formalities that some of the ancient regulations required.

Let us hope that the teachings of time will correct or justify these somewhat premature impressions. It is very dangerous to make prophesies beside the cradle; if they come true, it is almost always by chance.

CHAPTER XV

THE WORK OF THE COURT

254. The first task of the Permanent Court of International Justice was to answer requests of the League of Nations for advisory opinions. In this statement of the Court's work, these advisory opinions will be considered first, and then the judgments in litigated cases; in all cases the questions submitted, the facts that gave rise to the questions, and the decision reached by the Court are stated, and the theories of international law that are stated or implied in the opinions or judgments are discussed.

255. On May 12, 1922, the Council, on the request of the Governing Body of the International Labor Office, asked the Permanent Court for an advisory opinion on the question whether the Netherlands workers' delegate to the third session of the International Labor Conference had been nominated in accordance with Paragraph 3 of Article 389 of the Versailles Treaty.

Before this third session the Minister of Foreign Affairs of the Netherlands had invited five labor organizations to take part in a consultation as to the naming of the delegate; these five were:

(a) The Dutch Confederation of Trades Unions, with 218,596 members;

(b) The Confederation of Catholic Trades Unions, with 155,642 members;

(c) The Confederation of Christian Trades Unions, numbering 75,618 members;

(d) The General Confederation of Trades Unions, numbering 51,195 members; and

(e) The National Labor Secretariat, with 36,038 members.

The last organization refused to take part in the consultation. The first organization proposed its own candidate; the second, third and fourth supported a joint candidate, who was appointed as the workers' delegate to the Third Session. The Dutch Confederation of Trades Unions sent a letter of protest to the International Labor Office, maintaining that the candidate had not been selected in agreement with it, although it had a larger number of members than any other labor organization, and was consequently the "most representative organization" within the meaning of Article 389 of the Versailles Treaty; at any rate, it added later, it was one of the most representative, and it had not agreed to the chosen candidate. The Conference admitted the chosen delegate, on the condition that his admission was not to constitute a precedent, and asked the Governing Body to ask the Council to ask the Court for an advisory opinion on the interpretation of Article 389. The Council of the League then adopted a resolution asking the Court to give an advisory opinion upon the question "whether the workers' delegate for the Netherlands at the Third Session of the International Labor Conference was nominated in accordance with the provisions of Paragraph 3 of Article 389 of the Treaty of Versailles."

Notice of the request was sent, according to the Rules of the Court, to the members of the League and to the states mentioned in the Annex to the Covenant, and also, though the Rules did not require it, to Hungary and Germany. Notice was also sent to the International Association for the Legal Protection of Workers, the International Federation of Christian Trades Unions and the International Federation of Trade Unions. Legal arguments, documents and other information were submitted to the Court, and oral statements were made during the hearings, by the governments of Great Britain and the Netherlands and by the International Labor Office, the Dutch Confederation of Trades Unions and the International Federation of Christian Trades Unions.

The Court held unanimously, in an opinion delivered on

July 31, 1922, that the appointment in question had been made in accordance with the provisions of Article 389; this Article uses the term "organizations," in the plural, not the singular, and refers to organizations of both employers and employees; moreover this provision cannot be taken to mean that the most representative organization is the one with the greatest number of members; this interpretation would lead to the unreasonable result that one large organization could monopolize the nomination or could prevent agreement on a candidate that was satisfactory to the great majority of workers in the combined membership of the other organizations.

256. The first consideration this case suggests is very curious. The League of Nations, as such, and the Council and Assembly, had no direct interest in the question involved; it did not come up before them, and the solution of it did not affect them. The question related to one of the autonomous organisms of the League, the International Labor Organization, to which nations may belong that are still excluded from the League; when the Assembly and Council were considering the Court Statute, this Labor Organization had asked them to give it the right to consult the Court; they denied this request, because it did not come within the terms of Article 14 of the Covenant. Confronted now with a question of internal organization, inclined to answer it in the negative, but really evading giving an answer, the Labor Organization asked the Council to transmit the question, as an advisory matter, to the Court. The Council complied, thus acting as communicating agent; and the Court, paying more attention, probably, to the form than to the substance, saw no inconvenience whatever in examining and answering a request that, as a matter of fact, did not come from the Council and was not for the Council.

A detailed examination of the Permanent Court's answer shows that the concrete question was one of the strict literal interpretation of Article 389 of the Treaty of Versailles, and the reasoning therefore gave no opportunity for laying down any rules or principles of international law. As a matter of fact, the advisory opinion contains nothing whatever except a standard for interpretation: any interpretation that would result in an absurdity is not admissible. If the contention of the complaining trade union had been sustained, it would have meant that in a country with six labor organizations, one with 110,000 members and the others with 100,000 each, the first one, because it was the largest, could have insisted that the government had to agree with it on the nomination of a delegate, which would have meant that 110,000 workmen could impose their will on 500,000.

257. On the same day, May 12, 1922, the Council asked the Court to give it an advisory opinion on the following question, submitted by a motion of the representative of France on January 13, 1922: "Does the competence of the International Labor Organization extend to the regulation of the working conditions of agricultural laborers"? The question arose out of a request made first by the Swiss government and later by the French government that questions concerning agricultural labor be withdrawn from the agenda of the Third International Labor Conference, with which request the Labor Conference did not comply.

Notice of this second request was sent to the same states as in the first case, and also to the following associations or organizations: The International Labor Bureau, the International Federation of Agricultural Trade Unions, the International League of Agricultural Associations, the International Agricultural Commission, the International Federation of Christian Unions of Handworkers, the International Institute of Agriculture at Rome, the International Federation of Trades Unions, and the International Association for the Legal Protection of Workers. The French, British, Italian, Portuguese and Hungarian governments and the International Labor Bureau, the International Institute of Agriculture at Rome, the International Agricultural Commission, the Inter-

national Federation of Trades Unions, the International
Federation of Handworkers, the International Federation
of Christian Unions of Handworkers, the International
Federation of Agricultural Trades Unions, the Association
of Agriculturists of France and the Central Trade Union
of Agricultural Laborers of France, all took part in the
deliberations, by submitting cases or documents or making
oral statements.

The answer of the Court, based on a minute examination of the entire Part XIII of the Treaty of Versailles of
June 28, 1919, by which the International Labor Organization was established, was in the affirmative. This time,
however, the opinion was not unanimous; the opinion,
given on August 12, 1922, states that two of the eleven
judges reserved their vote, without stating the reasons
for their dissent.

258. In this case also it was not necessary to formulate
any fundamental theories of international law, and here
again there is nothing to mention except rules of construction. One of these, which needs no further comment, consists of the statement that in order to judge the meaning of
a treaty, it must be read as a whole, and not according to
the significance of various terms or phrases taken out of
their context and thus capable of being interpreted in more
than one sense. The other rule, equally obvious, and expressly recognized in the national laws of almost every
country, is that to determine the exact scope of a treaty,
the acts of the contracting nations after it was made have
a controlling force.

Thanks to the allegations of the parties in this case,
the Permanent Court had the opportunity to make a ruling,
from the point of view of international law, on one element
of construction that is very differently treated in different
national legal systems; this is the preparatory work for a
treaty, which Latin jurists rely on, but which Saxon jurists
refuse to take into account. The Court decided that it
was not necessary to consider the evidence on this point;
construing the text of the treaty itself, it came to the

conclusion that agricultural labor did come within the competence of the International Labor Organization. There was nothing in the preparatory work, the Court added, to disturb this conclusion.

259. With this advisory opinion the Court handed down another, on a related question, in answer to a request made on July 18, 1922, by the Council of the League of Nations. This opinion was unanimous. The question here was whether the examination of proposals for the organization and development of methods of agricultural production and of other questions of a similar nature fell within the competence of the International Labor Organization. France brought up this question, too; it arose out of a conflict that was beginning to develop between the functions of the International Institute of Agriculture at Rome and the International Labor Organization. The latter organization did not contest the matter; both before the Council and before the Court it stated, orally and in writing, that it had never thought of intervention of this kind, and that, in its opinion, the organizatic ⌐ and development of methods of agricultural production was outside of its competence.

Notice of the request was sent to the nations in the League of Nations and to the same non-member nations as before, and also to the International Institute of Agriculture at Rome; the Court had the opportunity to learn the opinions of this Institute and of the International Labor Organization, the International Federation of Agricultural Trades Unions and the governments of Esthonia, France, Haiti and Sweden.

The answer, in the negative, was unanimous, with certain reservations as to the other questions of the same nature, mentioned in the request; the answer was based on the analysis of Part XIII of the Treaty of Versailles, in the preceding opinion given on the same day.

260. The most significant thing in this advisory opinion is its definition of the object and the general lines of the

International Labor Organization. Its purpose, the Court says, is the improvement of the conditions of workers, by the regulation of hours of work, labor supply, the prevention of unemployment, an adequate living wage, protection of the worker against sickness, disease and injury arising out of his employment, the protection of children, young persons and women, old age pensions and health insurance, the protection of workers in countries other than their own, the right to organize, vocational and technical education, and, as the Treaty says, "other measures" designed to improve the condition of workers and to reduce the amount of injustice, misery and privation.

The organization and development of methods of continuous production does not come within its field. Perhaps, in some cases, the improvement of the lot of the laborers increases production, or increased production may result from improvement in vocational or technical training. The same thing, or the opposite thing, might result from shorter working hours or from other measures for the benefit of the workers. It does not follow that the International Labor Organization ought to refrain entirely from considering the effect upon production of the measures that may be adopted, but merely that the consideration of methods for the organization and development of production, from the economic point of view, are outside of its sphere of activity.

This gives a composite picture in which the lines or boundaries of the International Labor Organization are clearly drawn.

261. The fourth advisory opinion given by the Court is of an entirely different character. In a resolution adopted in Article 4, 1922, the Council of the League of Nations set forth that a dispute had arisen between France and Great Britain, caused by the nationality decrees promulgated in Tunis and in the French Zone of Morocco on November 8, 1921, and stating that, in agreement with the two governments, it asked the Permanent Court of International Justice to state whether this dispute was or was

not, by international law, solely a matter of domestic jurisdiction coming under Paragraph 8, Article 15, of the
Covenant. The Council added—thus giving to the advisory opinion in this case the special character mentioned
in the preceding chapter—that it had asked the two governments to take the question before the Permanent Court of
International Justice and to arrange a date with the Court
for the examination of the question and the procedure to
be followed. In the same resolution the Council stated that
the two governments had agreed that if the Court decided
the dispute was not a domestic question, they would submit the fundamental question involved in it either to
arbitration or to judicial decision, under conditions to be
fixed.

Notice of the request was sent to all the members of the
League of Nations and to the states mentioned in the
Annex to the Covenant; but only the British and French
governments appeared; cases and counter cases were filed,
and the oral proceedings, including arguments and public
hearings, lasted for five days.

The question arose out of the decrees published in Tunis
and in the French Zone of Morocco by the local authorities
and the French government, which holds a protectorate
over these regions; the decrees declared that all persons
born in this territory of foreign parents one of whom was
born there acquired local or French nationality; in other
words, they applied to this protectorate the present French
doctrine by which the nationality of origin *(jure sanguinis)*
cannot be maintained on foreign soil beyond the second
generation. England protested against these decrees, first
through its diplomatic service and then, not having come
to any agreement with the French government, laid the
matter before the League of Nations.

The Court decided unanimously that the dispute referred to in the Council resolution of October 4, 1922,
was not, by international law, a strictly domestic question
(Article 15, par. 8 of the Covenant) and therefore answered in the negative the question submitted. The two
powers in the litigation accepted the decision immediately

and soon afterward, through diplomatic means, reached a basis for the adjustment of the dispute.

262. The first assertion of a principle which occurs in this advisory opinion is the following, given here literally:

"The question whether a dispute is or is not solely within the domestic jurisdiction of a state is purely a relative question; it depends on the effect of its international relations."

The second principle, not less important, establishing an orientation that may have great influence in the future, is as follows:

"In the present state of international law, the Court is of opinion that questions of nationality, are, in principle, within this reserved domain"—*i.e.,* within the domain reserved for the exclusive competence of each nation. In other words, each nation has the right to decide who are its nationals and whom it will consider as aliens, without paying any attention to the interest, the opinion, or the desire of any other nation.

Although the subject matter is not, in principle, regulated by international law, the Court goes on to say that "it may happen that the right of a state to use its discretion is limited by engagements or obligations it may have contracted toward another or other states." In such a case the dispute that has arisen between the two states takes on an international character, without prejudicing, however, the right of the state to adopt the concrete measure in question.

And while, under Article 15 of the Covenant, any dispute between two of the contracting nations that is likely to lead to a rupture and that is not submitted to arbitration is to be brought before the Council, paragraph 8 of this Article limits the competence of the Council, by establishing the principle that the interest of the League in being able to recommend solutions it considers equitable and appropriate, for the sake of maintaining peace, yields before the equally primary interest of every state to maintain its unqualified independence in those matters that international law confides to its exclusive control. The Court says, however, that this exception cannot be given any extensive application.

This advisory opinion has established two limits as to the international character of a dispute. In accordance with one of them: the mere fact that a nation brings a dispute before the League of Nations is not enough of itself to give it an international character and withdraw it from the application of paragraph 8 of Article 15 of the Covenant. And according to the other: the mere fact that one of the parties invokes engagements of an international nature, to contest the exclusive competence of the other state, does not take the dispute out from under the application of paragraph 8. But when these engagements that are relied on are of a nature to permit the provisional conclusion that they are of juridical importance in connection with the dispute that has been submitted to the Council, and when the question whether a state is or is not competent to take any given action becomes subordinate to the consideration of the validity and the interpretation of these obligations, then the provisions of paragraph 8 of Article 15 cease to apply, and we pass from the exclusive domain of the nation into the field of international law.

The Court thought it necessary to consider the relations arising under a protectorate, and stated several points of doctrine on this subject. It held that the extent of the powers of the protecting state in the territory of the protected state depends partly on the treaties between them by which the protectorate was established, and partly on the conditions under which the protectorate has been recognized by other powers, as against which the provisions of these treaties are invoked. Although protectorates in general have certain characteristics in common under international law, they also possess individual juridical characteristics according to their origin and the degree of their development.

It is not necessary to emphasize the importance and the loftiness of some of these doctrines and declarations. The future will bring them out in bold relief, for subsequent actual cases, and for the scientific orientation of the law of nations.

263. The following request for an advisory opinion— the fifth of this series—was made by the Council on April 21, 1923, in these terms:

> "Do Articles 10 and 11 of the treaty of peace between Finland and Russia, signed at Dorpat on October 14, 1920, and the annexed declaration of the Russian delegation regarding the autonomy of Eastern Carelia, constitute engagements of an international character which place Russia under an obligation to Finland as to the carrying out of the provisions contained therein?"

Notice of the request was sent, in accordance with Article 73 of the Rules, to the members of the League of Nations, which includes Finland, and to the states mentioned in the Annex to the Covenant. Notice was also sent to the Union of Socialist Soviet Republics of Russia. The Soviet government, in a telegram to the President of the Court, refused to take any part in the proceedings before it or before the League of Nations, stating that it considered such proceedings as "without legal value either in substance or in form." The representative of the Finnish government made a statement, and submitted a written case; the Court also received a note from the Polish minister at The Hague and a telegram from the government of Esthonia.

The dispute was in relation to Eastern Carelia, to the measures taken by the Russian government toward its inhabitants, specified in Article 11 of the treaty of Dorpat, and to the promise of autonomy for this region, the latter contained not in the treaty but in a declaration annexed to it. The Court by a vote of 6 to 4, on July 3, 1923, declined to give an advisory opinion, believing that the refusal of the Russian government to lend its assistance made it impossible to complete the investigation of the case, which presupposed the consent and the coöperation of both parties.

264. In commenting on this refusal to give an opinion, and having in mind Article 17 of the Covenant, the Court stated that it is accepting and applying a principle which is the very base of international law: the independence of nations. No nation is under an obligation to submit its disputes with other nations to mediation, arbitration, or any other method of peaceful settlement, without its consent, which may be given once for all, or for one particular case without any previous or general obligation.

Outside of this one point, which, in the realm of principles, is sound, and must be recognized as just, it is possible to dissent from the Court's decision. The Court is the advisory organ of the League of Nations, and it is not easy to understand how it can refuse to give an opinion that is asked for, when it is a question of international law that is involved. It is not enough to say that one of the interested parties believes that its intervention is unjustified. A person who is consulted by an organism or a person that has the right to consult him, cannot fold his arms and sit back because of the will or the desire of some other person who may be affected by the consultation, whether or not he is the opponent of the consultant, and whether or not he has some legal or official connection with the person consulted.

The argument based on the lack of information on matters of fact, due to the defiant attitude of the Union of Socialist Soviet Republics of Russia, has no great weight. The Council of the League of Nations recommended that the information which could be furnished by the various interested countries be taken into consideration, but the request was not made in an obligatory or imperative form; as is usual, it authorized the Secretary-General to submit to the Permanent Court all the documents bearing on the question and to assist it in examining the case. He is the person that should have been called on for all the information on matters of fact that the Court considered useful or indispensable.

It may be that the Council, applying paragraph 8 of Article 11, of the Covenant, and in view of the attitude the Russian government took, wanted to know whether the question was or was not one of those left by international law to the exclusive competence of one of the parties. The answer would have served as the basis of its future action, which ought to have been decided according to its own convictions and not from the fact of the Russian government's assertions. It is not easy to understand what influence the intervention or the refusal of the Russian government could have had, if this had been the case.

265. The Council asked for another advisory opinion, the sixth, by a resolution adopted on February 3, 1923. The following facts were involved:

(a) A certain number of colonists, formerly German subjects, domiciled in territories that had formerly belonged to Germany but now were Polish, had acquired Polish nationality under Article 91 of the Treaty of Versailles. They occupied their lands under contracts *(Rentengutsverträge)*, which had been concluded between them and the German colonization commission before November 11, 1918, but had not been followed by an *Auflassung* [1] before that date. The Polish government, regarding itself as the legitimate owner of these lands by virtue of Article 256 of the Treaty of Versailles, considered that it had the right to declare these contracts annulled. The result was that the Polish authorities took certain measures against these colonists, ending in their being evicted from the lands they occupied.

(b) The authorities of Poland refused to recognize leases *(Pachtverträge)* made before November 11, 1918, between the German government and former German subjects, now Polish citizens. These leases were of lands that had belonged to the German Empire, the ownership of which was transferred to the Polish state by Article 256

[1] An indispensable formality required to perfect rights of ownership.

of the Treaty of Versailles. On these facts, the Court was asked:

(1) Whether the facts mentioned in (a) and (b) above involved international obligations of the kind contemplated by the treaty between the United States of America, the British Empire, France, Italy, Japan and Poland, signed at Versailles on June 28, 1919 (the Polish minorities treaty), and if these situations, as a consequence, came within the competence of the League of Nations, as defined in that Treaty;

(2) If the answer to the first question is in the affirmative, whether the position taken by the Polish government as set forth in (a) and (b) is in conformity with its international obligations.

Notice was sent to the members of the League of Nations, to the states mentioned in the Annex to the Covenant, and to the German government. After oral and written pleadings by the governments the Permanent Court gave a unanimous advisory opinion on September 10, 1923, answering the first question in the affirmative and the second in the negative.

266. The claim was made, during the argument, that the Court ought not to give an advisory opinion in this case, because the Polish minorities treaty provided not merely that the Court might be asked for an advisory opinion in the case of a dispute arising under it, but also that the dispute might be taken to the Court in the form of a litigation. The Court, however, expressly decided against this contention, thus settling one of the difficulties that have arisen in connection with the advisory function. The Court said that if it refused to settle a question brought before it under one of its powers, because it might be brought back to it under its other power, the result would be to make both powers useless.

The Court defined the aim of the treaty—and, it may be added, of the other minorities treaties—as being to close a dangerous source of oppression, conflict, and acts of revenge, and to raise a barrier against racial and religious hatred and to protect rights already acquired when it went into operation, by putting the minorities existing today under the impartial protection of the League of Nations.

Speaking from another point of view, the Court affirmed the general legal principle that private rights, acquired under legislation in force at the time they were acquired, did not become void and were not extinguished by the mere fact of a change in sovereignty. The contrary assertion, the Court said, has no legal foundation, and is against the almost universal opinion and practice.

267. On July 7 of the same year, the Council of the League of Nations adopted another resolution arising out of the following facts:

The Polish government decided to treat certain persons, who were formerly German nationals, as not having acquired Polish nationality and as continuing to possess German nationality, which exposed them in Poland to the treatment laid down for persons of non-Polish nationality, and in particular for those of German nationality.

It was maintained, on the one hand, on the ground that these persons were born in the territory which is now part of Poland, their parents having been habitually residents there at the date of their birth, that in virtue of Article 4, paragraph 1, of the treaty of June 28, 1919 between Poland and the Principal Allied and Associated Powers, they were *ipso facto* Polish nationals, and consequently enjoyed all the rights and guarantees granted by the provisions of this treaty to Polish nationals belonging to racial, religious or linguistic minorities.

The Polish government, on the other hand, considered itself entitled not to recognize these persons as Polish nationals, if their parents were not habitually resident in this territory both at the date of the birth of these persons, and also at the date of the entry into force of the treaty, on January 11, 1920.

The provision out of which the difficulty arose is worded

as follows: "Poland admits and declares to be Polish nationals, *ipso facto* and without the requirement of any formality, persons of German, Austrian, Hungarian or Russian nationality who were born in the said territory of parents habitually resident there, even if at the date of the coming into force of the present treaty they are not themselves habitually resident there."

On these facts, the League of Nations wished to know two things:

(1) Does the question regarding the position of these persons, in so far as they may belong to racial or linguistic minorities, arising out of the application by Poland of Article 4 of the Treaty of June 28, 1919, fall within the competence of the League of Nations under the terms of the treaty?

(2) If so, does Article 4 of this treaty refer solely to the habitual residence of the parents at the date of the birth of the persons concerned, or does it also require the parents to have been habitually resident there at the moment when the treaty went into force?

Notice of this request, as of the preceding one, was sent to the countries mentioned in Article 73 of the Rules, and to the German government. Only Germany and Poland appeared before the Court. Rumania also gave notice that it desired to be heard, and a date for this hearing was set; Rumania did not appear, however, but asked for an extension of time, which the Court did not grant. After the usual procedure had been complied with, the Court decided, on September 15, 1923, that the League of Nations was competent in this situation, and that Article 4 of the treaty referred to the habitual residence of the parents only at the time of the birth of these persons.

268. The first lesson to be drawn from this advisory opinion is the standard it sets up for deciding who belongs to a minority, so far as the collective protection of a minority is concerned,—which developed slowly in Europe, from the time when it was first organized until the end of the war of 1914. Poland maintained that this phrase, as used throughout the treaty, Article 4 of which was of special interest in this connection, could be applied to Polish citizens alone and in no sense to persons of other nationality, whether or not they had the right to be naturalized as Polish citizens, and that, as to these other non-Polish persons, Poland had the right to maintain all the particular rights generally admitted with reference to the persons not subject to the sovereignty of a nation by the fact of membership in it.

The Court, considering the entire situation, both as to the special position of Poland and as to the purpose and nature of these conventions for the protection of minorities, decided that they referred to all the inhabitants included in its population, without regard to the question of membership, provided only they differed from the general whole by their race, their religion, or their language.

Coming back to a specific principle which, as has already been stated, the Court had applied once before, the Court again affirmed that, aside from treaty provisions to the contrary, every sovereign nation has the general right to determine what persons it will regard as its nationals.

The specific point about the date on which the parents must have been habitually resident in Polish territory became the basis for a rule of interpretation,—that the thesis maintained by Poland would be contrary to the precedents of international practice, by which the domicile of the parents at the time when the child, having become of age, chooses his nationality, is not a requisite condition to their child's choice, and even is not relevant; moreover, if this condition were imposed, it would deprive persons whose parents were dead of the right to exercise this option. Moreover—and this is a very important consideration— the advisory opinion adds that the reason for imposing as a condition that the parents must have been habitual residents there at the time of the person's birth was to reduce to a minimum the effect of chance, and to prevent a fortuitous circumstance, such as a mere visit or trip, from having the same legal consequences as the permanent and regular residence of a family, which implies that they are domiciled there. This fixed residence of the parents, as the Court points out, with great wisdom, creates a moral bond between the child and his native land which justifies the award to him of its nationality; it merely completes the material bond already created by the fact of his birth.

269. Soon after having given its opinion on this question, on September 27, 1923, the Council of the League of Nations asked the Court for another opinion, on a question which had become the subject of a dispute between the states involved in it and which had been referred to the Council by the Conference of Ambassadors; this referred to the delimitation of the frontier between Poland and Czechoslovakia, and the question was whether the question was still open, and, if so, to what extent; or whether it must be considered as already settled by a final decision, subject to such modifications of detail as might result from the actual local marking of the boundaries.

Notice of the request was sent in strict compliance with the provisions of Article 73 of the Rules, which have already been explained; only the representatives of the Polish and Czechoslovakian governments appeared. After the written proceedings and hearings, the Court unanimously decided, on December 6, 1923, as follows:

(a) That the delimitation of the frontier between Poland and Czechoslovakia had been settled definitively by the decision of the Conference of Ambassadors on July 28, 1920, and that (b) this decision must be applied in its entirety, and that therefore that portion of the frontier in the region of Spisz topographically described therein remains subject to the modifications provided for in paragraph 3 of Article II of this decision (of the Conference of Ambassadors), apart from the modifications of detail which the customary procedure of marking boundaries locally may entail.

270. This advisory opinion, which was the longest handed down up to that time by the Court, discussed principally matters of fact and their significance as to legal results. It is not surprising, therefore, that the opinion contains very few legal considerations of general interest in international life. The only legal principle to be gathered from it is the statement that the mission of the Conference of Ambassadors had much in common with that of an arbitrator, as it was called upon, on account of the confidence of the nations concerned, to settle a dispute about the frontier between them, and that this mission was subject to the rule that, in the absence of an express agreement between the parties, an arbitrator has no power to interpret his award and still less to modify it by revising it.

271. The next request made to the Court, which had a certain analogy to the last one, was made by a resolution of the Council of the League of Nations adopted on June 17, 1924. It read as follows:

"Have the Principal Allied and Associated Powers, by the decision of the Conference of Ambassadors of December 6th, 1922, exhausted, in regard to the Serbo-Albanian frontier at the Monastery of Saint-Naoum, the mission which was recognized as belonging to them by the Assembly of the League of Nations on October 2, 1921?"

The resolution referred to in the preceding question was as follows:

"The Assembly, having considered the appeal of Albania to the Assembly, dated June 29th, 1921, and the reference by the Council to the Assembly of the allegation by Albania against the Serb-Croat-Slovene State, dated September 2nd, 1921;

"Recognizing the sovereignty and independence of Albania as established by her admission to the League;

"Taking note of the fact that the Serb-Croat-Slovene State and Greece have recognized the Principal Allied and Associated Powers as the appropriate body to settle the frontiers of Albania;

"Understanding that the Principal Allied and Associated Powers are very near agreement on this question submitted to them;

"Recommends Albania now to accept the forthcoming decision of the Principal Allied and Associated Powers."

After the usual notice had been sent to the members of the League of Nations and to the states mentioned in the Annex to the Covenant, the Court heard the two interested nations, Albania and the Serb-Croat-Slovene State, as well as Greece, in both oral and written procedure; the Court then examined the documents in the case, those submitted by the parties with their cases and those furnished at the request of the Court, and also the resolution of the Conference of Ambassadors, adopted on December 6, 1922, which read as follows:

"Resolved, to notify the Delimitation Commission and the Albanian and Serbian governments that the Conference of Ambassadors has decided to award the monastery of Saint-Naoum to Albania."

The advisory opinion was read in open Court on September 4, 1924. The Court held unanimously that the Principal Allied and Associated Powers, and the Conference of Ambassadors, acting in their name, had completely exhausted the mission with regard to the Serbo-Albanian frontier at the monastery of Saint-Naoum which was recognized as belonging to them by the Assembly of the League of Nations on October 2, 1921.

272. This ninth advisory opinion, like the preceding ones, does not contain any fundamental statements of a legal nature. The Court makes here a careful study of the facts, and arrives at the conclusion that when (*i.e.*, before) the Conference of Ambassadors reported its decision on December 6, 1922, the legal situation of the monastery of Saint-Naoum had not been decided, and that it could not be said that the monastery had been awarded, in any way not open to question, to one of the contracting parties.[1] The Court was of opinion, therefore, that the Conference had power to act as it had done, and that this

---

[1] The only provision said: "As far as the monastery of Saint-Naoum."

power was the express result of the agreement between Albania and the Serb-Croat-Slovene State. The opinion emphasizes this point, which is of particular interest.

Another point of a different nature in the opinion arises out of the contention made during the argument that the Conference's decision was subject to revision or annulment because of new evidence not known when the decision was made; the Court held that the existence of such new information had not been established.

And the Court was very careful not to go into the merits of the case, since they had not been submitted for its consideration. The question whether the monastery ought to be Albanian or Serbian was not before the Court, but only the question whether the decision that awarded it to Albania was definitive in its nature.

273. The tenth advisory opinion was requested by the Council of the League of Nations on December 13, 1925, in the following terms:

"The Council of the League of Nations, having been asked by the Mixed Commission for the Exchange of Greek and Turkish Populations to obtain from the Permanent Court of International Justice an advisory opinion on the dispute regarding the interpretation of Article 2 of the Convention on the Exchange of Greek and Turkish Populations, signed at Lausanne on January 30th, 1923, has decided to ask the Permanent Court of International Justice to give an advisory opinion on the following question:

"What meaning and scope should be attributed to the word 'established' in Article 2 of the Convention of Lausanne of January 30th, 1923, regarding the exchange of Greek and Turkish populations, in regard to which discussions have arisen and arguments have been put forward which are contained in the documents communicated by the Mixed Commission? And what conditions must the persons who are described in Article 2 of the Convention of Lausanne under the name of 'Greek inhabitants of Constantinople' fulfil in order that they may be considered as 'established' under the terms of the Convention and exempt from compulsory exchange?"

The Greek and Turkish governments, at the invitation of the Court, each submitted within the time fixed a memorandum on the question of the interpretation of Article 2 of the Convention regarding the exchange of Greek and Turkish populations signed at Lausanne on January 30th, 1923; and the Court heard, in the course of public sittings held on January 16th, 1925, oral statements upon the question made, on behalf of the government of the Greek Republic by H. E. M. Politis, Greek Minister at Paris, and, on behalf of the government of Turkey, by Dr. Tevfik Rouchdy Bey, President of the Turkish Delegation to the Mixed Commission at Constantinople.

The Court was of opinion:

"1. That the purpose of the word 'established' in Article 2 of the Convention of Lausanne of January 30th, 1923, regarding the exchange of Greek and Turkish populations, is to indicate the conditions in point of time and place on which depends the liability to exchange of Greeks and Moslems who respectively inhabit Constantinople or Western Thrace; that this word refers to a situation of fact constituted, in the case of the persons in question, by residence of a lasting nature;

2. That, in order that the persons referred to in Article 2 of the Convention of Lausanne as 'Greek inhabitants of Constantinople' may be considered as 'established' under the terms of the Convention and exempted from the compulsory exchange, they must reside within the boundaries of the Prefecture of the City of Constantinople as defined by the law of 1912; have arrived there, no matter whence they came, at some date previous to October 30th, 1918; and have had prior to that date intention of residing there for an extended period."

274. The most significant of the legal considerations appearing in this advisory opinion are stated below.

In the first place, the Court is satisfied that the difference of opinion which has arisen regarding the meaning and scope of the word "established," is a dispute regarding the interpretation of a treaty and as such involves a question of international law.   It is not a question of domestic concern between the administration and the inhabitants; the difference affects two States which have concluded a convention with a view to exchanging certain portions of their populations, and the criterion afforded by the word "established" used in Article 2 of this convention is especially intended to enable the contracting states to distinguish the part of their respective populations liable to exchange from the part exempt from it.

The choice of this word "established" serves to emphasize that, in order that a person may be considered as an inhabitant, his residence must be of a lasting nature and must have been so at the time in question.   Persons who at that time were only residing at Constantinople as mere visitors cannot therefore be regarded as exempt from exchange.

The degree of stability required is incapable of exact definition. The Court, however, considers that inhabitants who before October 30th, 1918, fulfilled the conditions enumerated as examples under heading (2) of the resolution adopted on October 1st, 1924, by the Legal Section of the Mixed Commission, are to be regarded as established within the meaning of the article and as consequently exempt from exchange, even if they have come to Constantinople with the intention of making their fortune and subsequently returning to their place of origin.

Heading 2 of the above mentioned resolution reads as follows:

"Any person possessing in these areas a fixed residence, with the intention of remaining there permanently. This intention may be inferred from a number of circumstances, such as, for instance, the permanent exercise of a profession, commerce or industry or the acquisition of a practice in conformity with the laws; further the fact of having concluded a contract for work of considerable duration, or of having entered upon a profession the nature of which would, in a general way, imply a residence of some length in the district, or any other fact tending to prove that the centre of such person's occupation and interests is situated in the area in question."

275.   The last advisory opinion given by the Court is the eleventh; it was requested by the Council of the League of Nations, who adopted on March 13, 1925, the following resolution:

"The Council of the League of Nations has received, in accordance with the terms of Article 39 of the Treaty of Paris between Poland and the Free City of Danzig, signed November 9th, 1920, an appeal by Poland against a decision given under the said article by the High Commissioner of the League of Nations on February 2nd, 1925.

"The said decision, the terms of which are communicated to the Court, deals with the following dispute between Poland and the Free City of Danzig.

"Under the terms of Article 104, paragraph 4, of the Treaty of Versailles, signed June 28th, 1919, Articles 29 to 32 (inclusive) of the Treaty of Paris between Poland and the Free City of Danzig, signed November 9th, 1920, and Articles 149 to 168 (inclusive) and Article 240 of the Agreement of Warsaw between Poland and the Free City of Danzig, signed October 24th, 1921, Poland is entitled 'to establish in the Port of Danzig a post, telegraph and telephone service communicating directly with Poland' (Article 29 of the Treaty of Paris).

"For the purpose of the above service Poland possesses postal premises in the Heveliusplatz at Danzig.

"On January 5th, 1925, in exercise of rights which she claims to derive from the above-mentioned international agreements, Poland set up letter-boxes at various points outside the Heveliusplatz premises. These boxes were intended to receive postal matter to be sent to Poland via the Polish postal service. The matter thus posted was to be collected and brought to the Heveliusplatz premises by postmen belonging to that service. Poland also claimed to be entitled to deliver outside the Heveliusplatz premises postal matter brought from Poland by the Polish postal service. The Free City of Danzig thereupon asked the High Commissioner to give a decision, in virtue of Article 39 of the Treaty of Paris, to the effect that the rights thus claimed by Poland were excluded by a decision or decisions given by the High Commissioner's predecessor in office, General Haking, which the Free City considered to preclude the Polish service from collecting or delivering postal matter outside the Heveliusplatz premises and to confine the use of the service to Polish authorities and officials and exclude its use by the public.

"The present High Commissioner's decision of February 2nd, 1925, declares (paragraph 6) that the dispute, 'stripped of all its technicalities, is whether the working area of the Polish postal service extends beyond the buildings allotted to that service.'

"The High Commissioner has examined this question in the light of certain decisions, or pronouncements, of his predecessor, General Haking.

"The High Commissioner considers that the questions now at issue between Poland and the Free City of Danzig are decided finally by a decision given by General Haking on May 25th, 1922, which in his opinion should be regarded as having been authoritatively interpreted and shown to be applicable by a decision given by General Haking on December 23rd, 1922, and a letter addressed by General Haking on January 6th, 1923, to the Commissioner-General of the Polish Republic at Danzig. He has accordingly (paragraph 18 of the decision of February 2nd, 1925) re-affirmed, in language intended to make explicit its application to the present dispute, the decision which he considers General Haking to have given.

"The Council has the honour to request the Permanent Court of International Justice, in conformity with Article 14 of the Covenant, to give an advisory opinion upon the following question:

"(1) Is there in force a decision of General Haking which decides in the manner stated in paragraph 18 of the present High Commissioner's decision of

February 2nd, 1925, or otherwise the points at issue regarding the Polish postal service, and, if so, does such decision prevent reconsideration by the High Commissioner or the Council of all or any of the points in question?

"(2) If the questions set out at *(a)* and *(b)* below have not been finally decided by General Haking:

"*(a)* Is the Polish postal service at the Port of Danzig restricted to operations which can be performed entirely within its premises in the Heveliusplatz, or is it entitled to set up letter-boxes and collect and deliver postal matter outside those premises?

"*(b)* Is the use of the said service confined to Polish authorities and officials, or can it be used by the public?"

The Court dealt with this question, at the request of the Council, in an extraordinary session, held from April 14 to May 16, 1925. The usual notice was given to the states in the League of Nations and to the states mentioned in the Annex to the Covenant, and also to the Senate of the Free City of Danzig. Each of the two governments directly concerned was allowed to submit written documents, by specified dates. No public hearing was held, as no government requested it.

The Court gave its opinion on May 25, 1925. It held that there was no decision in force covering the points at issue, as none of the High Commissioner's decisions dealt directly with the questions now raised in connection with the Polish mail service. It also held that there were no applicable restrictive provisions in the convention and agreement in force between the two governments. The opinion ends:

"In short, the Polish postal service may operate outside the premises at the Heveliusplatz, and its use is not confined to Polish authorities; but it should be observed that its operations are confined to the port of Danzig. This port is a territorial entity, the limits of which, however, as to the sphere of operation of the Polish postal service, have not been defined. The Court observes that it has not been asked to define and delimit the port of Danzig, but that, in its opinion, the practical application of the answers given by it to the Council depends on the question of the limits of the port of Danzig within the meaning of the treaty stipulations."

276. In this advisory opinion the Court has stated that the reasons contained in a decision, at least in so far as they go beyond the scope of the operative part, have no binding force as between the parties concerned. It is perfectly true that all the parts of a judgment concerning the points in dispute explain and complete each other and are to be taken into account in order to determine the precise meaning and scope of the operative portion. This is clearly stated in the award of the Permanent Court of Arbitration of October 14, 1902, concerning the Pious Funds of the Californias, which was repeatedly invoked by Danzig. The Court agreed with this statement, and added that it by no means followed that every reason given in a decision constitutes a decision itself.

277. The first litigated matter to come before the Court, for adjudication according to the ordinary procedure, was a very important case. It was a case coming up under the compulsory jurisdiction of the Court, on the application of the governments of Great Britain, France, Italy and Japan, against the German Empire, based on Article 380 of the Treaty of Versailles of June 28, 1919, according to the terms of which the Kiel Canal and its approaches are to be maintained free and open to the vessels of commerce and of war of all nations at peace with Germany on terms of entire equality.

The litigation arose out of the following facts: it was alleged that on March 21, 1921, in the morning, the British steamship *Wimbledon,* chartered by a French company, on its way to Danzig, with a cargo of 4,000 tons (of munitions of war), was refused passage through the Kiel Canal by the German authorities. The French ambassador at

Berlin protested against this action on March 23, and the German government repeated the refusal, alleging that the cargo of the *Wimbledon* consisted of munitions of war going to Poland; that the treaty of peace between Poland and Russia had not yet been ratified, and that there was therefore a state of war between those two countries; and that the German neutrality orders forbade the passage across German territory of war materials destined to either belligerent.

Consequently, in the demand, the first case, and the reply, the Court was asked to decree that the German government had wrongfully refused access to the Kiel Canal to the *Wimbledon* on March 21, 1921; that it was under obligation to make good the damages sustained by the ship and its charterers; that these damages should be set at 174,082 francs and 68 centimes, and that interest should be added, at 6% from March 21, 1921, unless the Court thought it more equitable to estimate in pounds sterling the part of the damages due to the period of idleness and the change of route; that the German government was to pay over that sum within one month from the decision to the French government; and that in case of default in the payment within the one month, interest should be payable at 10% from that time on.

The government of Poland took advantage of the right to intervene under the Statute because it was one of the contracting parties to the treaty; and the Court granted this application in a special resolution of June 28, 1923.

Germany, on its part, in its counter case and rejoinder, opposed the demand made by the other parties, and in its turn demanded that the Court decree that no indemnity was due, and further declare (a) that Article 380 of the Treaty of Versailles was not an obstacle to the application by Germany to the Kiel Canal, during the Russian-Polish war of 1920-1921, of a neutrality order admissible in itself, as was that of July 25, 1920, and (b) that the application of this order was not made impossible by the fact that preliminary negotiations for peace between Russia and Poland had been begun on November 2, 1920, but only on the coming into effect of the final treaty of peace on April 30, 1921.

After the written procedure, the representatives of the six interested governments were heard in public hearings. A German national judge, M. Walter Schücking, sat with the Court, in accordance with the Statute. The Court gave its decision on August 17, 1923, by a vote of 9 to 3. The opinion declared:

1. That the German authorities were wrong in refusing access to the Kiel Canal to the S. S. *Wimbledon* on March 21, 1921;

2. That Article 380 of the treaty signed at Versailles on June 28, 1919 between the Allied and Associated Powers and Germany prevented Germany from applying to the Kiel Canal the neutrality order promulgated by her on July 25, 1920;

3. That the German government is bound to make good the prejudice sustained by the vessel and her charterers/ as the result of this action;

4. That the prejudice sustained may be estimated at the sum of 140,749 francs 35 centimes, together with interest at 6% from the date of the present judgment;

5. That the German government shall therefore pay to the government of the French Republic, at Paris, in French francs, the sum of 140,749 francs 35 centimes with interest at 6% from the date of this judgment; payment to be effected within three months from this day; and

6. That each party shall pay its own costs.

278. In this *Wimbledon* decision there is more than one important statement, either about the Kiel Canal itself, or about the general doctrines concerning it, which it is important to bring together and emphasize.

In the first group, relating to the Canal, is a statement giving its actual legal definition. According to the judgment, since the Treaty of Versailles the Kiel Canal has ceased to be an internal and national navigable waterway, the use of which by the vessels of other than the riparian state is left entirely to the discretion of that state;

it has become an international waterway, intended to provide, under the treaty guarantee, easier access to the Baltic
for all nations of the world.

The Court affirms that the precedents of the Suez and
Panama Canals are merely illustrations of the general
opinion according to which, when an international waterway connecting two open seas has been permanently dedicated to the use of the whole world, such waterway is as-
similated to natural straits in the sense that even the passage of a belligerent man-of-war does not compromise the
neutrality of the sovereign state under whose jurisdiction
the waters in question lie. And even admitting that the
Article invoked by the complainants implied a limitation
of sovereignty and therefore ought to be construed re-
strictively, the examples of the Suez and Panama Canals,
though different in their international régime, proved to
the Court that the passage through the Kiel Canal did not
affect the duties of a neutral in this part of its jurisdiction.

Affirming once more the authority of treaties, and the
necessity that they be observed at any cost, the judgment
adds that Germany, by virtue of Article 380 of the Treaty
of Versailles, was under a formal duty to allow this ship
to pass, and could not set up its neutrality regulations as
against the engagements it had made. Germany was free
to declare and regulate her neutrality in the Russo-Polish
war, but subject to the condition that she respected and
maintained intact the contractual obligations she had entered into at Versailles on June 28, 1919.

279. Another complaint, also under the ordinary procedure, was submitted to the Permanent Court on May 13,
1924. This time Greece made the demand, against Great
Britain. M. M. A. Caloyanni sat on this occasion as a
national judge for Greece. The dispute arose over different
concessions made before and during the war of 1914 by
the Ottoman authorities in Palestine to a Greek subject,
M. Mavrommatis, which had never been recognized and
accepted by the British officials or by the British government. The applicant, therefore, basing its application on

Article 26 of the British mandate for Palestine, asked the Court to decide:

(a) As to the Jerusalem concessions:

1. That since work on them had been begun, the British government, as mandatory for Palestine, was under obligation to recognize them under condition that they be readapted to the new economic conditions of the country, or else to cancel them on payment of an equitable compensation;

2. That having as a matter of fact already made its choice by making it directly or indirectly impossible for the claimant to complete the work begun, it ought to pay him compensation;

3. That taking into consideration all the elements of the damages caused to the claimant, he should be allowed just and equitable compensation by awarding him the sum of £121,045, plus interest at 6% from July 20, 1923, until the date of the judgment;

(b) As to the Jaffa concessions:

1. That the fact that they were awarded after October 29, 1914, does not justify the British government in refusing to recognize them;

2. That the fact that they were not confirmed by an imperial *iradé,* a mere formality not constituting a decisive act, does not deprive them of their international value;

3. That if the British government, in its quality of mandatory power for Palestine, is free not to maintain them, it is none the less under an international obligation to compensate their beneficiary for the damages it has caused to him by refusing, as it has done, to allow him to carry them out;

4. That taking into consideration all the elements of the damages suffered by the complainant, he should be allowed just and reasonable compensation, by awarding him the sum of £113,294, plus interest at 6% from July 20, 1923 to the date of the judgment.

The representative of the British government raised a

preliminary question on the ground that the Court had no jurisdiction in the matter, because the case was not one under the mandate for Palestine of July 24, 1922, which went into effect September 29, 1923, and in accordance with Article 26 of which any dispute whatever that should arise between it and any other member of the League of Nations relating to the interpretation or application of its provisions that could not be settled by negotiation, was to be submitted to the Permanent Court of International Justice.

This exception was contested by the demandant, which entered formal opposition; after public hearings at which the two contesting parties stated their case, the Court decided, by a vote of 6 to 5, that it had no jurisdiction as to the Jaffa concessions, but did have jurisdiction over the part of the litigation based on the concessions in Jerusalem.

280. A careful examination of this decision discloses the following as its principal affirmations, so far as public international law, rather than the specific case in point, is concerned. It expressly defines the term dispute (*différend*), used often in international treaties, as consisting of a disagreement on a point of law or fact, or a conflict of legal views or of interests between two persons.

Referring to the problem arising from differences in two versions of a treaty in different languages, both authoritative, one of which appears to have a wider bearing than the other, the Court was of opinion that it was bound to adopt the more limited interpretation which can be made to harmonize with both versions and which, so far as it goes, is doubtless in accordance with the common intention of both parties.

The Court maintained, finally, that jurisdiction based on an international agreement embraces all disputes referred to it after its establishment, and that for the contrary to be true an express limitation is essential. Those who are drafting treaties, conventions and declarations hereafter that recognize or accept the jurisdiction of the Permanent Court will do well to remember this attitude.

The minority of the Court, composed of five judges who voted differently, handed down dissenting opinions maintaining that the Court was absolutely without jurisdiction in this case. In spite of their extraordinary interest, the details of the principles on which these dissenting opinions are based will not be given here.

281. The Court gave its second judgment in this case, the one on its merits, on March 26, 1925, in the following form:

"I. That the concessions granted to M. Mavrommatis under the agreements signed on January 27, 1914, between him and the City of Jerusalem regarding certain works to be carried out at Jerusalem, are valid;

"That the existence for a certain space of time of a right on the part of M. Rutenberg to require the annulment of the aforesaid concessions of M. Mavrommatis was not in conformity with the international obligations accepted by the mandatory for Palestine;

"That no loss resulting to M. Mavrommatis from this circumstance has been proved;

"That therefore the Greek government's claim for an indemnity must be dismissed;

"II. That Article 4 of the Protocol signed at Lausanne on July 23rd, 1923, concerning certain concessions granted in the Ottoman Empire, is applicable to the above mentioned concessions granted to M. Mavrommatis."

This decision consists of arguments based on the facts of the case, and contains no general principles of international law that call for special comment.

282. Another contentious proceeding, this time using the summary procedure, reached the Permanent Court on June 2, 1924. It arose out of a special agreement signed at Sofia on May 18, 1923, and ratified by the Greek and Bulgarian government on March 29, 1924. By its first Article, the contracting parties agreed to submit to the Permanent Court of International Justice, in accordance with the provisions of Rrticle 29 of the Statute and Articles 67 and 70 of the Rules (which contain the provisions for summary procedure) the dispute which had arisen between them as to the jurisdiction of the arbitrator appointed by M. Gustav Ador, by virtue of paragraph 4 of the annex to Section IV of Part XI of the treaty of peace signed at Neuilly on November 27, 1919.

Article 2 of the special agreement says that the Court shall determine the precise meaning of the last phrase of the first sub-paragraph of this paragraph 4, by answering two questions in particular:

1.   Does the text quoted above authorize claims for acts committed even outside Bulgarian territory as constituted before October 11, 1915, in particular in districts occupied by Bulgaria after her entry into the war?

2.   Does the text quoted above authorize claims for damages incurred by claimants not only as regards their property rights and interests, but also as regards their person, arising out of ill treatment, deportation, internment, or other similar acts?

The Court decided that the last sentence of the first sub-paragraph 4 of the annex to Section IV of Part IX of the Treaty of Neuilly should be interpreted as authorizing claims in respect to acts committed even outside Bulgarian territory as constituted before October 11, 1915, and in respect of damage incurred by claimants not only as regards their property rights and interests, but also as regards their person.

283. By a letter dated November 27, 1924, the agent representing the Greek government requested the Court, in accordance with Article 60 of the Statute, to furnish him with an authoritative and, as far as possible, detailed interpretation of the judgment of September 12, 1924, more especially in regard to the question whether, under that judgment, the claims in question may only be paid from the proceeds of the sale of Bulgarian property situated in Greek territory.

By another letter dated December 30, 1924, the Greek agent informed the Court that the interpretation desired by his government related to the exact scope of the second paragraph of the operative part of the judgment of September 12, 1924, and that in particular it was desired that the meaning of that portion of the judgment should be defined with regard to three aspects of the question, namely:

(a) "The possible existence, according to the terms of the judgment, of Bulgarian property in Greece which might be used to realize sums awarded by the arbitrator;

(b) The possibility, under the terms of the judgment, of liquidating Bulgarian landed property in Greece with a view to realizing such sums;

(c) The right of Greece, under the terms of the judgment, to apply to the Reparation Commission with a view to obtaining a redistribution between the Allied Powers of the total capital sum at which the obligation to make reparation imposed upon Bulgaria was fixed."

On March 26, 1925, the Court declared:

"That the request of the Greek government for an authoritative interpretation of the judgment of September 12, 1924, in accordance with Article 60 of the Statute, cannot be granted."

There is nothing in these two decisions of the chamber of summary procedure that calls for special comment.

284. The government of the German Reich, by an application instituting proceedings filed with the Registry of the Court on May 15, 1925, in conformity with Article 40 of the Statute and Article 35 of the Rules of Court, submitted to the Permanent Court of International Justice a suit concerning certain German interests in Polish Upper Silesia. These interests involved in the first place the taking over by a delegate of the Polish government of control of the working of the nitrate factory at Chorzow, the taking possession by him of the movable property and patents, licenses, etc., of the company which had previously worked the factory, and the removal from the land registers of the name of this company as owner of certain landed property at Chorzow and the entry of the Polish Treasury in its place. In the second place, these interests involved the notice given by the government of the Polish Republic to the owners of certain large agricultural estates of its intention to expropriate these properties.

It is submitted in the application:

1. (a) that Article 2 of the Polish law of July 14, 1920, constitutes a measure of liquidation as concerns property, rights and interests acquired after November 11, 1918, and that Article 5 of the same law constitutes a liquidation of the contractual rights of the persons concerned;

   (b) that, should the decision in regard to point (a) be in the affirmative, the Polish government in carrying out these liquidations has not acted in conformity with the provisions of Articles 92 and 297 of the Treaty of Versailles;

2. (a) that the attitude of the Polish government in regard to the *Oberschlesische Stickstoffwerke* and *Bayrische Stickstoffwerke* Companies was not in conformity with Article 6 and the following articles of the Geneva Convention;

   (b) should the decision in regard to point (a) be in the affirmative, the Court is requested to state what attitude should have been adopted by the Polish government in regard to the Companies in question in order to conform with the above-mentioned provisions;

3. that the liquidation of the rural estates belonging to Count Nikolaus Ballestrem; to the *Georg Giesches Erben Company;* to Christian Kraft, Fürst zu Hohenlohe-Oehringen; to the *Vereinigte Königs- und Laurahütte* Company; to the Baroness Maria Anna von Goldschmidt-Rothschild (née von Friedländer-Fuld); to Karl Maximilian, Fürst von Lichnowsky; to the City of Ratibor; to Frau Gabriele von Ruffer (née Gräfin Henckel von Donnersmarck); to the *Godulla* Company and to Frau Hedwig Voigt, would not be in conformity with the provisions of Article 6 and the following articles of the Geneva Convention.

In the course of the oral proceedings in Court, the German representative stated that he withdrew submission No. 3, in so far as it concerned the agricultural estate belonging to Madame Hedwig Voigt; this statement was duly recorded.

The application instituting proceedings was, in accordance with Article 40 of the Statute, communicated to the Polish government on May 16, 1925. That government informed the Court on June 12 and 18 that it felt obliged in this suit to make "certain preliminary objections of procedure, and, in particular, an objection to the Court's jurisdiction to entertain the suit"; these objections it intended to set out in a case which would be filed before the end of the month of June, that is to say in sufficient time "to enable the Court to commence the oral proceedings in regard to these objections of procedure on July 15."

The representative of the German government, on being informed of the Polish government's communication, also made a statement to the effect that the German reply to the Polish case on the question of jurisdiction would be filed in sufficient time, whereupon July 10 was fixed as the date for the filing of the German counter case in reply to the Polish government's case setting out the preliminary objections which that government intended to make.

The Polish case, which was headed *"Réponse exceptionnelle* to the application of the German government dated May 15, 1925," was filed with the registry and communicated to the representative of the German government on June 26. It was submitted in this document that:

>(a) in regard to suit No. 1 (the factory at Chorzow) the Court should declare that it had no jurisdiction or, in the alternative, that the application could not be entertained until the German-Polish Mixed Arbitral Tribunal had given judgment;

>(b) in regard to the suits grouped under No. II (the large agricultural properties), the Court should declare that it had no jurisdiction, or, in the alternative, that the application could not be entertained.

The Court,

I. (1) In *affaire I* referred to in the plea filed by the government of the Polish Republic:

dismissed this plea;

declared the Application to be admissible;

and reserved it for judgment on the merits.

(2) In *affaire II* referred to in the plea filed by the government of the Polish Republic:

dismissed this plea;

declared the application to be admissible;

and reserved it for judgment on the merits.

285. This decision, which was handed down on August 25 of this year, 1925, passes with great clarity on one question that had been discussed at length before it, on the relation between the fundamental issue involved and the competence of the Court, so far as its power of dealing with preliminary questions is concerned:

The Court said:

"A declaration by the Court that it has jurisdiction to deal with *Affaire I* mentioned in the first submission of the Polish objection must in no way prejudice the question of the extent to which the Court may see fit to deal with the questions contemplated by submission No. I of the German application in proceedings on the merits.

"The Court, therefore, for the purposes of the decision for which it is now asked, considers that it must proceed to the inquiry above referred to, even if this inquiry involves touching upon subjects belonging to the merits of the case; it is, however, to be clearly understood that nothing which the Court says in this present judgment can be regarded as restricting its entire freedom to estimate the value of any argument advanced by either side on the same subjects during the proceedings on the merits."

The Court also had occasion in this case to refer to the question of what is meant by a dispute between nations, and of how or when it may be determined that a dispute has arisen. The Court said:

"A difference of opinion does exist as soon as one of the

governments concerned points out that the attitude adopted by the other conflicts with its own views. Even if, under Article 23, the existence of a definite dispute were necessary, this condition could at any time be fulfilled by means of unilateral action on the part of the applicant party. And the Court cannot allow itself to be hampered by a mere defect of form, the removal of which depends solely on the party concerned."

286. This litigation, and various legal questions that have arisen in connection with the Mosul question between Great Britain and Turkey, are now pending before the Permanent Court. Other cases will follow; each day the Court's jurisprudence will become more comprehensive and its assistance will become more useful and be more desired. Until now it has apparently gone on from one successful issue to another; that the principal nations of the world, after watching it at work, continue to have confidence in it is shown by the recent London agreements between Germany, Belgium, France and Great Britain. Let us hope that its future action will justify these past triumphs, and will lend stability and security to its high mission of peace and justice.

CHAPTER XVI

CONCLUSION

287. The United States of North America has not ratified the Treaty of Versailles, and does not belong to the League of Nations. First in the latter part of Mr. Wilson's term, in the Senate and then in the presidential election campaign, won by the Republican party, and later through the discussions in newspapers and in conferences and meetings of political and professional societies, the belief became more general and more decided that any connection with the League would be completely against the traditional policies of this great North American power, and dangerous to its present and future needs in relation to European interests and disputes.

And because the Statute of the Permanent Court came through the Council and Assembly of the League of Nations, as they were charged by Article 14 of the Covenant with establishing it, the United States took no part whatever in the final discussions on the Statute, and did not ratify the protocol putting it into effect, although two eminent jurisconsults of the United States served in an unofficial capacity on the Advisory Committee that drafted this Statute.

There were, nevertheless—and there still are—a great many supporters and enthusiastic advocates of international justice in the United States; the World Court has their support and sympathy, and public opinion as a whole is in favor of it. A great many persons have shown extraordinary devotion in trying to make the advantages of the Court understood and in formulating conditions on which their country might participate in this work of peace and justice. James Brown Scott and Manley O. Hudson deserve special mention for their courage and persistence, in public and in private, toward this end.

This movement has become strong enough to reach official circles and to stir them to favorable action. The Court had hardly been opened when Mr. Hughes, then Secretary of State, came out openly in firm support of it, though suggesting that certain changes must be made in its election system and its operation. On February 24, 1923, President Harding sent a message to the Senate, officially calling its attention to the question of adherence to the Court, sending with the message a letter from Mr. Hughes proposing four conditions for the adherence of the United States to the Protocol.

These four conditions were as follows:

"1. That any such adhesion shall not be taken to involve any legal relation on the part of the United States to the League of Nations or the assumption of any obligation by the United States under the Covenant of the League of Nations constituting Part I of the Treaty of Versailles.

"2. That the United States shall be permitted to participate through representatives designated for that purpose, and upon an equality with the other states, members respectively of the Council and Assembly of the League of Nations, in any and all proceedings of either the Council or the Assembly for the election of Judges or Deputy Judges of the Permanent Court of International Justice, or for the filling of vacancies.

"3. That the United States will pay a fair share of the expenses of the Court as determined and appropriated from time to time by Congress of the United States.

"4. That the Statute for the Permanent Court of International Justice adjoined to the Protocol shall not be amended without the consent of the United States."

288. President Harding continued to fight against these pretended difficulties, some of a political nature and some technical, emphasizing in his semi-official speeches the conditions or changes that seemed indispensable to him for making the Court, in theory and in practice, in shape and substance, beyond the shadow of a doubt, an absolutely world-wide Court and not an organ of the League of Nations, and for ensuring that the United States would find itself on a perfectly equal footing with the other nations.

This last point did not merely involve participating in the work of the two electoral bodies, now named the Council and the Assembly; it included objection to the separate votes of the British Colonies and Dominions, because this, it was felt, gave five or six votes to Great Britain, which gave her an unjust preponderating influence.

In order to alter this condition, and to remove this aspect of this difficulty, President Harding suggested at St. Louis that in the future the Court itself should choose its new members by filling any vacancies itself; he further suggested that the financial administration of the Court be entrusted to the Bureau of the Permanent Court of Arbitration at The Hague, and that the right given to the League of Nations to request advisory opinions be suppressed, or else extended to all the adhering states, if that seemed preferable. It is not necessary to discuss these proposals here; most of them have been considered in other parts of this book.

289. Several Senators who took part in these decisions also formulated conditions and reservations. Senator Borah, for example, maintained that the codification of the law of nations should precede the creation of a court, that there must be a North American judge, and that the court must have compulsory jurisdiction. Senator Pepper limited his proposal [1] to the amendment of the Statute so that all the states mentioned in the Annex to the Covenant, whether members of the League or not, should be in the electoral body.

A joint resolution was introduced in the Senate by Senator Lodge on May 5, 1924, on this subject; it provided that the President should call a third Hague Conference and submit to it a plan incorporated in the resolution which, in addition to taking the election of the judges entirely out of the hands of the Council and Assembly, although the

[1] This refers to Senator Pepper's first proposal.

same procedure was kept, and making various changes in detail throughout the Statute, expressly took away from the Colonies and Dominions the right to take part in the elections, and then proposed a series of additional reservations, in its last three articles, which are reproduced below:

Article 65. The Court shall not have jurisdiction to give advisory opinions in questions relating to the admission of aliens into the United States or into educational institutions of the several states, or to the territorial integrity of the different states of the Union, or their public debts or financial obligations, or in any matter that concerns or involves the maintenance of the traditional policy of the United States with regard to American affairs, commonly called the Monroe Doctrine, or any other purely political principles of government, or on any matter which the United States considers to be a domestic question.

Article 66. The Court shall be subject to the rule recognized by international law that the authority of the United States applies within its own territory to aliens and to their property, in time of peace and in time of war.

Article 67. Before a case to which the United States is a party can be submitted to the Court, a special treaty must be made by the President of the United States, by and with the advice and consent of the Senate, between the United States and the other interested powers, defining clearly the subject matter of the dispute, the subject to be decided by the Court, and the times for the different stages of the procedure.

290. After December 6, 1923, President Coolidge, who then succeeded President Harding, urged the Senate to consider the subject favorably; on more than one occasion since then, official and unofficial, he has maintained this position. In May, 1924, the Senate Committee on Foreign Affairs, after numerous public hearings and long discussions, reported favorably, by a vote of 10 to 6, a resolution introduced by Senator Pepper, containing a new proposal made by him. It wiped out all connection as to the elections between the Court and the League of Nations, took away the vote from the Colonies and Dominions, excluded all questions relating to immigration from the jurisdiction of the Court, and proposed that the Monroe Doctrine be safeguarded by an international treaty. The Committee report also provided that the Court must be supported by all the nations of the world and that it should have a world code, prepared by the nations, which it was to interpret and apply.

After the Court had thus become a party question, it is only natural that the national conventions of the Republican and Democratic parties both advocated adherence to the Court in their party platforms, the Republican party advocating it on the Coolidge terms. All this agitation must result sooner or later, with amendments in the form or the substance of the Statute which, perhaps, the League of Nations would come forward to introduce, in the final adherence of the United States to this new institution which for so many reasons merits its enthusiastic support.

291. New evidence of the popularity and success of the Permanent Court may be gathered from the fact that the five Central American Republics, Guatemala, Salvador, Honduras, Nicaragua and Costa Rica, signed a treaty at Washington on February 7, 1923, with two annexes and two additional protocols setting up a Central American Court of Justice; the memory of their former Court, described in Chapter V of this book, and other powerful motives were, of course, among the reasons for their action.

In the first Article, the contracting parties agree to submit to the International Court established by this treaty any disputes now in existence between them, or any that may hereafter arise, of whatever nature or origin, if they have not been able to adjust them by diplomatic means nor to agree on some other form of arbitration, and if they have not agreed to submit such questions or controversies to some other Court. This last phrase implies an allusion, as evident as it is justified, to the permanent international organization that has been studied in this present book.

This Article adds that questions or litigations affecting the sovereign and independent existence of one of the contracting powers cannot be the subject of an arbitration or suit before this Court.

The parties agree that the judgments of their International Court, on points submitted to its jurisdiction, shall be final, irrevocable, without appeal and binding on all the parties to the suit, provided they are handed down within the time set in the protocol or in the rules of procedure applicable to the case, and provided they contain a detailed statement of the grounds in virtue of which the given judgment may become null or may give grounds for appeal.

The members of the Court, Article 2 says, are to be chosen from a list formed as follows: each of the contracting parties is to designate six persons, four of whom shall be its own nationals, chosen by the President of the Republic and approved by its national Congress or by the Senate, if that is its procedure, and two others, also chosen by the President, from two lists: one of fifteen names, made by the President of the United States, and another of five names, made by the government of whichever Latin-American Republic, outside of Central America, each of the contracting parties shall chose.

The four national members of the permanent list of jurists named by each republic must possess the qualifications required under the national laws for appointment as judges of its Supreme Court of Justice; they must be persons of the highest consideration, both for their moral qualities and for their professional ability. The others, according to Article 5, must also possess the following qualifications: they must be or have been heads or ministers of the state, or members of the highest court of justice in their country, or ambassadors or ministers plenipotentiary, but not to one of the Central American governments; or else they must be or have been members of an international arbitral tribunal, or of a permanent international court, or representatives of their governments before such a tribunal or court. The list drawn up by the President of the United States may also include lawyers admitted to practice before the Supreme Court of the United States and professors of international law.

To bring the Court into session, according to Article 4, the contracting party that wants it to sit notifies the nation or the nations against which it intends to bring an action, so that, within sixty days after they receive this notice, a protocol may be signed in which the precise questions to be settled are clearly set forth. Then each party chooses one jurisconsult from the list, and the parties together choose a third; if they cannot agree, the two already chosen select him, and if they cannot agree, the choice is made by lot.

Every judgment of the Court is sent to the governments of the five contracting states. The interested parties all agree to comply with the judgments, and to lend any naval assistance that may be necessary to obtain their complete execution, thus providing, in this form, a real and positive guarantee of respect for the treaty and for the Court it establishes.

The Court shall also have jurisdiction, as provided in the next article, over international questions submitted to it by special treaty between one of the Central American governments and the government of a foreign country. In such a case the parties are to agree, in the protocol, that the foreign government may choose its arbitrator freely, without regard to the lists; this does not prevent the application of the other provisions of the treaty.

The provisions on procedure, given in the annexes, are very detailed, and in general are commendable; it is not necessary to reproduce them here. Two protocols, one giving the details of the procedure to be observed at the signature of the treaty, and the other with the Government of the United States for the formation of the list of jurists, complete the treaty summarized here.

The establishment of this Court ought, as a matter of principle, to be regarded with favor, like anything else that contributes to bring about justice between the nations. Nevertheless, since there is a Permanent Court in existence already, it would be simpler to lend encouragement and support to it than to erect a new Court for each difficulty, with long and difficult procedure. And no one will deny that so far as impartiality and desire for justice are concerned, the existing Court offers all the guarantees and all the advantages that are sought for in this new one.

292. In preparing the program for the Fifth Pan-American Conference, which was held at Santiago, in Chile, in 1923, the following topic was inserted, as No. 10, on the motion of the Republic of Uruguay: "The consideration of the best methods for extending the application of the principle of judicial or arbitral settlement of disputes between the Republics on the continent of America."

M. Alejandro Alvarado Quirós presented a report and a plan for the creation of a Pan-American Court of Justice, in the name of the delegation of the Republic of Costa Rica. The following passages of the report deserve comment:

"In this order of ideas the Permanent Court of The Hague and the Permanent Court of International Justice, provided for in the Treaty of Versailles, have been created. Both have already rendered signal service; through the judicious choice of their distinguished judges, they will always be called upon to fix the principles of international law by their luminous decisions. But, on account of their location, and on account of the preponderating influence which the European element will necessarily have in the constitution of these courts, it is clear that their field of action will be limited to the problems, each day more difficult, that are involved in the restoration of order, political and economic, in the European powers, or, at most, to claims arising between them and an American country.

"The League of Nations admitted the validity of the Monroe Doctrine in the Covenant, in order to facilitate the entry of the United States into its membership. Subsequently, not to mention more than three cases as examples, the demands presented by the Republics of Peru and of Bolivia against Chile in the so-called Pacific question (*Cuestion del Pacifico*) and the conflict of territorial jurisdiction between Panama and Costa Rica have only confirmed the determination of European statesmen to have purely American affairs decided in America, on the ground that that is the most convenient location for a regional debate and for the most rapid and appropriate solutions."

293. The proposed treaty submitted with this significant report is as follows:

"Article 1. The high contracting parties agree to constitute and maintain a Permanent Court of Justice, to which they bind themselves to submit all the differences that may occur between them, in case their respective ministries of foreign affairs may not have been able to reach an agreement.

"Article 2. The Court will also hear international questions which any of the adhering governments and a non-adhering nation, by special convention, may have agreed to submit to it.

"Article 3. The Court will be formed by judges chosen by a majority of the members of the Supreme Court of each of the signatory states, one for each state, from among the jurists who may have the qualifications required for the office, and who are noted for their personal integrity, as well as for their knowledge of international law. The vacancies will be filled by substitute judges named at the same time and in the same way as the permanent judges, and must have the same qualifications as the former.

"Article 4. The International Court of Justice of America will have its seat at * * * *; but it may temporarily transfer its headquarters when the necessities of justice so require.

"Article 5. The permanent and substitute judges will be appointed for a period of ten years, counting from the day they assume their duties, and cannot be re-elected.

"In the case of death, resignation, or inability of any of them, the Supreme Court of the respective State shall proceed to name a substitute and the new judge will continue in the period of his predecessor.

"Article 6. The general expense of the Court will be shared equally by the signatory nations; and the expense arising from each particular case will be paid as may be decided by the Court. When a question be submitted to it in which one of the parties has not adhered to the treaty it will be admitted after it has been agreed that the State against which sentence may be given, obliges itself to pay the amount of the award and costs which the Court may deem necessary.

"The legislative authority of each of the high contracting parties will fix the salary of the respective judges at the beginning of the period referred to in the preceding article, and cannot alter the same until the following period.

"The signatory governments will assign the necessary items in their yearly budgets, as well as the amount required for the expenses of the Court, and they must remit in advance to the secretarial department of the same quarterly installments for the salaries and expenses.

"Article 7. The Court is authorized to establish the procedure to be followed by the parties, as well as causes for challenging, excusing or impeding the capacity of the judges. Likewise, it will appoint the members of its governing board and will establish its internal regulations, determining the formalities and time limits that may be necessary and which are not provided for in this treaty.

"Article 8. The Court sessions called to decide each particular case shall be composed of not less than three, nor more than seven judges, elected in a plenary session of the Court, excluding the judges who are natives or citizens of the state or states having a direct or indirect interest in the controversy.

"Article 9. The judges of the Court may not hold any other political or administrative office. Nor may they act as agents, counsellors or lawyers in any international questions. During their period of office they will enjoy diplomatic privileges and immunities.

"These dispositions shall not apply to substitute judges, except during active service.

"Article 10. The Court shall have a permanent status, and will always be ready to receive the claims, allegations and replies, which any of the signatory or other interested nations may desire to submit thereto, as provided in Articles 2 and 6.

"Article 11. The Court shall be competent to consider all questions that may be presented by the parties, provided that the controversy be of any of the following categories:

(a) The interpretation of a treaty.

(b) Any point of international law.

(c) The facts which brought about the violation of an international obligation.

"In case of doubt as to whether or not the Court is competent, it shall previously give its decision on that point.

"Article 12. The Court will apply:

1. International conventions and regulations expressly recognized by the litigating states;

2. International usage as proof of a practice accepted as a juridical precedent;

3. General principles of law recognized by civilized nations;

4. Previous decisions of the Court and doctrines of the most qualified publicists as auxiliaries to fix the rules of law; and

5. In addition, it will be a jury which shall conscientiously issue its verdicts.

"Article 13. The Court may not be requested to revise its decision except in virtue of the discovery of a fact which would have been able to influence it decisively, and which was unknown prior to that decision through no fault, error or omission of the party alleging it.

"Petition for revision may only be presented within six months after the notification of the decision and shall be examined by the Court in plenary session, excluding the judges appointed by the nation or nations interested in the litigation.

"Article 14. The present treaty will come into force as soon as at least twelve of the signatory states shall have ratified it and will not lapse for any reason whatever during a period of ten years from its last ratification, and thereafter it shall continue in force unless it has been denounced by at least half of the signatory Governments with a year's notice.

"Article 15. This treaty shall be ratified as soon as possible in accordance with the constitutional provisions of the high contracting parties, and will become effective by an exchange of ratifications through the Pan-American Union at Washington, in whose archives there will be deposited authentic copies in Spanish, English, Portuguese and French.

"The republics of America not ratifying this Covenant or which may not have been represented at the Fifth International Conference may adhere to the stipulations of the present treaty at any time by merely forwarding the official notification that their respective constitutional authorities have ratified it."

294. At the sixteenth meeting, at Santiago, on May 3, 1923, the following resolution was adopted:

"The Fifth Pan-American Conference resolves:

"To confide to the Commission of Jurists which is to meet at Rio de Janeiro in 1925 for the codification of international law the plan presented by the delegation of Costa Rica for the creation of a Permanent Court of Justice of America, as well as all other plans submitted by the different American governments on this subject."

The Commission referred to, which is composed of jurists, two of which are appointed by the government of each American republic, is to report on its work to the Sixth Pan-American Conference, which is to meet at Havana in 1926.

295. The general lines of this Costa Rican plan deserve great approbation. It has the merit of going straight at the question of compulsory jurisdiction, following the professional and even the diplomatic traditions of America, and it thus constitutes new and valiant support in both the field of opinion and of action for the existence of a Permanent International Court, and will help it to take

firm root. Moreover, in its essential characteristics, except for a few details, it conforms to the bases and the
rules that guide the movement and action of the institution
that has already been established, and thus illustrates the
uniformity of the aspirations and tendencies toward justice, one of the great objects of all civilized humanity.

Nevertheless, the point may be raised whether there
is any advantage in establishing a new Court instead of
making use of the one that already is in existence, and
which, with the necessary modifications, is in a position to
meet the just demands of America. The great majority of
the nations of the New World support today the existing
Court, and some have adhered to the additional (optional)
clause for compulsory jurisdiction.

Doubling or multiplying the number of courts may diminish the prestige of each of them, in addition to making
a very large increase in the financial burden placed on certain states, whose financial situation is rather restricted.

Add to this the fact that the existing Court has not so
much work to do yet that it can be said to need the
help of another court, and that it is impossible to predict
whether this will be the case some day, or at least to predict when that day will come. The international community is, as a matter of fact, composed of a small number of
states, about sixty only, and it is hardly credible that between sixty persons there would be enough legal questions
to call for lavish judicial power. As soon as the cases
begin to multiply between them, the questions begin to grow
fewer, because each judgment or determination of jurisprudence or every affirmation of a contested legal principle
makes a lawsuit unnecessary and useless when a new case
arises to which these principles can be applied.

And in relation to jurisprudence, to which reference has
just been made, there is another reason for not being very
enthusiastic about the existence of three separate and independent courts. There is a risk, graver in international
affairs than in domestic matters, of decisions asserting contradictory doctrines, which might cause conflicts between
the different parts of the globe and might imperil the

CONCLUSION 319

fundamental unity between moral conceptions and legal doctrines.

If there is one tribunal in Europe and another in America, to which one will Asia bring its questions today, and Africa and Oceanica tomorrow? The possible inconveniences that have been pointed out will be accentuated if each continent or each region has its own justice. An additional jurisdiction would immediately be proposed, between the different regions, which would be the true world organization; but the one now in existence, having on that account less to do today than the others, could undertake advantageously to perform the tasks of all the others.

It is true, as the delegation of Costa Rica asserts, that America is not used yet to the existence of the Permanent Court, and that, for this and other reasons, it is going to settle some of its great disputes in a different judicial form; but it is also true that it has taken some of its disputes before the old Court of Arbitration at The Hague, and that, so far as distance goes, there is no great difference between this part of the globe and the place where the disputes arose that are mentioned in the report of this delegation.

It is also true that a local atmosphere is essential for justice, and that certain questions of the New World ought to be argued and decided in an American atmosphere. But the actual Statute of the Permanent Court of International Justice is not sacrosanct and unalterable. It could very well be amended so that when the Permanent Court had American matters before it, it could hold two regular sessions a year, one at The Hague and the other in America, treating in each the affairs of that continent, and in either one or the other the matters that are between the two continents, as well as those from some other part of the world that are before it for examination and decision. The nationality of the judges that compose the Court would not cause any difficulty, because that depends in large part on the electoral assemblies in which the twenty-two American states have a large number of the votes, and will have a greater and more justifiable influence every day.

This American city might well be Havana, capital of the

Republic of Cuba. The means of communication between Havana and the whole universe are very easy and rapid, which is an element of particular importance in international matters. It is in the centre of America, equally accessible to the republics of North America and of South America. On account of its history and its special situation, all the important languages are in general use there, and all the necessary personal arrangements exist for the comfort and convenience of the Court. For these and other reasons, Havana is now in the process of becoming a great international city, where congresses and conferences of all kinds meet with remarkable frequency. Its designation as one of the seats of the Permanent Court would be a great honor for it, and would only place it under the pleasant duty of furnishing everything of a material nature that the meeting of the Court required.

And the Statute ought to make it possible, as it was necessary to arrange in the case of The Hague, for the majority of the judges to decide that the Court might be installed temporarily in some other place, either on account of general circumstances, or because of the particular circumstances of some specific litigation.

296. At the end of this book about this international jurisdiction, the writer, bolder every day in his hope for its future, desires to repeat once more what he said about it not long ago before the Academy of International Law at The Hague: it is no small thing for our generation to have witnessed its birth and to have seen it take its seat.

Hugo Grotius, who was the founder of the law of nations and its prophet, never dreamed of it. In the last century no one would have dared to state seriously that it would soon triumph. Without the World War, perhaps, and without the powerful movement against force that was developed in a good many nations, the governments would never have decided to put it into practice. This is human nature. It learns from preaching and from logic, but still more from unhappiness and grief. Always great and always progressive, it emerges, from success and disaster alike, stronger, nobler and more just. Let us rejoice over this lesson, which has been repeated often in the history of the world; and let us celebrate the fact that at last between nations, as for a long time between men, we can now, under the protection of a Permanent Court, speak of law and of justice, for the strong and for the weak.

BIBLIOGRAPHY

CHAPTER I

BARBEYRAC (J.).—*Supplément contenant l'histoire des anciens traités,* etc. Amsterdam et La Haye, 1739.

BARON (Julius).—*Peregrinenrecht und Ius gentium.* Leipzig, 1892.

BERARD (V.).—*De arbitrio inter liberas Graecorum civitates.* Thesi, Lutetiae Parisiorum, 1894.

BURGEL (H.).—*Die pylaeisch-delphische Amphiktyonie.* München, 1877.

DANTE ALIGHIERI.—*De Monarchia* (Édit. Tutte l. op. Dr. E. Moore). Oxford, 1904.

Geschichte (Allgemeine)—*In Einzeldarstellungen.* Unter Mitwirkung von Alex. Brückner, Felix Dahn und Wilhelm Oncken. Ts. I-III, Berlin, 1879-1893.

GROTIUS (H.).—*De iure belli ac pacis libri tres. In quibus ius naturae et gentium: item iuris publici praecipua explicantur.* Paris, 1625.
Le droit de la guerre et de la paix. Nouvelle traduction par Jean de Barbeyrac, aves les notes de l'auteur, etc. Amsterdam, 1724.

KAMAROWSKY (Comte de).—*Le Tribunal international.* Trad. française par Serge de Westman, précédé d'une introduction par Jules Lacointa. Paris, 1887.

LA FONTAINE (H.).—*Pasicrisie internationale.* Berne, 1903.

LANGE (Ch. I).—*Histoire de l'Internationalisme.* Tome I, Christiania, 1919.

LAURENT (F.).—*Études sur l'Histoire de l'Humanité.* Paris-Gand, 1879-1880: 1885-1870 (2ᵉ édition, Ts. I-III: V-VII).

LAVISSE (E.) et RAMBAUD (A.).—*Histoire générale du IVᵉ siècle à nos jours.* (Première et deuxième édition, Ts. I-VI), Paris, 1894, 1912.

NYS (Ernest).—*Le Droit international et la Papauté. Revue de droit international public et de législation comparée.* Tom X, 1878, p. 510.

NOVACOVITCH (M.).—*Les Compromis et les Arbitrages internationaux du XIIᵉ au XVᵉ siècle. Thèse.* Paris, 1905.

PHILIPSON (C.).—*The International Law and Custom of Ancient Greece and Rome.* London, 1911.

POIGNAND DE FONTENIOUX (H.).—*De l'évolution de l'idée du tribunal permanent à travers les âges et de son avenir. Thèse.* Poitiers, 1904.

RAEDER (A.).—*L'Arbitrage chez les Hellènes.* Christiania, 1912.

REINER (J.).—*Hugo Grotius und das Weltschiedsgericht.* Berlin, 1922.

REVON (M.).—*L'Arbitrage international: son passé, son présent, son avenir.* Paris, 1892.

ROCQUAIN (F.).—*La Papauté au moyen âge. Nicolas Ier, Grégoire VII, Innocent III, Boniface VIII.* Études sur le pouvoir pontifical. Paris, 1888.

ROUARD DE CARD (E.).—*L'Arbitrage international dans le passé, le présent et l'avenir.* Précédé d'une lettre par Ch. Giraud, etc. Paris, 1877.

SCHÜCKING (Walter).—*Die Organisation der Welt.* Leipzig, 1909.

TAÜBLER (E.).—*Imperium Romanum.* Studien zur Entwicklungsgeschichte des Römischen Reichs, Staatsverträge, 1913.—*Die Staatsverträge das Altertums.* Leipzig, 1894.

TOD, MARCUS NIEBUHR.—*International Arbitration Amongst the Greeks.* Oxford, 1913.

VINOGRADOFF (Sir Paul).—*Historical Types of International Law.* Bibliotheca Visseriana. Tome II. Leyden.

VOIGHT (M.).—*De fetialibus populi Romani questionis specimen.* Dissert. Lipsiae, 1852.

YORK (E.).—*Leagues of Nations. Ancient, mediaeval and modern.* London, 1919.

ZOUCHE (E.).—*Iuris et iudici fecialis, sive iuris inter gentes, etc.* Lugduni Batavorum, 1651.

CHAPTER II

ANDERSON (L.).—*The Relations between International Tribunals of Arbitration and the Jurisdiction of National Courts.* Proceedings of the American Society of International Law. Vol. III, 1909, p. 35.

APPLETON (L.).—*An International Tribunal for Europe.* London.

BALCH (Th.).—*International Courts of Arbitration.* Cambridge, 1874.
5th ed., with an Introduction and additional Notes by T. W. Balch. Philadelphia, 1914.
A World Court in the Light of the United States Supreme Court. Philadelphia, 1918.

BALDWIN (S. E.).—*Justice Between Nations,* Baltimore, 1914.
The New Era of International Courts. Baltimore, 1910.
The Membership of a World Tribunal for Promoting Permanent Peace. American Journal of International Law, 1918, p. 453.
BARBAULT (L.).—*Du Tribunal international.* Genève, 1872.
BARCLAY (Sir T.).—*New Methods of Adjusting International Disputes and the Future.* London, 1917.
BEICHMANN (F. V. N.).—*L'Établissement d'un Tribunal international permanent.* Bologne, 1917.
BENTHAM (J.).—*Principles of International Law. MS,* 1786-1787. Published by N. Tait, Edinburgh, 1843. *Essay IV.—A Plan for an Universal and Perpetual Peace.* Vol. III.
BEVILAQUA (C.).—*Projet d'organisation d'une Cour permanente de justice internationale.* Rio de Janeiro, 1921.
BLUNTSCHLI (J. C.).—*Die organisation des europäischen Staatenvereins. Gegenwart,* Nos 6, 8 und 9, 1878.
BORNER (W.).—*Das Weltstaatsprojekt des Abbé de Saint-Pierre. Ein Beitrag zur Geschichte der Weltfriedensidee.* Berlin und Leipzig, 1913.
BOSCO (Petrus de).—*De recuperatione terrae sanctae.* Édition Langlois, Paris, 1871.
BRIOUT (E.).—*L'idée de paix perpétuelle de Jérémie Bentham. Thèse.* Paris, 1905.
BRUNARD.—*Une Cour de cassation internationale.* 1873.
BUTLER (Nicholas Murray).—*The International Mind: an Argument for the Judicial Settlement of International Disputes.* New York, 1912.
The Road to Durable Peace. Saint Louis, 1918.
CASTEL (Ch. Ier) (Abbé de Saint-Pierre).—*Mémoire pour rendre la paix perpétuelle en Europe.* Cologne, 1712.
Projet pour rendre la paix perpétuelle en Europe. Tome III. Projet de traité pour rendre la paix perpétuelle entre les souverains chrétiens; pour maintenir toujours le commerce libre entre les nations; pour affermir beaucoup davantage les maisons souveraines sur le trône. Proposé autrefois par Henry le Grand, agréé par la reine Élisabeth, etc. Éclairci par l'abbé de Saint-Pierre. Utrecht, 1713-1716.
Abrégé du projet de paix perpétuelle, inventé par le roi Henry le Grand, approuvé par la reine Élisabeth, par le roi Jacques son successeur, par les Républiques et par divers autres potentats. Approprié à l'état présent des affaires générales de l'Europe.

Démontré infiniment avantageux pour tous les hommes nés et à naître, en général, et en particulier pour tous les souverains et pour les maisons souveraines. Rotterdam, 1729. Utrecht, 1728.

CHAVET (F.).—*Justice sociale et Justice internationale.* Paris, 1900.

CLARKE (F. R.).—*A Permanent Tribunal of International Arbitration: Its Necessity and Value. American Journal of International Law.* Vol. I, No. 2.

CROSBY (O.).—*The Constitution of an International Court of Decree and Enforcement, or a plea for the poor of all lands.* Tokyo, 1875.

DARBY (W. E.).—*International Tribunals: A Collection of the various schemes which have been propounded and of instances since 1815,* etc. London, 1897, 1899.
The Proved Practibility of International Arbitration, being an outline of modern pacific settlements. London, 1904.

DESCAMPS (E.).—*Essai sur l'organisation de l'arbitrage international. Mémoire aux Puissances, etc.* Bruxelles, 1896.

DREYFUS (F.).—*L'Arbitrage international.* Avec une préface de Fréd. Passy. Paris, 1892.

DUPLESSIX (E.).—*L'Organisation internationale.* Paris, 1900.

ELIOT (Charles W.).—*An International Force Must Support an International Tribunal.* Baltimore, 1914.

FERRER (A.).—*L'Ère nouvelle. Nécessité d'un Code international et d'un Tribunal arbitral des Nations.* Paris, 1863.

FIORE (P.).—*Le Droit international codifié.* Paris, 1911.

GENTILIS (Albericus).—*De jure belli libri tres.* Han, 1598.

GONDON (J.-B.).—*Du Droit public et du droit des gens.* Tom. III. Paris, 1808.

GRAM (G).—*Au sujet de projets d'un règlement pacifique des conflits internationaux présentés par la commission néerlandaise et M. Lammasch.* Christiania, 1917.

HAMMOND (J. H.).—*A world court. The Annals of the American Academy of Political and Social Science.* Vol. 96, July, 1921, p. 98.

HORNBY (Sir E).—*Constitution d'un Tribunal international.* Berne, 1893.

HOUZEAU DE LEHAI.—*Convention pour l'établissement d'une juridiction internationale,* 1895.

HUBBARD (G.).—*La Justice internationale. Revue juridique.* Paris, 1903, 1905.

HULL (W. I.).—*The International Grand Jury.* Baltimore, 1912.

KAMAROWSKY (Comte de).—*Le Tribunal international.* Trad. française par Serge de Westman, etc. Paris, 1887.

KATZ (Ed.).—*Der internationale Rechtshof.* Berlin und Leipzig, 1919.

LADD (W.).—*An Essay on a Congress of Nations for the adjustment of international disputes without resort to arms.* Reprinted from the original edition of 1840 (London) by James Brown Scott. New York, 1916.

LA FONTAINE (H.).—*The Existing Elements of a Constitution of the United States of the World.* New York, 1911.
The Great Solution: Magnissima Charta: An Essay on Evolutionary Constructive Pacificism. Boston, 1916.
International Judicature. Baltimore, 1915.

LAMMASCH (H.).—*Die Rechtskraft internationaler Schiedssprücke.* Christiania, 1913.

LAPRADELLE (A. DE).—*Les transformations de l'arbitrage international.* Almanach de la Paix. Paris, 1905, p. 56.

LARROQUE (P.).—*De la création d'un code de droit international et de l'institution d'un haut tribunal, juge souverain des différends internationaux.* Paris, 1875.

LAVELAYE (E. DE).—*On the Causes of War and the Means of Reducing Their Number.* London, 1872.

LEPERT (A.).—*Projet d'organisation de la justice internationale.* Paris, 1907.

LORIMER (J.).—*The Institutes of International Law.* Vol. II. Book V: *The Ultimate Problem of International Jurisprudence.* Edinburgh and London, 1884.
Proposition d'un Congrès international, basé sur le principe de facto: Revue de Droit international, 1871, p. 1.
Le problème final du droit international. Revue de Droit international, 1877, p. 161.

LORIA (A.).—*Les bases économiques de la Justice Internationale.* Christiania, 1913.

LOWELL (A. Lawrence).—*A League to Enforce Peace.* Boston, 1915.

MACFARLAND (H. B. F.).—*The Supreme Court of the World.* Baltimore, 1913.

MARBURG (Th.).—*Objections to the Present Hague Court.* Proceedings of the American Society for the Judicial Settlement of International Disputes. 1910, p. 94.
Law and Judicial Settlement. Baltimore, 1914.
The World Court and the League of Peace. Baltimore, 1915.

MARCHAND (P. R.).—*Nouveau projet de traité de paix perpétuelle.* Paris, 1842.

MILES (J. B.).—*Le Tribunal international.* Paris, 1875.

MILL (John Stuart).—*Considerations on Representative Governments.* London, 1861.

MOUGINS DE ROQUEFORT.—*De la solution juridique des conflits internationaux.* 1892.

NYHOLM (D. G.).—*Le Tribunal mondial.* Cairo, 1918.

NYS (Ernest).—*The Necessity of a Permanent Tribunal.* Baltimore, 1911.

PARNES (O.).—*Tribunal d'arbitrage armé.* Vienne, 1907.

PECQUEUR (R.).—*De la paix, son principe et de sa réalisation.* Paris, 1842.

PENFIELD (W. L.).—*International Courts of Justice.* Proceedings of the Pennsylvania Arbitration and Peace Conference. Philadelphia, 1908.

PENN (William).—*Essay on the Present and Future Peace of Europe.* London, 1693.

RALSTON (J. H.).—*Some Considerations as to International Arbitral Courts.* Proceedings of the American Society for Judicial Settlement of International Disputes. 1910, p. 151.

RICHARDSON (W.).—*A World Court. Advocate of Peace.* No. 5, 1911.

REEVES (J. S.).—*The Justiciability of International Disputes.* Baltimore, 1916.

ROOT (Elihu) and HAY (John).—*Instructions to the American Delegates to The Hague Conferences,* 1899 and 1907. Boston, 1913.

ROOT (Elihu).—*The Permanent Court of International Justice. Journal of the American Bar Association.* Vol. 6, No. 2, 1920.

SARTORIUS.—*Organon des Völkfriedens.* Zürich, 1837.

SCHLIEF (E.).—*Völkerrechtliche Organisationen und Schiedsgerichte. Friedenswarte,* 1906, p. 45.

SCIALOJA (V.).—*Per l'instituzione di tribunali internazionali. Revue de Droit international.* No. 1, 1909, p. 3.

SCOTT (James Brown).—*The Need of an International Court of Justice.* Proceedings of the Pennsylvania Arbitration and Peace Conference. Philadelphia, 1908, p. 98.

The Proposed International Court of Arbitral Justice. Report of the Mohonk Lake Conferences on international arbitration. 1909, p. 54.

Progress Toward an International Court of Arbitral Justice. Report of the Mohonk Lake Conferences. 1910, p. 67.

The American Society for the Judicial Settlement of International disputes: Its Scope and Work. Proceedings of same. Baltimore, 1910, p. 2.

A Court of the World. The Outlook, June 18, 1910.

Judicial Proceedings as a Substitute for War or International Self-redress. Baltimore, 1910.

A Permanent International Court of Justice. Editorial Review, April, 1911.

The Evolution of the Permanent International Judiciary. American Journal of International Law. 1912, p. 316.

An International Court of Justice. Letter and Memorandum to the Netherland Minister of Foreign Affairs, etc. New York, 1916.

L'évolution d'une juridiction internationale. Étude et documents. Paris, 1919.

An International Court of Justice, The United States Supreme Court: A Prototype of an International Court. Carnegie Endowment for International Peace Year Book, 1920, pp. 96, 99.

Project of an International Court of Justice. Baltimore, 1917.

SEEBOHM (F.).—*On International Reform.* London, 1871.

SEELY (Sir J. R.).—*The Possible Means of Preventing War in Europe.* See Darby, *International Tribunals,* p. 92.

SETH LOW.—*International Arbitration.* Proceedings of the National Arbitration and Peace Congress. New York, 1907.

SIGAUD (A.).—*Confédération européenne.* Paris, 1859.

SPRAGUE (A. B.).—*Internationalism* (by A. de Marcoartu). London, 1876.

SMITH (H. A.).—*The American Supreme Court as an International Tribunal.* Oxford, 1920.

SNOW (A. H.).—*Judicative Conciliation.* Baltimore, 1916.

TAFT (William H.).—*The American Supreme Court, the Prototype of a World Court.* Baltimore, 1915.

TRYON (J. L.).—*The Proposed High Court of Nations.* Boston, 1910.

VAN DER MANDERE (H.).—*Eine reorganisatie van het permanente hof van Arbitrage. Vragen des Tijds,* Sept., 1910.

VANCE (W. R.).—*The Supreme Court of the United States as an International Tribunal.* Baltimore, 1915.

The Vision of a World Court. Baltimore, 1917.

VESNITCH (M. R.).—*Cardenal Alberoni: An International Precursor of Pacifism and International Arbitration,* etc. New York, 1913.

Deux précurseurs français du pacifisme et l'arbitrage international: P. Dubois et E. Crucé. Paris, 1911.

WEHBERG (Hans).—*Das Problem eines internationalen Staatengerichtshofes.* München u. Leipzig, 1912.

The Problem of an International Court of Justice. Transl. by Charles G. Fenwick. Oxford, 1918.

WESTLAKE (J.).—*International Law. Peace* (Part I). Cambridge, 1904.

WHEELER (Everett P.).—*A World Court and International Police.* Baltimore, 1916.

WHITE (Thomas Raeburn.).—*Underlying Principles which Should Govern Appointment of Judges of the International Court. Advocate of Peace,* 1911, No. 7.

CHAPTER III

American Society for the Judicial Settlement of International Disputes. Proceedings: Meetings at Washington, Baltimore and Cincinnati: 1910-1914. See under Wilson, Wheeler, Eliot, Ginn, Foulke, Macfarland, Marburg, etc.

American Society of International Law.—Proceedings: Meetings of 1909, 1912, 1915. See under Scott, Root, Burton, Montague, Ion, Harris, MacVeagh, etc. Washington, D. C.

Arbitration and Peace Congress. New York, 1907, 1909.

Association internationale de l'arbitrage et de la paix, de la Grande-Bretagne.—Procès-verbal de la Conférence de Bruxelles de 1882. Londres, 1883.

Assemblée (Première) générale de la Ligue internationale et permanente de la Paix. Juin, 1868. Paris, 1868.

Bar Association of the State of New York. Memorial adopted, January 22, 1896. See under Darby, *International Tribunals,* p. 167.

Congrès des Amis de la Paix universelle. Bruxelles, Sept., 1848. *Compte rendu,* Bruxelles, 1849.

Congrès des Amis de la Paix universalle. Paris, 1849. *Compte rendu,* Paris, 1850.

Congrès de Genève. Sept., 1867. *Annales,* Genève, 1868.

Congrès de la Ligue internationale de la paix et de la liberté. Recueil officiel des résolutions votées par les vingt et un premiers Congrès. Genève, 1888.

Congrès de la Paix (6e). Anvers, 1894. *Bulletin,* Anvers, 1894.

Congrès international de la Paix. Compte rendu, Paris, 1889.

Congrès international des Sociétés des Amis de la Paix. Paris, Sept., 1878. *Compte rendu,* Paris, 1880.

Congrès (1er, 2e) *national des Sociétés françaises de la Paix.* Toulouse, 1903-4.

Congrès universels de la paix tenus de 1843 à 1910 *et des quatre assemblées générales substituées aux congrès de* 1898, 1899, 1909 *et* 1911. Berne, 1912.

Congrès (20e)*universel de la paix.* La Haye, 1913.

Délégation autrichienne-allemande à la Conférence de la Paix (Annexes A et B à la note de la).—See Documents présentés au comité consultatif de juristes et relatifs à des projets déjà existants pour l'établissement d'une Cour permanente de justice internationale. La Haye, 1920, p. 130.

Droit international (*Association de*).—Observations présentées par Alexandre Corsi, avec l'adhésion de C. F. Gabba, de l'Université de Pise, sur un projet de convention internationale pour l'exécution des jugements étrangers. Pisa, 1901.

Durable Peace (*Central Organisation for a*).—*Recueil des rapports sur les différents points du programme minimum.* La Haye, 1916.

General Peace Conventions (The).—1st, 2nd and 3rd. London, 1843.

Gouvernement danois (*Projet élaboré par le comité institué par le.*—See under Documents présentés au comité consultatif de juristes, etc. La Haye, 1920, pp. 202.

Gouvernement de l'Italie (*Extrait d'un projet présenté à la Conférence préliminaire de la Paix par le*).—See under Documents présentés au comité consultatif de juristes, etc. La Haye, 1920, p. 120.

Gouvernements du Suède, du Danemark et de Norvèg (*Avant-projet concernant une organisation juridique internationale élaboré par les trois comités nommés par les*).—See under Documents présentés au comité, etc. La Haye, 1920, p. 150.

Gouvernement norvégien (*Rapport élaboré par le comité institué par le*).—See under Documents présentés au comité, etc. La Haye, 1920, p. 210.

Groupe interparlementaire suèdois. Recueil de documents. Rédigé par P. G. Widegren. Stockholm, 1915.

Instituto Americano de Derecho Internacional.—Acta final de la Sesion de la Habana. Washington, D. C., 1917.

Institute (*American*) *of International Law.*—The recommendations of Habana concerning international organization, adopted by the American Institute of International Law at Habana, January 23, 1917. Address and commentary by James Brown Scott. New York, 1917.

Institut de droit international.—Annuaires. Sessions de Bruxelles, 1877; de Christiania, 1912; de Rome, 1921.

*Interparlementaire Conférence.—*Rapport sur l'organisation d'une Cour internationale permanente d'arbitrage. Par Lord Weardale (P. J. Stanhope). Bruxelles, 1894.

International Peace (Carnegie Endowment for).—Division of International Law. James Brown Scott, Director. Nos. 1-35, Washington, D. C., 1915-1920.

International Peace (Carnegie Endowment for).—Pamphlet 1, 28, 30, 35, 39. Washington, 1914-1921.

International Peace (Carnegie Endowment for).—Epitome. Washington, 1919.

International Peace (Carnegie Endowment for).—International Conciliation. *Official documents looking toward peace.* 4 Series. New York, 1917.

Knox (Philander G.).—Note to the Powers. Advocate of Peace. No. 2. 1910.

Lake Mohonk Conferences on International Arbitration.—Reports: 1896, 1898, 1899, 1907, 1910, 1911; Logan, Chester, Bassett Moore, Tripp, Wheeler, James Brown Scott (1909), Kirchwey, Humphrey, d'Estournelles de Constant, Foulke, Marburg, etc. Also Reports of 1908, 1914 and 1915.

National (1st and 2nd) *Peace Congress.—*New York, 1907; Boston, 1909.

National (3rd) *Peace Congress.—*Baltimore, 1910.

Pazifistenkongress. Berlin, 13 bis 15 Juni, 1919, mit einen Sonderschreiben von A. H. Fried. Charlottenburg, 1919.

*Pennsylvania.—*See under *Arbitration and Peace Conference.—Official Report.* Philadelphia, 1908.

*Projet (Extrait d'un) présenté à la Conférence de la paix par la délégation allemande.—*See under Documents présentés au comité consultatif de juristes, etc. La Haye, 1920, p. 124.

Projet de convention élaboré par une commission suédoise gouvernementale, 1919.—See under Documents présentés au comité, etc. La Haye, 1920, p. 236.

*Projet (avant-) suisse.—*See under Documents présentés au comité, etc. La Haye, 1920, p. 252.

Projet néerlandais de règlement relatif à l'établissment de la Cour permanente, etc.—See under Documents présentés au comité, etc. La Haye, 1920, p. 278.

Projet des cinq puissances neutres relatif à l'établissement de la Cour permanente, etc.—See under Documents présentés au comité, etc. La Haye, 1920, p. 300.

Schweizerische Vereinigung für Internationales Recht. Zürich, 1917.

The International Law Association.—See Reports of the 16th, 17th and 18th Conferences. London, 1893, 1895, 1899.

Union Interparlementaire.—See Résolutions des conférences et décisions principales du Conseil. 2e édition, Leipzig, 1911.

Union Interparlementaire.—19e conférence. Stockholm, août, 1914 (Documents préliminaires).

Union Juridique Internationale.—See under Documents présentés au comité, etc. La Haye, 1920, p. 344.

CHAPTER IV

Acts (The final) of the First and Second Hague Peace Conferences, together with the Draft Convention of a Judicial Arbitration Court. Washington, 1915 (Carnegie Endowment Publications).

Addresses of the New York State Bar Association to His Imperial Majesty Nicholas II, Emperor of all the Russias, and to the President of the United States, on the occasion and in commendation of the Peace Congress at the Hague, and recommending the creation of an international Court. New York, 1899.

ADLER (A.).—*Die Haager Friedenskonferenz des Jahres 1907 und die Fortbildung des Völkerrechtes.* Berlin, 1909.

BUSTAMANTE Y SIRVEN (A. S. de).—*La segunda Conferencia de la Paz reunida en El Haya en 1907.* Madrid, 1908, 2 vols.
   La seconde Conférence de la Paix réunie a La Haye en 1907. Trad. de l'espagnol par Georges Scelle. Paris, 1909.

Conférence internationale de la Paix. La Haye, 18 mai-29 juillet, 1899. Publié par le ministère des Affaires étrangères. La Haye, 1899.

DUMAS (Jacques).—Pourrait-on donner aux États un droit d'action directe devant la Cour de La Haye? *La Paix par le Droit,* No. 6, 1907.

ERNST (A.).—*L'Œuvre de la deuxième Conférence de la Paix.* Exposé juridique et texte des conventions. Bruxelles, 1908.

FOX (F. W.).—*Some Historical Incidents in Connexion with the Es-*

tablishment of the International Tribunal of Arbitration at the Hague in 1899, and International Arbitration. London, 1901.

FRIED (A. H.).—*Die zweite Haager Konferenz. Ihre Arbeiten, ihre Ergebnisse und ihre Bedeutung.* Leipzig, 1909.

HAY (John) and ROOT (Elihu).—*Instructions to the American Delegates to the Hague Conferences,* 1899 and 1907. Boston, 1913.

HOLLS (F. W.).—*The International Court of Arbitration at the Hague.* Albany, 1901.

The Peace Conference at the Hague and Its Bearings on International Law and Policy. New York, 1914.

HUBER (Max).—*Die Fortbildung des Völkerrechtes auf dem Gebiete des Prozes und Landkriegsrechts durch die II internationale Friedenskonferenz im Haag,* 1907. Tübingen, 1908.

LAWRENCE (T. J.).—*International Problems and Hague Conferences.* London, 1908.

LÉMONON (E.).—*La seconde Conférence de la Paix.* La Haye, juin-octobre, 1907. Préface de Léon Bourgeois, 2e éd. Paris, 1912.

MARTENS (F. de).—*La Conférence de la Paix à La Haye. Études d'histoire contemporaine.* Trad. du russe par N. de Sancé. Paris, 1900.

MÉRIGNHAC (A).—*La Conférence internationale de la Paix.* Avec une préface de Léon Bourgeois. Paris, 1900.

RENAULT (L.).—*Les deux Conférences de la Paix, 1899 et 1907. Recueil des textes arretés par ces conférences et de différents documents complémentaires.* Paris, 1909, 2e éd.

SCOTT (James B.).—*The Hague Conventions and Declarations of 1899 and 1907,* accompanied by tables of signatures, ratifications and adhesions of the various Powers, and texts of reservations. New York, 1915 (Carnegie Endowment Publications).

Texts of the Peace Conference at the Hague, 1899 and 1907, with English translation and appendix of related documents. A prefatory note by Elihu Root. Boston, 1908.

American Addresses at the 2nd Hague Conference, delivered by J. H. Choate, General Horace Porter, James Brown Scott.

The Project Relative to a Court of Arbitral Justice: draft convention and report adopted by the Second Hague Peace Conference of 1907: with an introductory note. Washington, 1920 (Carnegie Endowment Publications).

The Reports of the Hague Conferences of 1899 and 1907: with an introduction. Oxford, 1917 (Carnegie Endowment Publications).

Instructions to the American Delegates to the Hague Peace Conferences and Their Official Reports: with an introduction. New York, 1916 (Carnegie Endowment Publications).

The Hague Peace Conferences of 1899 and 1907: a series of lectures delivered at Johns Hopkins University in 1908. Vol. I, *Conferences;* Vol. II, *Documents.* Baltimore, 1909.

S. DE FUENTES (Fernando).—*Informe relativo a la 2a Conferencia de la Paz reunida en el Haya,* etc. Vol. II. Habana, 1908.

SCHÜCKING (Walter).—*Das Werk von Haag. Unter Mitwirkung von L. von Bar u. A. Herausgegeben von W. S. Serie I-II, Bd. 1/3.* München-Leipzig, 1912-14.

Der Staatenverband der Haager Konferenzen. München u. Leipzig, 1912.

WEHBERG (H.).—*Kommentar zum dem Haager Abkommen "betreffend die friedliche Erledigung internationaler Streitigkeiten,"* von 18 Okt., 1907. Tübingen, 1911.

CHAPTER V

Anales de la Corte de Justicia Centroamericana. Director Ernesto Martin. 1911-1917. San José, Republica de Costa-Roca.

Demanda del Gobierno de El Salvador contra el de Nicaragua ante la Corte de Justicia Centroamericana. San Salvador, 1916 (Libro rosado de El Salvador).

MUNRO (D. G.).—*The Five Republics of Central America:* Their Political and Economical Development and Their Relations with the United States. New York, 1918 (Carnegie Endowment Publications).

Pacto de Union de Centroamerica celebrado en San José de Costa-Rica, el 19 de Enero de 1921. Tegucigalpa, 1921.

Protocolo de la Conferencia de Plenipotenciarios centroamericanos reunida en San José de Costa-Rica el 4 diciembre de 1920. Tegucigalpa, 1921.

SCOTT (James B.).—*The Closing of the Central American Court of Justice, American Journal of International Law.* 1918, p. 453.

CHAPTER VI

ALVAREZ (Alejandro).—*L'Organisation internationale d'après le traité de Versailles.* Paris, 1920.

BAKER (Ray Stannard).—*Woodrow Wilson and World Settlement.* New York, 1923, 3 vols.

What Wilson Did at Paris. Garden City, New York, 1919.

BARTLET (Vernon).—*Behind the Scenes at the Peace Conference.* London, 1919.

BARTHOU (Louis).—*Le Traité de paix.* Paris, 1919.

BEICHMANN (Fred V. N.).—*Le Pacte de la Société des Nations dans le traité de paix de Versailles.* Scienta, p. 210, 1920.

BOURGEOIS (Léon).—*Le Pacte de 1919 et la Société des Nations.* Paris, 1919.

Le Traité de paix de Versailles. Rapport présente au Sénat le 3 octobre 1919. Paris, 1919.

BUSTAMANTE Y SIRVEN (A. S. de).—*Informe oral y publico sobre el Tratado de Paz con Alemania, ante las Comisiones de Relaciones Exteriores del Senado y de la Camara.* V. Discursos, Habana.

DILLON.—*The Peace Conference.* London, 1919.

LORD GREY OF FALLODON.—*The Peace Conference.* London, 1919, 2 vols.

HANOTAUX (Gabriel).—*Le Traité de paix de Versailles du 28 juin 1919,* etc. Paris, 1919.

HASKINS (C. H.) et LORD (R. H.).—*Some Problems of the Peace Conference.* Cambridge, 1920.

HOUSE (Edward M.) and SEYMOUR (C.)—*What Really Happened at Paris:* The Story of the Peace Conference. New York, 1921.

KEEN (F. N.).—*The League of Nations Covenant.* Text of the proposed Covenant with speech of President Wilson, etc. London, 1919.

KEYNES (J. M.).—*A Revision of the Treaty.* London, 1922.

LAMMASCH (H.).—*Woodrow Wilson's Friedensplan.* Mit ausgewählten Briefen, Schriften und Reden des Präsidenten Wilson. Leipzig u. Wien, 1919.

LANSING (R.).—*The Peace Negotiations.* A Personal Narrative. Philadelphia, 1921.

LEVY (R. G.).—*La juste paix ou la vérité sur le traité de Versailles.* Paris, 1920.

LUGAN (A.).—*Les problèmes internationaux et le Congrès de la Paix.* Paris, 1919.

MEURER (Christian).—*Die Grundlagen des Versailler Friedens und der Völkerbund.* Würzburg, 1920.

PILLET (A.).—*Le traité de Versailles.* Paris, 1920.

SMUTS (General Jan C.).—*The League of Nations.* A Practical Suggestion. London, 1918.

TARDIEU (A.).—*La Paix* (Nouvelle édition). Paris, 1921.

TEMPERLY (H. W. V.).—*A History of the Peace Conference of Paris.* London, 1920, 5 vols.

THOMPSON (C. T.).—*The Peace Conference Day by Day.* New York, 1920.

Tratado de Paz celebrado por las Naciones Aliadas y asociadas con Alemania. Habana, 1920 (Republica de Cuba).

Traité de Paix entre les puissances alliées et l'Allemagne, et protocole, signés à Versailles le 28 juin, 1919. Paris, 1919. (*Publications du ministère des Affaires étrangères.*)

Traité de Paix entre les puissances alliées et associées et l'Allemagne, et protocole, signés à Versailles le 28 juin, 1919. *Édition pour les délégués à la Conférence de la Paix* (textes anglais et français). Paris, Imprimerie Nationale, 1919.

Treaty of Peace between the allied associated Powers and Germany. Signed at Versailles, June 28, 1919. London, 1919 (Parliamentary Papers. Treaty Series, No. 4, 1919).

WUNDISCH (Friedr.).—*Der Friedensvertrag von 28 Juni, 1919,* etc. Mannheim, 1919.

ZANOLLI-BRANCO (V.) e Andrea CAFFI.—*La pace di Versailles.* Note e documenti, etc. Roma, 1919.

CHAPTER VII

ALTAMIRA (Rafael).—*La Sociedad de las Naciones y el Tribunal permanente de Justicia internacional.* Madrid, 1920.
El proceso ideologico del Proyecto de Tribunal de Justicia Internacional. Madrid, 1920.

BELLOT, HUGH (H. L.).—*Texts Illustrating the Constitution of the Supreme Court of the United States and the Permanent Court of International Justice* (Grotius Society texts, etc. No. 8, London, 1921).

BEVILAQUA (Clovis).—*Projet d'organisation d'une Cour permanente de justice internationale.* Rio de Janeiro, 1921.

Comité consultatif de juristes.—Documents présentés au Comité et relatifs à des projets déjà existants pour l'établissement d'une Cour permanente de justice internationale. La Haye, 1920.

Communiqués officiels du comité consultatif de juristes pour l'institution de la Cour permanente de justice internationale, visée à l'article 14 du pacte de la Société des Nations, réuni au Palais de la Paix, etc.: *Der Völkerbund,* Aug., 1920.

Creating a World Court of Justice.—Journal of the American Bar Association. Sept., 1920.

Cronaca.—*La Società delle Nazione. Per una Corte permanente di Giustizia internazionale. Rivista di diritto internazionale.* Anno VIII, Settembre, 1920.

DELHORBE (Florian).—*La Cour permanente de justice internationale. Mercure de France.* Juillet 15, 1920.

DIENA (Giulio).—*La Cour permanente de justice internationale.* Trad. de G. B. Torino, 1921.

Discours du ministre des Affaires étrangères néerlandais, le Jonkheer Dr. H. A. van Karnebeek, de M. Léon Bourgeois, délégué du Conseil de la Société des Nations, et du baron Descamps, président de la commission, lors de l'installation de la commission des juristes chargés de préparer, etc. *Der Völkerbund,* Juli, 1920. V. *Bulletin de l'Institut intermédiaire international.* Tom. III, octobre, 1920, p. 304.

DUGGANN (Ed.).—*The League of Nations: The Principle and the Practice.* London, 1921.

EYQUEM (D.).—*La Cour de justice internationale. La Paix par le Droit.* Nos. 11-12, novembre, décembre, 1920.

GUTIÉRREZ (Gustavo).—*La Liga de las Naciones. Cuba Contemporanea.* Oct., 1919, p. 151; nov., 1919, p. 289.

HARLEY (J. E.).—*The League of Nations and the New International Law.* London, 1921.

HILL (David J.).—*The Permanent Court of International Justice. American Journal of International Law.* Vol. 14, 1920, p. 387.

La Cour de justice internationale. Communiqué à la presse: 15 Sept., 1920. *Journal du Droit international* (Clunet): juill.-oct., 1920.

La Corte de giustizia internazionale. Vita italiana. Settembre 15, 1920.

LAPRADELLE (A. de).—*Le Retour à La Haye. Vie des Peuples.* Juillet 25, 1920.

LARNAUDE (M. F.).—*La Société des Nations.* Paris, 1920.

LÉMONON (Ernest).—*La Cour permanente de Justice internationale. Journal du Droit international.* Août-oct., 1922.

LIEPMANN (M.).—*Der Friedensverträg und das Völkerbund.* Hamburg, 1920.

MORELLET (J.).—*L'Organisation de la Cour permanente de Justice internationale.* Paris, 1921.

MOORE (John Bassett).—*The Organization of the Permanent Court of International Justice. Columbia Law Review,* June, 1922. See International Conciliation, No. 186, May, 1923, p. 380.

Mr. Root's World Court. Nation (New York). Sept. 25, 1920.

PANNUZIO (Siergio).—*Introduzione alla Società delle Nazione.* Ferrara, 1920.

Permanent Court of International Justice. The Law Times. Vol. 150, No. 13, 1920. No. 4050, p. 293.

PHILLIMORE (Lord).—*An International Criminal Court and the Resolutions of the Committee of Jurists.* British Year Book (1922-23), p. 79. (The second *vœu* of the Committee: High Court of International Justice.)

Rapport présenté sur la Cour permanente de Justice. V. *Annuaire de l'Institut de Droit international.* Session de Rome, 1921, p. 110.

The Permanent court of international justice. Journal of the British Institute of International Affairs. July, 1922.

Procès-verbaux des séances du Comité (Comité consultatif de jurists), 16 juin-24 juillet, 1920, avec annexes. La Haye, 1920. *Publications de la Cour permanente de Justice internationale.*

Resolution concerning the establishment of the Permanent Court of International Justice, passed unanimously by the Assembly of the League of Nations. *American Journal of International Law.* April, 1923.

Revista de Derecho Internacional.—Estatuto y Reglamento del Tribunal Permanente de Justicia Internacional. Tomo II, No. 3, Habana, 1922.

ROOT (Elihu).—*The Permanent Court of International Justice. Journal of the American Bar Association.* December, 1920.

The Constitution of an International Court of Justice. Remarks before the Advisory Committee of Jurists at the Hague. June, 1920. *American Journal of International Law.* January, 1921.

SCOTT (James Brown).—*The Election of Judges for the Permanent Court of International Justice. American Journal of International Law.* October, 1921. p. 556.

The Project of a Permanent Court of International Justice and Resolutions of the Advisory Committee of Jurists. Carnegie Endowment for International Peace. No. 35. Washington, 1920.

A Permanent Court of International Justice. Editorial comments: *American Journal of International Law.* October, 1920.

The Permanent Court of International Justice: Analysis of the project adopted by the Assembly. *American Journal of International Law.* April, 1921.

Société des Nations.—Cour permanente de Justice internationale. Documents relatifs aux mesures prises par le Conseil de la Société des Nations, aux termes de l'article 14 du pacte et à l'adoption par l'Assemblée du statut de la Cour permanente, etc. (16 juin-24 juillet). *Publications de la Société des Nations,* Genève.

Statute for the Permanent Court of International Justice, provided by Article 14 of the Covenant of the League of Nations. *American Journal of International Law. Official documents.* April, 1923.

TAYLE (E.).—*The 14th Point. A Study of the League of Nations.* London, 1919.

Text of Root Plan for Permanent Court of International Justice. Commercial and Financial Chronicle, New York. October, 1920.

The Conference of Jurists at the Hague. The Nation (New York). July 25, 1920.

The World's Most Significant Document. Advocate of Peace. Sept.-Oct., 1920.

The Proposed Court of International Justice. Advocate of Peace. Sept.-Oct., 1920.

The Permanent Court of International Justice. By a late Whewell scholar in international law. *The Covenant.* July, 1920.

The Supreme Court of the World. Advocate of Peace. July, 1920.

The Permanent Court of International Justice. Advocate of Peace, Oct., 1920.

World Peace Foundation: The Permanent Court of International Justice: Protocol of signature, optional clause and Statute, etc. *The League of Nations,* Vol. IV, No. 3, Boston, 1921.

WILSON (G. G.).—*The First Year of the League of Nations.* Boston, 1921.

CHAPTER VIII

BOURGEOIS (Léon).—*L'Œuvre de la Société des Nations* (1920-1923). Paris, 1923.

BUSTAMANTE Y SIRVÉN (Antonio S. de).—*La 2a Conferencia de la Paz, reunida en El Haya en 1907.* Madrid, 1908. 2 vols.
La seconde Conférence de la Paix réunie à La Haye en 1907. Trad. par Georges Scelle. Paris, 1909.

La Cour permanente de Justice internationale. Conférence à l'Académie de Droit international de La Haye le 1ᵉʳ aout, 1923. La Haye, 1923.

Cour permanente de Justice internationale.—Actes et documents relatifs à l'organisation de la Cour. Série D. Leyden, 1921.

Curtiss (W. J.).—*The Permanent Court of International Justice: Its Organization, etc. Journal of the American Bar Association,* March, 1922.

Houston (H. S.).—*The World Court at Work* (with bibliographical sketches of the Judges). *Our World,* New York. September, 1922.

Kamarowsky (Comte de).—*Le Tribunal international.* Trad. de Serge de Westman. Paris, 1887.

League of Nations Association, Japan.—*A propos de l'élection des juges de la Cour permanente de Justice internationale.* Tokyo, 1921.

Permanent Court of International Justice, a Fact. Advocate of Peace, Oct., 1921.

Rougier (Antoine).—*L'Organisation de la Cour permanente de Justice internationale. Revue politique et parlementaire,* 10 août 1921.

Scelle (Georges).—*L'Institution d'une Cour de Justice internationale. Les difficultés. L'Action nationale,* aout, 1920.

Scott (James Brown).—*The Election of Judges for the Permanent Court of International Justice. American Journal of International Law.* Oct., 1921.

Torriente (Cosme de la).—*Cuba, Bustamante y el Tribunal Permanente de Justicia Internacional.* Discurso en la Sociedad Cubana de Derecho Internacional. Habana, 1922.

Cuba, Bustamante and the Permanent Court of International Justice. International Conciliation, No. 178. New York, Sept., 1922.

La Ligas de las Naciones. Trabajos de la 2a Asamblea. Habana, 1922.

The League's Court Started. Literary Digest. Oct. 8, 1921.

The World Court of Justice. Editorial notes. *Illinois Law Review.* November, 1921.

Who's Who of the Permanent Court of International Justice. Headway, Nov., 1921.

Yamada (Dr.).—*Establishment of the Permanent Court of International Justice. Japanese Review of International Law.* Feb.-July, 1922.

CHAPTER IX

Actes et documents relatifs à l'organisation de la Cour. (Cour permanente de Justice internationale.) Série D, No. 2, Leyden, 1922.

BOURQUIN (Maurice).—La Cour de Justice internationale. *Revue de Droit international et de législation comparée.* No. 1-2, 1921.

LODER (B. C. J.).—*La différence entre l'Arbitrage international et la Justice internationale.* Conférence à l'Académie de Droit international de La Haye, 1923.

MANDERE (H. C. G. J.).—*Het permanente hof van internationale justitie te's Gravenhage.* Leyden, 1921.

MORELLET (J.).—*L'Organisation de la Cour permanente de Justice internationale.* Paris, 1921.

Procés-verbaux des séances du Comité (Cour permanente de Justice internationale. Comité consultatif de juristes). 16 juin-24 juillet, 1920. Avec *Annexes.* La Haye, 1920.

SCOTT (James Brown).—*The Permanent Court of International Justice.* Carnegie Endowment for International Peace Year Book, 1921, pp. 104-34, 149-92.

CHAPTER X

BUSTAMANTE Y SIRVÉN (Antonio S. de).—*La Cour permanente de Justice internationale.* Conférence, etc. La Haye, 1923.

MORELLET (J.).—*L'Organisation de la Cour permanente de Justice internationale.* Paris, 1921.

Société des Nations.—Comptes vérifiés pour le quatrième exercice, 1922. *Memorandum du secrètaire général.* Genève, 14 mai 1924.

TORRIENTE (Cosme DE LA).—*La Cuarta Asamblea de la Liga de las Naciones.* Habana, 1923.

The Statesman's Year Book. London, 1924.

CHAPTER XI

BLOCISZEWSKI (J.).—*De la compétence de la Cour permanente de Justice internationale. Revue générale de Droit international public.* Paris, janvier-avril, 1922.

BIBLIOGRAPHY 343

Cour permanente de Justice internationale (Publications de la).— Collection des textes gouvernant la compétence de la Cour. Série D, No. 3. Leyden, 1924.

Cour permanente de Justice internationale (Publications de la).— Actes et documents relatifs à l'organisation de la Cour, etc. Leyden, 1922.

International Law Association. Report of the 31st Conference held at the Palace of Justice, Buenos Aires. London, 1923.

LODER (B. C. J.)—*The Permanent Court of International Justice and Compulsory Jurisdiction.* British Year Book (1921-1922), p. 6.

POLITIS (N.)—*La Justice internationale.* Paris, 1924.

Procès-verbaux des séances du Comité (Comité consultatif des Juristes), etc. La Haye, 1920.

RICHARDS (Sir H. E.).—*The Jurisdiction of the Permanent Court of International Justice.* British Year Book (1921-1922), p. 1.

SALDAÑA (Quintiliano).—*La justicia penal internacional.* Madrid, 1923.

SALVIOLI (Gabriele).—*La Corte permanente de Giustizia internazionale.* Roma, 1924.

CHAPTER XII

Cour permanente de Justice internationale.—Règlement de la Cour. Adopté par la Cour le 24 mars 1922. La Haye, 1922 (and English text).

HAMMARSKJÔLD (A.).—Le réglement de la Cour permanente de Justice internationale. *Revue de Droit international et de Législation comparée.* No. 2-3, 1922.

Institut intermédiaire international.—La Cour permanente de Justice internationale. Statut et règlement. Leyden, 1922.

Revista de Derecho Internacional. Estatuto y Reglamento del Tribunal Permanente de Justicia Internacional. Tomo II, No. 3. Habana, Sept., 1922.

CHAPTER XIII

BUSTAMANTE Y SIRVÉN (Antonio S. de).—*La Cour permanente de Justice internationale.* Conférence, etc. La Haye, 1923.

Can a Court Prevent War? Editorial. The Outlook, February 28, 1923.

344 THE WORLD COURT

FERRERO (G.).—*Discours aux sourds.* Paris, 1924.

HUDSON, MANLEY (O.).—*The Permanent Court of International Justice (Reprinted from Harvard Law Review.* Vol. XXXV, No. 3).

Procés-verbaux des séances du Comité (Comité consultatif de juristes), etc. La Haye, 1920.

WEHBERG (H.).—*The Problem of an International Court of Justice.* Transl. by Charles G. Fenwick. Oxford, 1918.

CHAPTER XIV

Actes et documents relatifs à l'Organisation de la Cour (Publications de la Cour permanente de Justice internationale), etc. Leyden, 1922.

Procès-verbeaux des séances du Comité (Comité consultatif de juristes), etc. La Haye, 1920.

SALVIOLI (Gabriele).—*La Corte Permanente de Giustizia Internationale.* Roma, 1924.

CHAPTER XV

BLUELL (R. L.).—*The World Tribunal in Action. Current History,* December, 1922.

Coleccion de Dictamenes. Revista de Derecho Internacional. Año I, Nos. 3 y siguientes. La Habana, 1922.

Cour permanente de Justice internationale.—Le différend franco-anglais relatif à la nationalité des étrangers en Tunisie et au Maroc. *Journal du Droit international,* janvier-février, 1923.

Cour permanente de Justice internationale.—Avis consultatif No. 4 (13 février 1923). *Revue de Droit international et de législation comparée.* Nos. 2-3, 1923.

Cour permanente de Justice internationale.—Deuxième session extraordinaire. *Journal du Droit international.* Mars-avril, 1923.

DU PREZ (William A.).—*The New Hague Court at Work. Current History,* October, 1922.

DU PUY (W. A.).—*The New Hague Court at Work. Current History,* October, 1922.

FOUQUES DUPARC (J.).—*La Protection des minorités de race, de langue et de religion.* Paris, 1922.

GREGORY (Charles Noble).—*An Important Decision by the Permanent Court of International Justice.* American Journal of International Law. April, 1923.

HMMARSKJÖLD (A.).—*The Early Work of the Permanent Court of International Justice, Harvard Law Review.* April, 1923.

HARRIS, WILSON.—*Nations at Law. Great Britain and France at The Hague.* Société des Nations, janvier-février, 1923.

HUDSON, MANLEY (O.).—*The First Year of the Permanent Court of International Justice.* American Journal of International Law. January, 1923.
The Work and the Jurisdiction of the Permanent Court of International Justice. Proceedings of the Academy of Political and Social Science, July, 1923.
Les décrets de nationalité devant la Cour permanente de Justice internationale. Afrique Française, supplément de mars 1923.
Les décrets du 8 novembre 1921 sur la nationalité d'origine en Tunisie et au Maroc (zone française) devant la Cour permanente de Justice internationale. Revue de Droit international privé. No. 1, 1922-1923.

MAHAIM (E.).—*Les avis de la Cour permanente de Justice internationale au sujet de l'interprétation de certains articles de la partie XIII du Traité de Versailles.* Revue de Droit international et législation comparée, Nos. 5-6, 1922.
Nationality Decrees and the International Court. Law Journal. Febr. 29, 1923.

PICARD (Maurice)—*Le différend franco-anglais relatif aux décrets du 8 novembre 1921 sur la nationalité d'origine en Tunisie et au Maroc devant la Cour permanente de Justice internationale de la Haye.* Journal du droit international, mars-avril, 1923.
Publications de la Cour permanente de Justice internationale, Recueil des Avis consultatifs. Série B. Nos. 1, 2, 3, Leyden, 1922. Nos. 4, 5, 6, 7, 8, Leyden, 1923. No. 9, Leyden, 1924.
Publications de la Cour permanente de Justice internationale.—Recueil des Arrêts. Série A. No. 1, Leyden, 1923. Nos. 2 et 3, Leyden, 1924.

SCOTT (James Brown).—*Sovereign States before Arbitral Tribunals and Courts of Justice.* Six lectures delivered at New York University. New York, 1924.
The Permanent Court of International Justice. Carnegie Endowment for International Peace Year Book, 1922, pp. 152-157.
The Permanent Court of International Justice at Work. Advocate of Peace, November, 1922.

TUMEDEI (Cesare).—*La Corte dell' Aja e la nazionalita in Tunisia. Politica,* 31 Marzo, 1923.

VINEUIL (Paul de).—*Les Leçons du quatrième avis consultatif de la Cour permanente de Justice internationale. Revue de Droit international et de législation comparée.* Nos. 2-3, 1923.

VINEUIL (Paul de).—*L'Affaire de la Jaworzina devant la Cour permanente de Justice internationale. Revue de Droit international et de législation comparée.* Nos. 1-2, 1924.

CHAPTER XVI

A Court of International Justice. Advocate of Peace, May, 1923.

A Typical American Utterance. National Review, August, 1923.

America, United States of.—Department of State: International Court of Justice at the Hague—a letter from the Secretary of State relative to the proposed adherence to the Protocol establishing an international Court of Justice at The Hague. Washington, D. C., 1923. See Congressional Record, 67th Congress, Vol. 64.

America, United States of.—President Harding, 1921. Permanent Court of International Justice. Message—transmitting a letter from the Secretary of State and asking the consent of the Senate to the adhesion of the United States to the protocol. Washington, 1923. Letter of the President to the Foreign Relations Committee. March 2, 1923. Congressional Record, 67th Congress, Vol. 64.

BORCHARD (E. M.).—*Limitations on the Functions of International Courts. Annals of the Academy of Political and Social Science.* July, 1921.
The Permanent Court of International Justice. North American Review, July, 1923.

BORCHARD (E. M.). and MANLEY O. HUDSON.—*The International Court. Addresses delivered on December 29, 1923.* Chicago, 1923.

BOREL (Eugène).—*The United States and the Permanent Court of International Justice. American Journal of International Law.* July, 1923.

Bringing America to the International Court. Advocate of Peace. May, 1923.

BROWN (Philip Marshall).—*The Classification of Justiciable Disputes. American Journal of International Law.* April, 1922.

BUTLER (Nicholas Murray).—*The International Court Favors Our Joining It.* Letter to *The New York Herald.* Congressional Record (daily ed.). March 2, 1923, p. 5190.

Consensus (The).—*The Vote of the National Council of the National Economical League on the World Court.* Boston, 1924.

CHARTERIS (A. H.).—*The Permanent Court of International Justice. New Outlook.* June 9, 1923.

DAVIS (John W.).—*International Justice. Journal of the American Bar Association.* Feb., 1922.

Drei Spurche des städigen internationalen Gerichtshofs. Niemeyer Zeitschrift internationales recht. Heft 5-6, 1923.

FENWICK (Charles G.).—*Law the Prerequisite of an International Court. Annals of the Academy of Political and Social Science.* July, 1921.

FINCH (George A.)—*The United States and the Permanent Court of International Justice. American Journal of International Law.* July, 1923.

FOREIGN POLICY ASSOCIATION (New York).—*The Permanent Court of International Justice. New Bulletin,* March 2 and 16, 1923.

FRIERSON (William).—*The Permanent Court of International Justice.* Address delivered before the Maryland State Bar Association, June 29, 1922. Congressional Record, March 10, 1923 (daily ed.), p. 5583.

HAMMOND (J. H.).—*A World Court. Annals of the Academy of Political and Social Science.* July, 1921.

HARD (William).—*The Borah Court versus The Root Court. The Nation.* May 2, 1923.

HUDSON (Manley O.).—*The United States and the New International Court.* New York, 1922.

The United States and the International Court. Advocating participation in the Court, Manley O. Hudson: opposing participation in the Court, William E. Borah. Chicago, 1923.

The First Year of the Permanent Court of International Justice. American Journal of International Law, January, 1923.

The Second Year of the Permanent Court of International Justice. American Journal of International Law. January, 1924.

A Challenge to American Lawyers. Journal of the American Bar Association. February, 1922.

The Permanent Court of International Justice. Advocate of Peace. January, 1923.

Shall America Support the New World Court? *Atlantic Monthly.* January, 1823.

The Problem of the International Court Today. An address before the Missouri Bar Association, Dec. 14, 1923.

The Work of the Permanent Court of Justice during its first two years, World Peace Foundation, Vol. IV, No. 6, 1923.

The Permanent Court of International Justice, An Indispensable Step. Annals of the Academy of Political and Social Science. July, 1923.

HUGHES (Charles Evans).—*The Permanent Court of International Justice.* Proceedings of the Academy of Political and Social Science. July, 1923.

JOHNSON (W. Fletcher).—*The Story of the World Court. The Outlook.* Aug. 1, 1923.

JOHNSON (Hiram).—*Splendid Isolation for the United States. National Review.* Sept., 1923.

La Corte Permanente di giustizia internazionale. Vita internazionale, 30 Maggio, 1922.

LAPREDELLE (A. de).—*La nouvelle Cour de Justice internationale. Vie des Peuples.* 10 mars, 1922.

LATEY (William).—*The Court of International Justice. Journal of comparative legislation and international law.* February, 1922.

League of Nations.—Former Justice John H. Clarke; W. G. Harding, The President and the Court; Herbert Hoover, America's Next Step; Edward M. House, The Running Sands; Charles E. Hughes, The Secretary and the Critics; Elihu Root, Elihu Root and the Court. World Peace Foundation, 6, No. 1.

Let us join the World Court, Editorial, *Nation,* New York, March 7, 1923.

MACNAIR (H. F.).—*The United States and the Permanent Court of International Justice. Weekly Review.* May 19, 1923.

MILLS, OGDEN (L.).—*The Relation of the United States to the Permanent Court of International Justice.* Proceedings of the Academy of Political and Social Science. July, 1923.

New York State Bar Association.—Report of Committee on International Arbitration. Presented at the 46th annual meeting. New York, 1923.

Our Administration's Proposal on the Permanent Court (basic documents). The President's Message: Secretary Hughes's letter, etc. *Advocate of Peace.* March, 1923.

PACIFICUS.—L'œuvre de la Société des Nations: l'œuvre juridique. *Grande Revue,* février, 1922.

PEPPER (George W.).—*The Permanent Court of International Justice.* Proceedings of the Academy of Political and Social Science. July, 1923.

President Harding and the Permanent Court of International Justice. The Economist. March 3, 1923.

President Harding and the Permanent Court of International Justice. Advocate of Peace. August, 1923.

President Harding's Plea for the World Court, Current History. April, 1923.

President Harding Reiterates Stand of United States against League of Nations: renews plea for joining of World Court. *Commercial and Financial Chronicle.* New York. April, 1923.

Protocol of signature and statute establishing the Permanent Court of International Justice. International Conciliation, No. 186. May, 1923.

Quinta Conferencia Internacional Americana. Programa, Actas. Santiago de Chile, 1923.

Quinta Conferencia Internacional Americana. Hacia la Solidaridad Americana, por Samuel Guy Inman. Madrid, 1924.

Quinta Conferencia Internacional Americana. Revista de Derecho Internacional. No. 9, Tomo V, 31 Marzo, 1924. Habana.

RALSTON (J. H.).—*The Limitations of Courts. Advocate of Peace.* March, 1922.

ROOT (Elihu).—*The Law of an Unruly World. Advocate of Peace.* February, 1921.

RUFFIN (Henry).—*Coup d'œil sur la Cour permanente de Justice internationale, L'Europe nouvelle,* 25 février, 1922.

Senator Borah and the World Court.—Our World, August, 1923.

SHEPPARD (Morris).—*The Permanent Court of International Justice.—Congressional Record* (daily ed.). February 25, 1923, p. 4631.

SHIELDS (John K.).—*The International Court.* Address delivered in the Senate, March 3, 1923. *Congressional Record* (daily ed.), March 10, 1923, p. 5581.

Starting the Fight to Join the Peace Court. Literary Digest, March 10, 1923.

Statements by President Harding, Mr. Hughes, Mr. Root and Mr. Hoover with regard to the adherence of the United States to the Protocol. International Conciliation. No. 186, May, 1923.

The United States and the World Court. Editorial, *World's Work.* April, 1923.

The Tribunal of the World. Advocate of Peace. February, 1922.

The United States and the International Court of Justice. Advocate of Peace, March, 1923.

TORRIENTE (Cosme DE LA).—*Labor internacional.* Habana, 1924.

TOWNER (Horace M.).—*The Permanent Court of International Justice.* Address in the Senate, March 4, 1923. *Congressional Record* (daily ed.), March 15, 1923, p. 5815.

U. S. Congress.—*Senator Lodge's Joint Resolution.* 68th Congress. May 5-8, 1924.

WEHBERG (Hans).—*L'Amérique et la Cour permanente de Justice internationale. Revue de Droit international et de législation comparée.* Nos. 23, 1923.

OTHER RECENT WORKS

AMERIKA UND DER VÖLKERBUND.—*Die Frieden Warte.* Mârz, 1923, p. 73.

BARKER (Ernest).—*A Confederation of the Nations: Its Powers and Constitution.* Oxford, 1918.

BELLOT, HUGH (H. L.).—*Colons allemands en Pologne. Journal du Droit international* (Clunet). Mars-avril, 1924, p. 321.

BERRY (T. T.).—*The Hope of the World. An Appreciation of the League of Nations Scheme.* London, 1919.

ERZBERGER (Matthias).—*Der Völkerbund. Der Weg zum Weltfrieden.* Berlin, 1918.

GUGGENHEIM (Paul).—*Das Gutachten des Haager Gerichtshofes über die Rechte deutscher Ansiedler in Posen.* Die Frieden Warte. Jan.-März, 1924.

HOBSON (J. A.).—*Towards International Government.* London, 1915.

HUDSON (Manley O.).—The Permanent Court of International Justice and World Peace. *The Annals of the Academy of Social and Political Science.* July, 1924.
Advisory Opinions of National and International Courts. Cambridge, 1924.

HUGHES (Charles E.).—*The Permanent Court of International Justice. American Society of International Law.* Proceedings, 1923.

HYDE (H. E.).—*The International Solution.* London, 1907.

LAWRENCE (T. J.).—*Lectures on the League of Nations, delivered at the University of Bristol.* London, 1919.

LISZT (Franz V.).—*Von Staatenverband zur Völkergemeinschaft,* etc. München u. Berlin, 1917.

MOORE (John Bassett).—*International Law and Some Current Illusions, and other essays.* New York, 1924.

OPPENHEIM (L.).—*The League of Nations and its Problems.* 3 lectures. London, 1919.

Our Country and the World Court.—Advocate of Peace. No. 6. June, 1924.

PAULUS (J.).—*La revision du pacte de la Société des Nations. Revue générale de Droit international public.* Nov.-déc., 1923, p. 525.

PICCIONI (G.).—*La sanction militaire des décisions de la Société des Nations. Revue générale de Droit international public.* Nos. 3-4, 1923, p. 242.

PRESIDENT COOLIDGE.—On World Peace.—International documents. *Advocate of Peace.* No. 6. June, 1924.

ROOT (Elihu).—*The Permanent Court of International Justice.* Proceedings of the American Society of International Law, 1923, p. 1.

SCELLE (Georges).—*Le Pacte des Nations et sa liaison avec le Traité de Paix.* Préface de Léon Bourgeois. Paris, 1919. Extrait de l'origine et l'œuvre de la Société des Nations. Copenhagen, 1924.

SCHÜCKING (Walter).—*Kommentar zum Friedenvertrage,* etc. Berlin, 1920.

Sociedad Cubana de Derecho Internacional. Añuarios de la 5a, 6a, y 7a Reunión añual. Habana, 1922, 1923, 1924.

Société des Nations.—Actes de la première assemblée. *Séances plénières.* Genève, 1920.

Société des Nations.—Actes de la deuxième assemblée. Genève, 1921.

VÖLLMAR (H. F. A.).—*Les finances de la Société des Nations.* La Haye, 1924.

WEHBERG (Hans).—*Die internationale Gerechtigkeit. Die Frieden Warte.* Nov.-Dec., 1923, p. 389.

WITHERS (Hartley).—*The League of Nations; Its Economical Aspect.* London, 1918.

WLASSICS (Baron Jules).—*Deux avis de la Cour permanente de Justice internationale de La Haye. Revue de Hongrie.* 15 mars, 1924, p. 97.

WOODBURY (Gordon).—*The Permanent Court of International Justice in Relation to American Tradition.* Proceedings of the American Academy of Political and Social Science. Philadelphia, 1923.

THE STATUTE

For the Permanent Court of International Justice provided for by Article 14 of the Covenant of the League of Nations

ARTICLE 1. A Permanent Court of International Justice is hereby established, in accordance with Article 14 of the Covenant of the League of Nations. This Court shall be in addition to the Court of Arbitration organized by the Conventions of The Hague of 1899 and 1907, and to the special Tribunals of Arbitration to which States are always at liberty to submit their disputes for settlement.

CHAPTER I

ORGANIZATION OF THE COURT

ART. 2. The Permanent Court of International Justice shall be composed of a body of independent judges, elected regardless of their nationality from among persons of high moral character, who possess the qualifications required in their respective countries for appointment to the highest judicial offices, or are jurisconsults of recognized competence in international law.

ART. 3. The Court shall consist of fifteen members: eleven judges and four deputy-judges. The number of judges and deputy-judges may hereafter be increased by the Assembly, upon the proposal of the Council of the League of Nations, to a total of fifteen judges and six deputy-judges.

ART. 4. The members of the Court shall be elected by the Assembly and by the Council from a list of persons nominated by the national groups in the Court of Arbitration, in accordance with the following provisions.

In the case of Members of the League of Nations not represented in the Permanent Court of Arbitration, the lists of candidates shall be drawn up by national groups appointed for this purpose by their Governments under the same conditions as those prescribed for members of the Permanent Court of Arbitration by Article 44 of the Convention of The Hague of 1907 for the pacific settlement of international disputes.

ART. 5. At least three months before the date of the election, the Secretary-General of the League of Nations shall address a written request to the Members of the Court of Arbitration belonging to the States mentioned in the Annex to the Covenant or to the States which join the League subsequently, and to the persons appointed under paragraph 2 of Article 4, inviting them to undertake, within a given time, by national groups, the nomination of persons in a position to accept the duties of a member of the Court.

No group may nominate more than four persons, not more than two of whom shall be of their own nationality. In no case must the number of candidates nominated be more than double the number of seats to be filled.

ART. 6. Before making these nominations, each national group is recommended to consult its Highest Court of Justice, its Legal Faculties and Schools of Law, and its National Academies and national sections of International Academies devoted to the study of Law.

ART. 7. The Secretary-General of the League of Nations shall prepare a list in alphabetical order of all the persons thus nominated. Save as provided in Article 12, paragraph 2, these shall be the only persons eligible for appointment.

The Secretary-General shall submit this list to the Assembly and to the Council.

ART. 8. The Assembly and the Council shall proceed independently of one another to elect, firstly the judges, then the deputy-judges.

ART. 9. At every election, the electors shall bear in mind that not only should all the persons appointed as members of the Court possess the qualifications required, but the whole body also should represent the main forms of civilization and the principal legal systems of the world.

ART. 10. Those candidates who obtain an absolute majority of votes in the Assembly and in the Council shall be considered as elected.

In the event of more than one national of the same Member of the League being elected by the votes of both the Assembly and the Council, the eldest of these only shall be considered as elected.

ART. 11. If, after the first meeting held for the purpose of the election, one or more seats remain to be filled, a second and, if necessary, a third meeting shall take place.

ART. 12. If, after the third meeting, one or more seats still remain unfilled, a joint conference consisting of six members, three appointed by the Assembly and three by the Council, may be formed, at any time, at the request of either the Assembly or the Council, for the purpose of choosing one name for each seat still vacant, to submit to the Assembly and the Council for their respective acceptance.

If the Conference is unanimously agreed upon any person who fulfils the required conditions, he may be included in its list, even though he was not included in the list of nominations referred to in Article 4 and 5.

If the joint conference is satisfied that it will not be successful in procuring an election, those members of the Court who have already been appointed shall, within a period to be fixed by the Council, proceed to fill the vacant seats by selection from among those candidates who have obtained votes either in the Assembly or in the Council.

In the event of an equality of votes among the judges, the eldest judge shall have a casting vote.

Art. 13. The members of the Court shall be elected for nine years.

They may be re-elected.

They shall continue to discharge their duties until their places have been filled. Though replaced, they shall finish any cases which they may have begun.

Art. 14. Vacancies which may occur shall be filled by the same method as that laid down for the first election. A member of the Court elected to replace a member whose period of appointment had not expired will hold the appointment for the remainder of his predecessor's term.

Art. 15. Deputy-judges shall be called upon to sit in the order laid down in a list.

This list shall be prepared by the Court and shall have regard firstly to priority of election and secondly to age.

Art. 16. The ordinary Members of the Court may not exercise any political or administrative function. This provision does not apply to the deputy-judges except when performing their duties on the Court.

Any doubt on this point is settled by the decision of the Court.

Art. 17. No Member of the Court can act as agent, counsel or advocate in any case of an international nature. This provision only applies to the deputy-judges as regards cases in which they are called upon to exercise their functions on the Court.

No Member may participate in the decision of any case in which he has previously taken an active part, as agent, counsel or advocate for one of the contesting parties, or as a Member of a national or international Court, or of a Commission of inquiry, or in any other capacity.

Any doubt on this point is settled by the decision of the Court.

ART. 18. A member of the Court can not be dismissed unless, in the unanimous opinion of the other members, he has ceased to fulfill the required conditions.

Formal notification thereof shall be made to the Secretary-General of the League of Nations, by the Registrar.

This notification makes the place vacant.

ART. 19. The members of the Court, when engaged on the business of the Court, shall enjoy diplomatic privileges and immunities.

ART. 20. Every member of the Court shall, before taking up his duties, make a solemn declaration in open Court that he will exercise his powers impartially and conscientiously.

ART. 21. The Court shall elect its President and Vice-President for three years; they may be re-elected.

It shall appoint its Registrar.

The duties of Registrar of the Court shall not be deemed incompatible with those of Secretary-General of the Permanent Court of Arbitration.

ART. 22. The seat of the Court shall be established at The Hague.

The President and Registrar shall reside at the seat of the Court.

ART. 23. A session of the Court shall be held every year.

Unless otherwise provided by rules of Court, this session shall begin on the 15th of June, and shall continue for so long as may be deemed necessary to finish the cases on the list.

The President may summon an extraordinary session of the Court whenever necessary.

ART. 24. If, for some special reason, a member of the Court considers that he should not take part in the decision of a particular case, he shall so inform the President.

If the President considers that for some special reason one of the members of the Court should not sit on a particular case, he shall give him notice accordingly.

If in any such case the member of the Court and the President disagree, the matter shall be settled by the decision of the Court.

ART. 25. The full Court shall sit except when it is expressly provided otherwise.

If eleven judges can not be present, the number shall be made up by calling on deputy-judges to sit.

If, however, eleven judges are not available, a quorum of nine judges shall suffice to constitute the Court.

ART. 26. Labor cases, particularly cases referred to in Part XIII (Labor) of the Treaty of Versailles and the corresponding portion of the other Treaties of Peace, shall be heard and determined by the Court under the following conditions:

The Court will appoint every three years a special chamber of five judges, selected so far as possible with due regard to the provisions of Article 9. In addition, two judges shall be selected for the purpose of replacing a judge who finds it impossible to sit. If the parties so demand, cases will be heard and determined by this chamber. In the absence of any such demand, the Court will sit with the number of judges provided for in Article 25. On all occasions the judges will be assisted by four technical assessors sitting with them, but without the right to vote, and chosen with a view to insuring a just representation of the competing interests.

If there is a national of one only of the parties sitting as a judge in the chamber referred to in the preceding paragraph, the President will invite one of the other judges to retire in favor of a judge chosen by the other party in accordance with Article 31.

The technical assessors shall be chosen for each particular case in accordance with rules of procedure under Article 30 from a list of "Assessors for Labor cases" composed of two persons nominated by each Member of the League of Nations and an equivalent number nominated by the Governing Body of the Labor Office. The Governing Body will nominate, as to one half, representatives of the workers, and as to one half, representatives of employers from the list referred to in Article 412 of the Treaty of Versailles and the corresponding Articles of the other Treaties of Peace.

In Labor cases the International Labor Office shall be at liberty to furnish the Court with all relevant information, and for this purpose the Director of that Office shall receive copies of all the written proceedings.

ART. 27. Cases relating to transit and communications, particularly cases referred to in Part XII (Ports, Waterways and Railways) of the Treaty of Versailles and the corresponding portions of the other Treaties of Peace shall be heard and determined by the Court under the following conditions:

The Court will appoint every three years a special chamber of five judges, selected so far as possible with due regard to the provisions of Article 9. In addition, two judges shall be selected for the purpose of replacing a judge who finds it impossible to sit. If the parties so demand, cases will be heard and determined by this chamber. In the absence of any such demand, the Court will sit with the number of judges provided for in Article 25. When desired by the parties or decided by the Court, the judges will be assisted by four technical assessors sitting with them, but without the right to vote.

If there is a national of one only of the parties sitting as a judge in the chamber referred to in the preceding paragraph, the President will invite one of the other judges to retire in favor of a judge chosen by the other party in accordance with Article 31.

The technical assessors shall be chosen for each particular case in accordance with rules of procedure under Article 30 from a list of "Assessors for Transit and Communications cases" composed of two persons nominated by each Member of the League of Nations.

ART. 28. The special chambers provided for in Article 26 and 27 may, with the consent of the parties to the dispute, sit elsewhere than at The Hague.

ART. 29. With a view to the speedy dispatch of business, the Court shall form annually a chamber composed of three judges who, at the request of the contesting parties, may hear and determine cases by summary procedure.

ART. 30. The Court shall frame rules for regulating its procedure. In particular, it shall lay down rules for summary procedure.

ART. 31. Judges of the nationality of each contesting party shall retain their right to sit in the case before the Court.

If the Court includes upon the Bench a judge of the nationality of one of the parties only, the other party may select from among the deputy-judges a judge of its nationality, if there be one. If there should not be one, the party may choose a judge, preferably from among those persons who have been nominated as candidates as provided in Articles 4 and 5.

If the Court includes upon the Bench no judge of the nationality of the contesting parties, each of these may proceed to select or choose a judge as provided in the preceeding paragraph.

Should there be several parties in the same interest, they shall, for the purpose of the preceding provisions, be reckoned as one party only. Any doubt upon this point is settled by the decision of the Court.

Judges selected or chosen as laid down in paragraphs 2 and 3 of this Article shall fulfil the conditions required by Articles 2, 16, 17, 20, 24 of this Statute. They shall take part in the decision on an equal footing with their colleagues.

ART. 32. The judges shall receive an annual indemnity to be determined by the Assembly of the League of Nations upon the proposal of the Council. This indemnity must not be decreased during the period of a judge's appointment.

The President shall receive a special grant for his period of office, to be fixed in the same way.

The Vice-President, judges and deputy-judges shall receive a grant for the actual performance of their duties, to be fixed in the same way.

Traveling expenses incurred in the performance of their duties shall be refunded to judges and deputy-judges who do not reside at the seat of the Court.

Grants due to judges selected or chosen as provided in Article 31 shall be determined in the same way.

The salary of the Registrar shall be decided by the Council upon the proposal of the Court.

The Assembly of the League of Nations shall lay down, on the proposal of the Council, a special regulation fixing the conditions under which retiring pensions may be given to the personnel of the Court.

ART. 33. The expenses of the Court shall be borne by the League of Nations, in such a manner as shall be decided by the Assembly upon the proposal of the Council.

CHAPTER II

COMPETENCE OF THE COURT

ART. 34. Only States or Members of the League of Nations can be parties in cases before the Court.

ART. 35. The Court shall be open to the Members of the League and also to States mentioned in the Annex to the Covenant.

The conditions under which the Court shall be open to other States shall, subject to the special provisions contained in treaties in force, be laid down by the Council, but in no case shall such provisions place the parties in a position of inequality before the Court.

When a State which is not a Member of the League of Nations is a party to a dispute, the Court will fix the amount which that party is to contribute toward the expenses of the Court.

ART. 36. The jurisdiction of the Court comprises all cases which the parties refer to it and all matters specially provided for in Treaties and Conventions in force.

The Members of the League of Nations and the States mentioned in the Annex to the Covenant may, either when signing or ratifying the protocol to which the present Statute is adjoined, or at a later moment, declare that they recognize as compulsory, *ipso facto* and without special agreement, in relation to any other Member or State accepting the same obligation, the jurisdiction of the Court in all or any of the classes of legal disputes concerning:

(*a.*) The interpretation of a Treaty.

(*b.*) Any question of International Law.

(*c.*) The existence of any fact which, if established, would constitute a breach of an international obligation.

(*d.*) The nature or extent of the reparation to be made for the breach of an international obligation.

The declaration referred to above may be made unconditionally or on condition of reciprocity on the part of several or certain Members or States, or for a certain time.

In the event of a dispute as to whether the Court has jurisdiction, the matter shall be settled by the decision of the Court.

ART. 37. When a treaty or convention in force provides for the reference of a matter to a tribunal to be instituted by the League of Nations, the Court will be such tribunal.

ART. 38. The Court shall apply:

1. International conventions, whether general or particular, establishing rules expressly recognized by the contesting States;

2. International custom, as evidence of a general practice accepted as law;

3. The general principles of law recognized by civilized nations;

4. Subject to the provisions of Article 59, judicial decisions and the teachings of the most highly qualified publicists of the various nations, as subsidiary means for the determination of rules of law.

This provision shall not prejudice the power of the Court to decide a case *ex aequo et bono,* if the parties agree thereto.

CHAPTER III

PROCEDURE

ART. 39. The official languages of the Court shall be French and English. If the parties agree that the case shall be conducted in French, the judgment will be delivered in French. If the parties agree that the case shall be conducted in English, the judgment will be delivered in English.

In the absence of an agreement as to which language shall be employed, each party may, in the pleadings, use the language which it prefers; the decision of the Court will be given in French and English. In this case the Court will at the same time determine which of the two texts shall be considered as authoritative.

The Court may, at the request of the parties, authorize a language other than French or English to be used.

ART. 40. Cases are brought before the Court, as the case may be, either by the notification of the special agreement or by a written application addressed to the Registrar. In either case the subject of the dispute and the contesting parties must be indicated.

The Registrar shall forthwith communicate the application to all concerned.

He shall also notify the Members of the League of Nations through the Secretary-General.

ART. 41. The Court shall have the power to indicate, if it considers that circumstances so require, any provisional measures which ought to be taken to preserve the respective rights of either party.

Pending the final decision, notice of the measures suggested shall forthwith be given to the parties and the Council.

ART. 42. The parties shall be represented by Agents.

They may have the assistance of Counsel or Advocates before the Court.

ART. 43. The procedure shall consist of two parts: written and oral.

The written proceedings shall consist of the communication to the judges and to the parties of cases, counter-cases and, if necessary, replies; also all papers and documents in support.

These communications shall be made through the Registrar, in the order and within the time fixed by the Court.

A certified copy of every document produced by one party shall be communicated to the other party.

The oral proceedings shall consist of the hearing by the Court of witnesses, experts, agents, counsel and advocates.

ART. 44. For the service of all notices upon persons other than the agents, counsel and advocates, the Court shall apply direct to the Government of the State upon whose territory the notice has to be served.

The same provision shall apply whenever steps are to be taken to procure evidence on the spot.

ART. 45. The hearing shall be under the control of the President or, in his absence, of the Vice-President; if both are absent, the senior judge shall preside.

ART. 46. The hearing in Court shall be public, unless the Court shall decide otherwise, or unless the parties demand that the public be not admitted.

ART. 47. Minutes shall be made at each hearing, and signed by the Registrar and the President.

These minutes shall be the only authentic record.

ART. 48. The Court shall make orders for the conduct of the case, shall decide the form and time in which each party must conclude its arguments, and make all arrangements connected with the taking of evidence.

ART. 49. The Court may, even before the hearing begins, call upon the agents to produce any document or to supply any explanations. Formal note shall be taken of any refusal.

ART. 50. The Court may, at any time, intrust any individual, body, bureau, commission or other organization that it may select, with the task of carrying out an inquiry or giving an expert opinion.

ART. 51. During the hearing any relevant questions are to be put to the witnesses and experts under the conditions laid down by the Court in the rules of procedure referred to in Article 30.

ART. 52. After the Court has received the proofs and evidence within the time specified for the purpose, it may refuse to accept any further oral or written evidence that one party may desire to present unless the other side consents.

ART. 53. Whenever one of the parties shall not appear before the Court, or shall fail to defend his case, the other party may call upon the Court to decide in favor of his claim.

The Court must, before doing so, satisfy itself, not only that it has jurisdiction in accordance with Articles 36 and 37, but also that the claim is well founded in fact and law.

ART. 54. When, subject to the control of the Court, the agents, advocates and counsel have completed their presentation of the case, the President shall declare the hearing closed.

The Court shall withdraw to consider the judgment.

The deliberations of the Court shall take place in private and remain secret.

ART. 55. All questions shall be decided by a majority of the judges present at the hearing.

In the event of an equality of votes, the President or his deputy shall have a casting vote.

ART. 56. The judgment shall state the reasons on which it is based.

It shall contain the names of the judges who have taken part in the decision.

ART. 57. If the judgment does not represent in whole or in part the unanimous opinion of the judges, dissenting judges are entitled to deliver a separate opinion.

ART. 58. The judgment shall be signed by the President and by the Registrar. It shall be read in open Court, due notice having been given to the agents.

ART. 59. The decision of the Court has no binding force except between the parties and in respect of that particular case.

ART. 60. The judgment is final and without appeal. In the event of dispute as to the meaning or scope of the judgment, the Court shall construe it upon the request of any party.

ART. 61. An application for revision of a judgment can be made only when it is based upon the discovery of some fact of such a nature as to be a decisive factor, which fact was, when the judgment was given, unknown to the Court and also to the party claiming revision, always provided that such ignorance was not due to negligence.

The proceedings for revision will be opened by a judgment of the Court expressly recording the existence of the new fact, recognizing that it has such a character as to lay the case open to revision, and declaring the application admissible on this ground.

The Court may require previous compliance with the terms of the judgment before it admits proceedings in revision.

The application for revision must be made at latest within six months of the discovery of the new fact.

No application for revision may be made after the lapse of ten years from the date of the sentence.

ART. 62. Should a State consider that it has an interest of a legal nature which may be affected by the decision in the case, it may submit a request to the Court to be permitted to intervene as a third party.

It will be for the Court to decide upon this request.

ART. 63. Whenever the construction of a convention to which States other than those concerned in the case are parties is in question, the Registrar shall notify all such States forthwith.

Every State so notified has the right to intervene in the proceedings; but if it uses this right, the construction given by the judgment will be equally binding upon it.

ART. 64. Unless otherwise decided by the Court, each party shall bear its own costs.

RULES OF COURT

PREAMBLE

The Court
By virtue of Article 30 of Its Statute
Adopts the Present Rules:

CHAPTER I

THE COURT

HEADING 1.—*Constitution of the Court.*

SECTION A.—*Judges and Assessors.*

ARTICLE 1. Subject to the provisions of Article 14 of the Statute, the term of office of judges and deputy-judges shall commence on January 1st of the year following their election.

ART. 2. Judges and deputy-judges elected at an earlier session of the Assembly and of the Council of the League of Nations shall take precedence respectively over judges and deputy-judges elected at a subsequent session. Judges and deputy-judges elected during the same session shall take precedence according to age. Judges shall take precedence over deputy-judges.

National judges chosen from outside the Court, under the terms of Article 31 of the Statute, shall take precedence after deputy-judges in order of age.

The list of deputy-judges shall be prepared in accordance with these principles.

The Vice-President shall take his seat on the right of the President. The other Members of the Court shall take their seats to the right and left of the President in the order laid down above.

ART. 3. Deputy-judges whose presence is necessary shall be summoned in the order laid down in the list referred to in the preceding Article, that is to say, each of them will be summoned in rotation throughout the list.

Should a deputy-judge be so far from the seat of the Court that, in the opinion of the President, a summons would not reach him in sufficient time, the deputy-judge next on the list shall be summoned; nevertheless, the judge to whom the summons should have been addressed shall be called upon, if possible, on the next occasion that the presence of a deputy-judge is required.

A deputy-judge who has begun a case shall be summoned again, if necessary out of his turn, in order to continue to sit in the case until it is finished.

Should a deputy-judge be summoned to take his seat in a particular case as a national judge, under the terms of Article 31 of the Statute, such summons shall not be regarded as coming within the terms of the present Article.

ART. 4. In cases in which one or more parties are entitled to choose a judge *ad hoc* of their nationality, the full Court may sit with a number of judges exceeding eleven.

When the Court has satisfied itself, in accordance with Article 31 of the Statute, that there are several parties in the same interest and that none of them has a judge of its nationality upon the bench, the Court shall invite them, within a period to be fixed by the Court, to select by common agreement a deputy-judge of the nationality of one of the parties, should there be one; or should there not be one, a judge chosen in accordance with the principles of the above-mentioned Article.

Should the parties have failed to notify the Court of their selection or choice when the time limit expires, they shall be regarded as having renounced the right conferred upon them by Article 31.

ART. 5. Before entering upon his duties, each member of the Court, under the terms of Article 31 of the Statute, shall make the following solemn declaration in accordance with Article 20 of the Statute:

"I solemnly declare that I will exercise all my powers and duties as a judge honourably and faithfully, impartially and conscientiously."

A special public sitting of the Court may, if necessary, be convened for this purpose.

At the public inaugural sitting held after a new election of the whole Court the required declaration shall be made first by the President, secondly by the Vice-President, and then by the remaining judges in the order laid down in Article 2.

ART. 6. For the purpose of applying Article 18 of the Statute, the President, or if necessary the Vice-President, shall convene the judges and deputy-judges. The member affected shall be allowed to furnish explanations. When he has done so the question shall be discussed and a vote shall be taken, the member in question not being present. If the members present are unanimously agreed, the

Registrar shall issue the notification prescribed in the above mentioned Article.

ART. 7. The President shall take steps to obtain all information which may be helpful to the Court in selecting technical assessors in each case. With regard to the question referred to in Article 26 of the Statute, he shall, in particular, consult the Governing Body of the International Labour Office.

The assessors shall be appointed by an absolute majority of votes, either by the Court or by the special Chamber which has to deal with the case in question.

ART. 8. Assessors shall make the following solemn declaration at the first sitting of the Court at which they are present:

"I solemnly declare that I will exercise all my powers and duties as an assessor honourably and faithfully, impartially and conscientiously, and that I will scrupulously observe all the provisions of the Statute and of the Rules of Court."

SECTION B.—*The Presidency.*

ART. 9. The election of the President and Vice-President shall take place at the end of the ordinary session immediately before the normal termination of the period of office of the retiring President and Vice-President.

After a new election of the whole Court, the election of the President and Vice-President shall take place at the commencement of the following session. The President and Vice-President elected in these circumstances shall take up their duties on the day of their election. They shall remain in office until the end of the second year after the year of their election.

Should the President or the Vice-President cease to belong to the Court before the expiration of their normal term of office, an election shall be held for the purpose of appointing a substitute for the unexpired portion of their term of office. If necessary, an extraordinary session of the Court may be convened for this purpose.

The elections referred to in the present Article shall take place by secret ballot. The candidate obtaining an absolute majority of votes shall be declared elected.

ART. 10. The President shall direct the work and administration of the Court; he shall preside at the meetings of the full Court.

ART. 11. The Vice-President shall take the place of the President, should the latter be unable to be present, or, should he cease to hold office, until the new President has been appointed by the Court.

ART. 12. The President shall reside within a radius of ten kilometers from the Peace Palace at The Hague.

The main annual vacation of the President shall not exceed three months.

ART. 13. After a new election of the whole Court and until such time as the President and Vice-President have been elected, the judge who takes precedence according to the order laid down in Article 2, shall perform the duties of President.

The same principle shall be applied should both the President and the Vice-President be unable to be present, or should both appointments be vacant at the same time.

SECTION C.—*The Chambers.*

ART. 14. The members of the Chambers constituted by virtue of Article 26, 27 and 29 of the Statute shall be appointed at a meeting of the full Court by an absolute majority of votes, regard being had for the purposes of this selection to any preference expressed by the judges, so far as the provisions of Article 9 of the Statute permit.

The substitutes mentioned in Articles 26 and 27 of the Statute shall be appointed in the same manner. Two judges shall also be chosen to replace any member of the Chamber for summary procedure who may be unable to sit.

The election shall take place at the end of the ordinary session of the Court, and the period of appointment of the members elected shall commence on January 1st of the following year.

Nevertheless, after a new election of the whole Court the election shall take place at the beginning of the following session. The period of appointment shall commence on the date of election and shall terminate, in the case of the Chamber referred to in Article 29 of the Statute, at the end of the same year, and in the case of the Chambers referred to in Articles 26 and 27 of the Statute, at the end of the second year after the year of election.

The Presidents of the Chambers shall be appointed at a sitting of the full Court. Nevertheless, the President of the Court shall, *ex officio,* preside over any Chamber of which he may be elected a member; similarly, the Vice-President of the Court shall, *ex officio,* preside over any Chamber of which he may be elected a member, provided that the President is not also a member.

ART. 15. The special Chambers for labour cases and for communications and transit cases may not sit with a greater number than five judges.

Except as provided in the second paragraph of the preceding Article, the composition of the Chamber for summary procedure may not be altered.

ART. 16. Deputy-judges shall not be summoned to complete the special Chambers or the Chamber for summary procedure, unless sufficient judges are not available to complete the number required.

SECTION D.—*The Registry.*

ART. 17. The Court shall select its Registrar from amongst candidates proposed by members of the Court.

The election shall be by secret ballot and by a majority of votes. In the event of an equality of votes, the President shall have a casting vote.

The Registrar shall be elected for a term of seven years commencing on January 1st of the year following that in which the election takes place. He may be re-elected.

Should the Registrar cease to hold his office before the expiration of the term above-mentioned, an election shall be held for the purpose of appointing a successor.

ART. 18. Before taking up his duties, the Registrar shall make the following declaration at a meeting of the full Court:

"I solemnly declare that I will perform the duties conferred upon me as Registrar of the Permanent Court of International Justice in all loyalty, discretion and good conscience."

The other members of the Registry shall make a similar declaration before the President, the Registrar being present.

ART. 19. The Registrar shall reside within a radius of ten kilometers from the Peace Palace at The Hague.

The main annual vacation of the Registrar shall not exceed two months.

ART. 20. The staff of the Registry shall be appointed by the Court on proposals submitted by the Registrar.

ART. 21. The Regulations for the Staff of the Registry shall be adopted by the President on the proposal of the Registrar, subject to subsequent approval by the Court.

ART. 22. The Court shall determine or modify the organization of the Registry upon proposals submitted by the Registrar. On the proposal of the Registrar, the President shall appoint the member of the Registry who is to act for the Registrar in his absence or, in the event of his ceasing to hold his office, until a successor has been appointed.

ART. 23. The registers kept in the archives shall be so arranged as to give particulars with regard to the following points amongst others:

1. For each case or question, all documents pertaining to it and all actions taken with regard to it in chronological order; all such documents shall bear the same file number and shall be numbered consecutively within the file;

2. All decisions of the Court in chronological order, with references to their respective files;

3. All advisory opinions given by the Court in chronological order, with references to their respective files.

4. All notifications and similar communications sent out by the Court, with references to their respective files.

Indexes kept in the archives shall comprise:

1. A card index of names with necessary references;

2. A card index of subject matter with like references.

ART. 24. During hours to be fixed by the President the Registrar shall receive any documents and reply to any enquiries, subject to the provisions of Article 38 of the present Rules and to the observance of professional secrecy.

ART. 25. The Registrar shall be the channel for all communications to and from the Court.

The Registrar shall ensure that the date of despatch and receipt of all communications and notifications may readily be verified. Communications and notifications sent by post shall be registered. Communications addressed to the official representative or to the agents of the parties shall be considered as having been addressed to the parties themselves. The date of receipt shall be noted on all documents received by the Registrar, and a receipt bearing this date and the number under which the document has been registered shall be given to the sender, if a request to that effect be made.

ART. 26. The Registrar shall be responsible for the archives, the accounts and all administrative work. He shall have the custody of the seals and stamps of the Court. He shall himself be present at all meetings of the full Court and either he, or a person appointed to represent him with the approval of the Court, shall be present at all sittings of the various Chambers; he shall be responsible for drawing up the minutes of the meetings.

He shall further undertake all duties which may be laid upon him by the present Rules.

The duties of the Registry shall be set forth in detail in a List of Instructions to be submitted by the Registrar to the President for his approval.

HEADING 2.—*Working of the Court.*

ART. 27. In the year following a new election of the whole Court the ordinary annual session shall commence on the fifteenth of January.

If the day fixed for the opening of a session is regarded as a holiday at the place where the Court is sitting, the session shall be opened on the working day following.

ART. 28. The list of cases shall be prepared and kept up to date by the Registrar under the responsibility of the President. The list for each session shall contain all questions submitted to the Court for an advisory opinion and all cases in regard to which the written proceedings are concluded, in the order in which the documents submitting each question or case have been received by the Registrar. If in the course of a session, a question is submitted to the Court or the written proceedings in regard to any case are concluded, the Court shall decide whether such question or case shall be added to the list for that session.

The Registrar shall prepare and keep up to date extracts from the above list showing the cases to be dealt with by the respective Chambers.

The Registrar shall also prepare and keep a list of cases for revision.

ART. 29. During the sessions the dates and hours of sittings shall be fixed by the President.

ART. 30. If at any sitting of the full Court it is impossible to obtain the prescribed quorum, the Court shall adjourn until the quorum is obtained.

ART. 31. The Court shall sit in private to deliberate upon the decision of any case or on the reply to any question submitted to it.

During the deliberation referred to in the preceding paragraph, only persons authorized to take part in the deliberation and the Registrar shall be present. No other person shall be admitted except by virtue of a special decision taken by the Court, having regard to exceptional circumstances.

Every member of the Court may request that a question which is to be voted upon shall be drawn up in precise terms in both the official languages and distributed to the Court. A request to this effect shall be complied with.

CHAPTER II

PROCEDURE

HEADING 1.—*Contentious Procedure.*

SECTION A.—*General Provisions.*

ART. 32. The rules contained under this heading shall in no way preclude the adoption by the Court of such other rules as may be jointly proposed by the parties concerned, due regard being paid to the particular circumstances of each case.

ART. 33. The Court shall fix time limits in each case by assigning a definite date for the completion of the various acts of procedure, having regard as far as possible to any agreement between the parties.

The Court may extend time limits which it has fixed. It may likewise decide in certain circumstances that any proceeding taken after the expiration of a time limit shall be considered as valid.

If the Court is not sitting the powers conferred upon it by this article shall be exercised by the President, subject to any subsequent decision of the Court.

ART. 34. All documents of the written proceedings submitted to the Court shall be accompanied by not less than thirty printed copies certified correct. The President may order additional copies to be supplied.

SECTION B.—*Procedure before the Court and before the special Chambers (Articles 26 and 27 of the Statute).*

I. INSTITUTION OF PROCEEDINGS

ART. 35. When a case is brought before the Court by means of special agreement, the latter, or the document notifying the Court of the agreement, shall mention the addresses selected at the seat of the Court to which notices and communications intended for the respective parties are to be sent.

In all other cases in which the Court has jurisdiction, the application shall include, in addition to an indication of the subject of the dispute and the names of the parties concerned, a succinct statement of facts, an indication of the claim and the address selected at the seat of the Court to which notices and communications in regard to the case are to be sent.

Should the notice of a special agreement, or the application, contain a request that the case be referred to one of the special Chambers mentioned in Articles 26 or 27 of the Statute, such request shall be complied with, provided that the parties are in agreement.

Similarly, a request to the effect that technical assessors be attached to the Court, in accordance with Article 27 of the Statute, or that the case be referred to the Chamber for summary procedure shall also be granted; compliance with the latter request is, however, subject to the condition that the case does not refer to any of the questions indicated in Articles 26 and 27 of the Statute.

ART. 36. The Registrar shall forthwith communicate to all members of the Court special agreements or applications which have been notified to him.

II. WRITTEN PROCEEDINGS

ART. 37. Should the parties agree that the proceedings shall be conducted in French or in English, the documents constituting the written procedure shall be submitted only in the language adopted by the parties.

In the absence of an agreement with regard to the language to be employed, documents shall be submitted in French or in English.

Should the use of a language other than French or English be authorized, a translation into French or into English shall be attached to the original of each document submitted.

The Registrar shall not be bound to make translations of documents submitted in accordance with the above rules.

In the case of voluminous documents the Court, or the President if the Court is not sitting, may, at the request of the party concerned, sanction the submission of translations of portions of documents only.

ART. 38. The Court, or the President, if the Court is not sitting, may, after hearing the parties, order the Registrar to hold the cases and counter-cases of each suit at the disposal of the Government of any State which is entitled to appear before the Court.

ART. 39. In cases in which proceedings have been instituted by means of a special agreement, the following documents may be presented in the order stated below, provided that no agreement to the contrary has been concluded between the parties:

A case, submitted by each party within the same limit of time;

A counter-case, submitted by each party within the same limit of time;

A reply, submitted by each party within the same limit of time.

When proceedings are instituted by means of an application, failing any agreement to the contrary between the parties, the documents shall be presented in the order stated below:

5. Any declarations made by the parties;

6. All decisions taken by the Court during the hearing.

ART. 56. Before the oral proceedings are concluded each party may present his bill of costs.

IV. INTERIM PROTECTION

ART. 57. When the Court is not sitting, any measures for the preservation in the meantime of the respective rights of the parties shall be indicated by the President.

Any refusal by the parties to conform to the suggestions of the Court or of the President, with regard to such measures, shall be placed on record.

V. INTERVENTION

ART. 58. An application for permission to intervene, under the terms of Article 62 of the Statute, must be communicated to the Registrar at latest before the commencement of the oral proceedings.

Nevertheless, the Court may, in exceptional circumstances, consider an application submitted at a later stage.

ART. 59. The application referred to in the preceding Article shall contain:

1. A specification of the case in which the applicant desires to intervene;

2. A statement of law and of fact justifying intervention;

3. A list of the documents in support of the application; these documents shall be attached.

Such application shall be immediately communicated to the parties, who shall send to the Registrar any observations which they may desire to make within a period to be fixed by the Court or by the President, should the Court not be sitting.

ART. 60. Any State desiring to intervene, under the terms of Article 63 of the Statute, shall inform the Registrar in writing at latest before the commencement of the oral proceedings.

The Court, or the President if the Court is not sitting, shall take the necessary steps to enable the intervening State to inspect the documents in the case, in so far as they relate to the interpretation of the convention in question, and to submit its observations thereon to the Court.

VI. AGREEMENT

ART. 61. If the parties conclude an agreement regarding the settlement of the dispute and give written notice of such agreement to the Court before the close of the proceedings, the Court shall officially record the conclusion of the agreement.

Should the parties by mutual agreement notify the Court in writing that they intend to break off proceedings, the Court shall officially record the fact and proceedings shall be terminated.

VII. Judgment

Art. 62. The judgment shall contain:
1. The date on which it is pronounced;
2. The names of the judges participating;
3. The names and style of the parties;
4. The names of the agents of the parties;
5. The conclusions of the parties;
6. The matters of fact;
7. The reasons in point of law;
8. The operative provisions of the judgment;
9. The decision, if any, referred to in Article 64 of the Statute.

The opinions of judges who dissent from the judgment, shall be attached thereto should they express a desire to that effect.

Art. 63. After having been read in open Court the text of the judgment shall forthwith be communicated to all parties concerned and to the Secretary General of the League of Nations.

Art. 64. The judgment shall be regarded as taking effect on the day on which it is read in open Court, in accordance with Article 58 of the Statute.

Art. 65. A collection of the judgments of the Court shall be printed and published under the responsibility of the Registrar.

VIII. Revision

Art. 66. Application for revision shall be made in the same form as the application mentioned in Article 40 of the Statute.

It shall contain:
1. The reference to the judgment impeached;
2. The fact on which the application is based;
3. A list of the documents in support; these documents shall be attached.

It shall be the duty of the Registrar to give immediate notice of an application for revision to the other parties concerned. The latter may submit observations within a time limit to be fixed by the Court, or by the President should the Court not be sitting.

If the judgment impeached was pronounced by the full Court, the application for revision shall also be dealt with by the full Court. If the judgment impeached was pronounced by one of the Chambers mentioned in Articles 26, 27 or 29 of the Statute, the application for revision shall be dealt with by the same Chamber. The provisions of Article 13 of the Statute shall apply in all cases.

If the Court, under the third paragraph of Article 61 of the Statute, makes a special order rendering the admission of the application conditional upon previous compliance with the terms of the judgment impeached, this condition shall be immediately communicated to the applicant by the Registrar and proceedings in revision shall be stayed pending receipt by the Registrar of proof of previous compliance with the original judgment and until such proof shall have been accepted by the Court.

SECTION C.—*Summary Procedure.*

ART. 67. Except as provided under the present section the rules for procedure before the full Court shall apply to summary procedure.

ART. 68. Upon receipt by the Registrar of the document instituting proceedings in a case which, by virtue of an agreement between the parties, is to be dealt with by summary procedure, the President shall convene as soon as possible the Chamber referred to in Article 29 of the Statute.

ART. 69. The proceedings are opened by the presentation of a case by each party. These cases shall be communicated by the Registrar to the members of the Chamber and to the opposing party.

The cases shall contain reference to all evidence which the parties may desire to produce.

Should the Chamber consider that the cases do not furnish adequate information, it may, in the absence of an agreement to the contrary between the parties, institute oral proceedings. It shall fix a date for the commencement of the oral proceedings.

At the hearing, the Chamber shall call upon the parties to supply oral explanations. It may sanction the production of any evidence mentioned in the cases.

If it is desired that witnesses or experts whose names are mentioned in the case should be heard, such witnesses or experts must be available to appear before the Chamber when required.

ART. 70. The judgment is the judgment of the Court rendered in the Chamber of summary procedure. It shall be read at a public sitting of the Chamber.

HEADING 2.—*Advisory Procedure.*

ART. 71. Advisory opinions shall be given after deliberation by the full Court.

The opinions of dissenting judges may, at their request, be attached to the opinion of the Court.

ART. 72. Questions upon which the advisory opinion of the Court is asked shall be laid before the Court by means of a written request, signed either by the President of the Assembly or the President of the Council of the League of Nations, or by the Secretary-General of the League under instructions from the Assembly or the Council.

The request shall contain an exact statement of the question upon which an opinion is required, and shall be accompanied by all documents likely to throw light upon the question.

ART. 73. The Registrar shall forthwith give notice of the request for an advisory opinion to the members of the Court, and to the Members of the League of Nations, through the Secretary-General of the League, and to the States mentioned in the Annex to the Covenant.

Notice of such request shall also be given to any international organizations which are likely to be able to furnish information on the question.

ART. 74. Any advisory opinion which may be given by the Court and the request in response to which it was given, shall be printed and published in a special collection for which the Registrar shall be responsible.

HEADING 3.—ERRORS.

ART. 75. The Court, or the President if the Court is not sitting, shall be entitled to correct an error in any order, judgment or opinion, arising from a slip or accidental omission.

Done at The Hague, the twenty-fourth day of March, one thousand nine hundred and twenty-two.

(S) LODER,
President.

(S) A. HAMMARSKJÖLD,
Registrar.